TRADING SECRETS

Based on actual events

SPEAKING VOLUMES, LLC

NAPLES, FLORIDA

2011

TRADING SECRETS

ISBN 978-1-61232-931-4

TRADING SECRETS

Tadeusz R. Sas

Being a double agent is not difficult.
It's being a treble or quadruple agent that is hard.
— KGB defector

This book, based on events that actually took place, has been fictionalized, and, as they say, the names have been changed to protect the innocent—with the exception of major figures—although how many of the characters portrayed in this book were truly "innocent" is another question.

About the Author

The author of this based-on-real-life novel was born in the United Kingdom to Polish parents in 1941 and participated in many of the events that are described in this book.

The owner of a company that traded extensively in Eastern Europe, in the days when it was not fashionable to do so, he travelled widely to all the countries comprising "The Soviet Bloc". His business activities brought him into contact with senior government officials in the military and security services as well as politicians and businessmen not only in the United Kingdom but in many of the Eastern European Countries.

Having completed two terms as an elected member of Westminster City Council, Mr. Sas also served for many years as a Magistrate at Marylebone Magistrates Court in London. He also lectured in public speaking for the Conservative party.

Relocating to the USA in 1988, he opened a new defense equipment company where he is President and a supplier of sophisticated security equipment to the U.S Federal Government and exports widely.

The story recounted in this novel is based on events that actually occurred and people that lived and breathed.

The narrative ranges widely over the 20th century following events that interconnected affecting many aspects of political and intelligence life.

The man depicted as Pretender to the Throne of Russia worked within the KGB to attain his goal of becoming Czar but actually "ran out of years" as old age overtook him before he could safely achieve his goal.

The interaction between the British Secret Service and the KGB using businessmen plus the involvement of the CIA makes an interesting read, focusing on how business has been used as an intelligence tool by many countries and their Security Services. Businessmen have free ranging access to all levels of society and the money that they generate opens doors that are usually closed fostering emotions ranging from greed to jealousy as is revealed in this book.

Names have been changed in this fictionalized book, with the exception of well-known political figures.

Dedicated to my long-suffering wife Carmen,
who discovered the knack of putting up with me.
To my wonderful children,
Elizabeth (and Colin),
Edward (and Svetlana),
Sophia, and my Late son, Richard.
Also to Giula and Scott
and my grandchildren,
Isabella, Katelyn, and Polina.

CHAPTER ONE

1991
Day One
Kuwait

Fire and brimstone, Christian mused as he watched the burning oil wells. It was as if the very gates of Hell had been opened.

When Christian Hardaway was fourteen years old and an indifferent pupil at Harrow School, the teacher had assigned the reading of Dante's *Inferno*. It was an assignment Christian completed without enthusiasm, but today the images that the book invoked returned.

Standing in the Kuwaiti desert, hearing the blowtorch roar from the oil wells, watching the flames of the great fires, the enormous plumes of heavy smoke arching into the sky, turning day into sulfurous twilight, Christian felt, for the first time, that he grasped what Dante had intended. If indeed there was a Hell on Earth, it was here and now.

Major General Raymond Philips—retired from the U.S. Army Corps of Engineers—twisted his moustache and squinted towards the cataclysm as if it were a brigade formed for inspection. "It smells bloody awful, Christian," he allowed.

Philips might no longer wear a uniform, but his gray suit was tailored such that it fitted him like one. He habitually stood at parade rest and in manner and appearance resembled no one as much as Field Marshal Bernard Montgomery. He was happy when people pointed this out to him, but less happy if he heard anyone whistling "the very model of a modern major general" from the Gilbert and Sullivan operetta *The Pirates of Penzance*.

Yes, Christian thought, television cameras never capture the heat, humidity, or smell, and in its own way the stench of burning oil, or the caustic dust rising from the pulverized expanse of desert.

"That it does, Raymond," he said. "That it does. All that money going up in fire and smoke.

Not that the Arabs lose much sleep over it."

Philips grunted, taking in both his reaction to the comment and his opinion of Arabs. "It's Friday, sir. You won't be seeing the emir tonight." Thursday and Friday were the "weekend" in Arab countries.

Christian grimaced. Emir Jabir Al Sabah had returned to Kuwait just days before and had already reestablished his weekly practice of marrying a virgin on the eve of the Muslim holy day. Today, he would divorce her, as he had the hundreds who had gone before, then send the honored teenage girl back to wherever she came from along with the agreed royal gift and his noble seed.

"Yes, we wouldn't want anything to interrupt his routine. When is our appointment?"

"Everything is ready for tomorrow afternoon, assuming that His Highness does not decide that an evening in Paris or London would distract him from the mess they made of his palaces."

It had been apparent to Christian the moment he stepped from his plane that the former desert dwellers of Kuwait were struggling as they roughed it in the shells of their ransacked palaces and homes. Charter flights filled with interior designers clutching fabric swatches were already winging their way from Paris, London, and Rome. Support aircraft bearing gold-plated faucets, porcelain doorknobs, and silk bed sheets were also on their way to Kuwait City. Emergency supplies for the nomads of yesteryear.

Carpetbaggers of one kind or another all but lined the streets of the city, patiently waiting or jockeying for their turn to speak to those in positions of influence. The Palestinian and Jordanian secretaries and assorted Arab middlemen were in full battle cry, smelling not the acrid fires of Kuwait but the alluring scent of dollars and pounds.

"Then we'll see him tomorrow, *Insha'Allah*," said Christian, using the Arabic "if God wills it" catchall phrase that throws the blame for almost anything on God's will as opposed to man's actions or, in this part of the world, more usually, inactions.

No, the anti-war crowd had it right, in Christian's opinion. The war was about oil because oil greased the world economy, made a decent livelihood possible for countless millions, heated homes in the dead of winter, made it possible to escape the congestion of cities on the weekend, and provided the countless necessities the West now took for granted. Protecting oil struck Christian as precisely the kind of motive required of great nations to wage war. Better to fight for the raw energy to keep the wheels of industry going than to ask young men to die in some cynical crusade to "make the world safe for democracy."

And, of course, war was always good for business—especially Christian's business.

Though his fifty-first birthday was just a few weeks behind him, Christian scarcely looked his age. He was tall and slim with the kind of rugged good looks once required of leading men in movies, with just a touch of gray now appearing in his hair. He was always meticulously dressed, a walking advertisement for Savile Row and its expert tailors. Always at ease, whether with a king, a general, or a foot soldier, Christian was the product of generations of aristocratic breeding and the best schools that money could buy. Even so, no trace of arrogance was visible; in fact, genuinely, there was none. Christian was the man that others, especially women, found attractive in all senses of the word.

A man's man and a woman's man, to boot.

"I'm told it could take two years to put them all out," Philips said, rubbing the inside of his cheeks with his tongue as if to remove the taste of the smoke.

"I'd like that contract," Christian answered. "If we were in that line of business."

International Military Support Services Ltd., or IMSS, as it was commonly known, founded by his father, was now one of the largest privately held companies in the United Kingdom.

Philips grunted. He had come to work for IMSS five years earlier upon the personal recommendation of the then Conservative Party foreign secretary, and, overall, Christian had been pleased. Philips was now the company's general manager and one of Christian's few confidants in a line of work in which subterfuge was stock in trade.

"I've had enough," Christian said as he turned towards the black Mercedes in which they'd arrived. Private planes weren't using the Kuwait airport as yet, so they'd used a military airfield in Saudi Arabia then driven over, since travel within Kuwait was possible only by road.

Their Kuwaiti driver squatting in the shade of the idling car stood up and brushed the desert sand from his robes and opened the door for them. Christian noted again the patched bullet holes in the back of the car and idly wondered what the story was.

As the heavy Mercedes smoothly accelerated towards Kuwait City, Christian observed once again the debris of war. Scattered, burned-out trucks and cars of all description lined the road. Intermixed were the twisted remains of various military vehicles, many of them so deformed that it often took even his practiced eye more than a few seconds to determine what the vehicle had been before it and its occupants had been changed from complex mechanical and living organisms to a pile of junk by the roadside.

Philips reached forward and raised the glass divider between them and the driver, whose command of English was limited, but Philips was nothing if not cautious.

"Yes?" Christian asked.

"Have you, ahh, decided what to do about Mrs. Hardaway?"

Evelyn Hardaway was Christian's wife of twenty-two years. When Philips had joined Christian in Riyadh a few days earlier, he had brought with him confirmation of Christian's suspicions that his wife was not only having yet another affair, but was now involved with a commercial attaché to the Russian embassy in London.

"What's the man's name again?" Christian asked.

"Alexei Zakusov, sir."

"How badly compromised is she?"

Philips cleared his throat. "It's not as if the Cold War were hard at it. A couple of years ago, this would have been an utter disaster. Still, the Russian Communists remain in power, for now, at least. And you well know that the KGB has always used commercial attachés as standard cover. I have no doubt he's still up to the same old job, just a new boss. It's not good."

"Has anyone at the Foreign Office commented?"

"Not as yet. I learned this privately, but you know that anyone going into the embassy in London is filmed and cross checked. Your good lady also knows that, as does everyone else."

Christian winced at the expression "good lady." "Everyone," in Philips's jargon, would include the Security Service, commonly known as MI5 for short—and The Secret Intelligence Service better known as SIS or MI6, as well as the Joint Intelligence Committee, which oversaw them both and was the cornerstone of British security. In other words, it almost was "everyone."

"*What about The Times*, sir?" Philips asked.

"I spoke with Hawkins." Martin Hawkins was deputy director of the SIS. "He assured me the article will be suppressed." The London *Times* reporter had been sniffing around IMSS and had interviewed a few disgruntled former employees. No matter how carefully anyone was vetted, no matter how highly recommended, there were always a few; however, Hawkins had been a reliable friend of the firm for a decade.

Christian had no idea what the article's slant was going to be, but from what he'd learned, it was not favorable, and in his line of work, any publicity was bad. IMSS functioned, and prospered, unofficially sponsored and discreetly supported by the British government, but without any doubt, a disposable asset should the heat become too much to bear.

"Then there's nothing to worry about in that regard, is there, sir?" Philips asked, cocking an eyebrow.

Christian did not answer, but a vein in his temple started to throb as he looked out of the car window at the unending desert sands stretching into the far distance.

The heavy car wound its way through the debris of the broken city. The shops on the main boulevards were looted and stood empty with gutted windows. Christian could see owners and their staff sweeping the mess out of the buildings and away from their frontage.

The Mercedes slowed then eased to a stop. The Sheraton was functioning, after a fashion, and was crowded with reporters from two dozen nations as well as businessmen who had arrived to strike deals now that the Kuwait government was back in business and so much was needed.

Christian was a well-known and honored guest at the hotel and had received one of the best suites. The whole hotel resounded with the sounds of workers hammering, cutting, and drilling as they repaired the destruction. The Iraqis had stripped the hotel of everything it didn't take dynamite to break loose, but bathroom fixtures had been hastily installed in his suite, so Christian at least had running water. Meanwhile, Philips had casually mentioned he was bathing in water poured from jugs, though he did have a functioning toilet and was on the cooler side of the building with his open windows catching a stray breeze now and again.

The reporters were in their uniform of tan slacks and safari jackets. They were interspersed with Western businessmen in suits and small groups of Japanese businessmen, cut from the same mold and all looking equally sweaty and uncomfortable.

Among the throng in the lobby, Christian caught sight of a Westerner flanked by two subordinates, moving towards the non-working elevators where he would be disappointed to learn that he would need to climb the stairs to his room. He felt a sudden rush of adrenaline as he recognized the man.

"Why would Mitch Seaver be here?" he asked Philips quietly.

"He is?"

"Yes. Don't turn around, but he and his heavies are heading for the staircase right now."

Seaver was a deputy director of the U.S. Central Intelligence Agency. Christian could not recall seeing him in the field since he'd been promoted to that position some six months earlier.

"I suppose it has something to do with American security interests here," Philips drawled.

"Maybe. He could also be running interference for ITP." International Trading Partners was a quasi-official U.S. company and one of IMSS's biggest competitors. It was crammed with former CIA agents, had a former presidential candidate as chairman, and was routinely promoted by the U.S. State Department to foreign countries. It was also a very generous contributor to both political parties in the United States, and its lobbyists were the cream of the crop. Seaver was on its board of directors, representing CIA interests.

"I suppose that's it, Christian. They've never had a strong toehold here before," Philips said.

"No, but then the Americans have never driven the Iraqis out of Kuwait before. They must be expecting repayment. See what you can sniff out, will you, Raymond?"

"Yes, sir!" Philips straightened his tie and marched off at a brisk pace. Christian had no doubt that within the next couple of hours he would learn from Philips what the "Company" was here to accomplish.

As he mounted the stairs, Christian tried to shake old memories but found he could not. Too many personal problems awaited him in England. He wondered how it could ever have come to this. Christian had met Evelyn DeLysle at the Newbury Hunt Ball when he had been a very randy and highly available twenty-eight-year-old bachelor. Her father, the duke of Berkshire, was vaguely and unfavorably known to him. A compulsive gambler, the duke had squandered most of the family fortune at Monte Carlo baccarat tables, and then, losing all sense of dignity, had blown the rest at horse and dog racing tracks in England. All he had bequeathed to his only daughter was an education and a title.

Their former stately home was now a museum supported by The National Trust in which the duke had spent his last years, living in the former servants' quarters and tending the vegetable garden. Some of the visitors who became lost and stumbled upon him often asked the stooped figure if he had ever worked for the duke and if he knew him. The duke's faded blue eyes would twinkle for a moment as he regaled them with stories of the duke and the life he had led in that grand house, never informing them that he was, in fact, the duke.

Evelyn was tall for a woman of her generation at 5'10", but still a few inches shorter than Christian. She had been on the arm of a man almost old enough to be her father, both of them laughing loudly as their eyes first met. Christian was not vain but knew he looked good in his red hunting dinner jacket, and though his father did not use the family title, Christian was, after all, due to become earl upon his father's death. Wealth and social position were the two things the English respected above all else, perhaps not necessarily in that order, but definitely in that juxtaposition.

When Evelyn saw Christian on the dance floor, her heart began to race. When Christian saw Evelyn, his pulse stayed steady, but warmth in his groin prompted him to approach her and ask, "Care to dance?"

"I would love to," she answered with a smile that suggested he could have anything he wanted from her. She left the arm of the ruddy-cheeked local landowner who had just sparked the flint of his gold lighter to ignite her cigarette. As she floated off with Christian, he stood in place, abandoned without a word, with the flame of his lighter a beacon to her departure.

"Do you tango, Lady DeLysle?"

"Does a foxhound hunt?"

Over the next hour of delicious exertion, Christian learned that Evelyn, like himself, had hunted avidly since early youth. She especially loved the chase— the horns blaring, the hounds baying, the cold morning mist, the cut and dash of the men's red hunting jackets, the pursuit and cornering of the quarry, and finally the near orgasmic moment when she reared her mount in triumph over the bloodied carcass of the dead fox.

Evelyn, or Evvy, as he came to call her, was a stunning beauty, with long blond hair, round blue eyes, and lips set in a perpetual pout. The slit up the side of her black velvet dress that first night stopped only just this side of indecency. Perhaps at another time Christian might have been more cautious, a bit more discerning to the warning signals, but then perhaps not. She was a delicious package that he could not wait to unwrap—in fact, the two of them were in bed within twenty-four hours.

Of course, he'd had his share of lusty women, more than his share, since the possibility of becoming the wife of a handsome and wealthy earl was a terrific libido stimulant, but he had never met one whom he had thought of as marriage material, at least not until now. And that realization came as more of a shock than any other aspect of his heated relationship with Lady Evelyn. Until he'd bedded her, he had no idea he was even thinking of marriage, but the months spent in orgasmic ecstasy led him to propose almost in spite of himself. Only later, much later, when he knew his wife better, did he wonder if she hadn't planted the seeds of that idea in ways too subtle for him to notice.

Now, twenty-two years later, she was making a fool of herself and of him, and in the process placing in peril all that his father and he had worked their lifetimes to build. Well, marry because your wife could play the part of a slut so well and this is what you get, he thought, suddenly feeling very tired.

CHAPTER TWO

1991
Day Two
Kuwait City

Emir Jabir Al Sabah reminded Christian of a cadaver more than he did of a living man.

It might have been his weekly virgin, although he understood that the Tao taught that intercourse with a virgin added to a man's life. Well, the emir was a Muslim, and in his case, the teenage girls seemed to be killing him.

At the moment, the emir was talking quietly on the telephone, the fifth or sixth such interruption since Christian and Philips had been ushered into his presence almost two hours earlier. Though they had at last concluded the pleasantries and were prepared to discuss business, the emir was not ready, and as his attention span was, in any case, short, such meetings were like pulling teeth.

The palace had been hastily restored and was in much better condition than the Sheraton, but the signs of Iraqi occupation were still visible, though not here in the emir's private office. The all-male staff was back on duty, and the palace appeared to be running as before.

The emir, reclining on satin pillows, was dressed in traditional *thobe* and *ghutra*. He was joined by his secretary of management, a bookish Palestinian named Moussa Khaldun, similarly attired in traditional robes, and another man who had been introduced to Christian as secretary to the influential foreign minister, Sheik Sabah Al Ahmad, the emir's brother, who was said to run Kuwait's day-to-day affairs. Also in the room were the Kuwaiti army chief of staff and the head of internal security, each with matching mustaches and in immaculately tailored khaki uniforms, their shiny boots a counterpoint to the sandals worn by the other Kuwaitis.

Every few moments, a servant appeared as if from nowhere to offer the heavy, traditionally sweet Arab coffee or bottled Evian. Christian poured a glass of water and took a small sip. Can't drink too much, he had once told one of his employees, if you go out to have a pee, they will all be gone when you get back. It takes a long time to get them to the conference table, longer still to get to business, but turn your back for an instant and they vanish.

The emir replaced the telephone and nodded at Khaldun, who resumed, in his precise voice, at the exact point he had paused almost thirty minutes earlier. "And what equipment is IMSS able to immediately provide us with?" Khaldun was forty-three years old with a degree in engineering from the Sorbonne in Paris and an MBA from Harvard.

Having seen Mitch Seaver at the hotel, Christian was increasingly concerned about the CIA's presence here. IMSS had always enjoyed a competitive advantage over the American security companies because of Kuwait's long association with Britain, which had, in fact, been the first Western power to recognize its independence and had extended protection to it until 1961. In addition, the emir and his government simply preferred doing business with British companies, especially as they would rather fly to London than New York almost anytime.

But now that the Americans had saved their asses and assets, there was certainly going to be payback. It was his job to see to it that it did not take place at the expense of his company nor at the expense of the traditional strength demonstrated by the British security services in the Gulf.

"We have secured assurances from the ministry of defense that we will have unimpeded access to the very latest technology," Christian said. "Items that until now had been reserved solely for the elite British SAS and other special forces now can be offered to your forces, Your Highness. None of us desires a repeat of these past unfortunate months. What we have immediately available includes the latest-generation night-vision equipment, which proved so invaluable to your armed forces." A handful of Kuwaitis had actually fought in the Gulf War, and Christian took the tack of suggesting they had won the war singlehandedly. "Detectors for chemical agents will warn you of any chemical attacks, and we have, as well, antidotes in the event of a chemical or biological attack. We have also a wide range of special communications equipment. Also available is a selection of the very finest ex-military training officers, a number of them being former SAS, as well as highly experienced bomb-disposal officers. These are the best of the best, Your Highness, and available to train the military of Kuwait to the highest of standards and," he added, foreseeing the needs of the generals, "they can stay here for as long as you need them to serve as advisors."

This had been a problem in the past, especially in regards to bomb disposal, as the local Kuwaitis were never very keen to approach an unexploded device, so the advisor or instructor usually dismantled the device himself while the Kuwaiti officers looked on in relief from afar. All this was not cheap. Life insurance and a tax-free salary could buy the best candidates for a short while, but to keep them in country took more than that. The boredom for the Brits and their wives soon became unbearable.

The Joint Intelligence Committee, or JIC, to whose chairman Christian regularly reported his activities, was always eager to have human resources on hand since they were invaluable in providing accurate intelligence. Khaldun, being no fool, understood that loyal British subjects, particularly those who had served in its military, could only be expected to report what they did and what was going on, even if through informal channels. It was a game thousands of years old. Khaldun himself owed no loyalty to the Kuwaitis, as he was a Palestinian and was always regarded as a hired hand no matter what his status as Mr. Fixit to the emir could bestow in the short term.

Khaldun smiled and tipped his head slightly and asked, "Her Majesty's government is in the pipeline, of course?" Christian acknowledged it was by gesture, and then said, "There can be no question but when it comes to the security of Kuwait, your interests and those of Her Majesty's government are one and the same. I would never act other than in those interests and with complete government approval."

At that moment, the emir answered still another telephone call, and everyone sat in silence. The humming of the air-conditioning and the flapping of a servant's sandals as he poured more coffee or set out bottles of water were the only sounds in the room. Christian glanced at Philips, who sat ramrod straight in his chair, seemingly relaxed and attentive at the same time. He wondered how the man did it.

Christian knew that what he proposed was a small piece of the largesse Kuwait was about to spend on its future security needs. His technical advisers and salesmen would be here within a few days with detailed proposals for tanks, armored vehicles, and anti-tank weapons, but special forces equipment was what the emir had expressed immediate interest in, and that was what they would talk about today. While Iraq had ultimately been expelled, its large, if inept, army had shown how ridiculously easy it was to overrun tiny Kuwait. Even now, the emir's government could not hope to add defenses that would stop an invasion from either Iraq or nearby Iran, but clearly it had to do a better job of slowing them down initially, until such time as the Western powers could act to protect it.

The emir replaced the telephone in its cradle, spoke a few moments in generalities, then started positively recounting Kuwait's long history with Britain and the wonderful things he knew about Christian, his father Julian, and their company. Coming from anyone but an Arab, it would have been enough to turn his head. Emanating from the emir of Kuwait, it was, in actuality, a story related in the tradition of the Bedouin, a story that might end with a surprise.

When the emir stopped speaking, Philips cleared his throat — Christian looked at him to give permission for him to speak. "Given recent events, we would be distressed to learn such business as we've historically had here had gone over to the Americans," Philips said. They had decided he would raise the issue. "If we aren't careful, they'll grab up the world. A large contingent of very brave British lads is still in service here, and you know that you can count on your long ties with Her Majesty's government; not to mention, the Americans give strong support to the Israelis at all times." The implication being that one never knew about the Americans, and indeed one never did, and there was also the question of their unstinting support for Israel, which may one day become a huge problem in the Middle East.

Khaldun spoke. "Of course, the decision rests with the Emir and no one else, but at this moment, he sees no reason why we will not be doing business together. We need only work out the details." The suave Palestinian was the voice of the emir in such matters, and Christian sighed with relief—no change.

"And the training officers, mine clearance, and bomb-disposal teams? Will they be required?" Christian asked. JIC would press on this, he knew.

"Without question." Khaldun smiled. "We would have a major problem without them, wouldn't we?"

The gleam in the eyes of Moussa Khaldun reassured Christian that all was well in this small corner of the world. He had no doubt but that Khaldun was already counting his two-percent commission.

CHAPTER THREE

1991
Day Two
Kuwait City

There was no bar in the hotel, as Islam prohibited drinking alcohol. Christian and Philips lingered at their table after dinner. Christian poured himself another glass of bottled water. Across the table, Philips removed a thin flask from his suit's inner pocket and discreetly spiked his drink and raised his eyebrows in question. "Christian?"

Christian shook his head.

Philips smiled as he slipped the flask into place. "Cheers!" Philips smiled broadly, and then took a pull from his drink as his eyes wandered the increasingly crowded room, coming to rest finally on a lithe Filipino waiter.

Christian spotted Mitch Seaver just taking a seat a few tables away with his entourage. "The Company is gracing us with its presence."

Philips slowly took in the room and then pursed his lips when he found the table. "Perhaps Mr. Seaver would care to join you for a cup of coffee," he suggested.

"Ask, will you?"

Philips smiled a bit mischievously. "My pleasure." He rose and crossed in a regimental strut to the CIA table. He stood off a respectful distance for a moment or two, then approached when invited, leaned down, whispered in Seaver's ear, and nodded once towards Christian, who smiled invitingly. Seaver gave directions to his men, no doubt telling them to stay put, and then surrendered his seat to Philips before crossing the room to join Christian.

The still rather new deputy director for Central Intelligence presented that broad, phony, over-white-toothed smile affected by so many Americans, in Christian's view, then extended his hand and said, "Good to see you, Chris! Really good to see you. You sure got in country in a hurry." He took the seat vacated by Philips.

"I could say the same for you. Congratulations on your promotion. This is the first time I've seen you since."

"And how is the queen's empire these days?"

"You'll have to ask her. I'm just an honest purveyor of modest security services."

"In a pig's eye," Seaver said, his smile losing its energy for a moment.

The initial sparring done for now, Seaver visibly relaxed a bit. He was fit, as all the senior CIA types tended to be, with a full head of close-cut graying hair and thin-lens glasses. His hands were manicured, and his face well massaged. His accent placed him from one of the rectangular-shaped states in Middle America. His suit was tasteful Brooks Brothers.

"Let me ask you a question, Chris."

"Certainly. It's Christian, by the way. We Brits don't share your American fascination with shortening given names."

"You don't say? I never noticed." He cleared his throat, then said, "It's looking increasingly as if our late great Soviet empire is about to crumble. Would you agree?"

Christian nodded. From what he'd heard, and his sources were impeccable, it was all over in Moscow except for the shouting. What remained was the question of what kind of Russia would emerge from the mess

"Here's the question: Let's say you work in a company where it's dog eat dog, nobody trusts anybody, and the only way the bosses can keep the thing going is to direct everyone's attention outward against the competition. Are you with me?"

"Just barely."

"And I heard you didn't have a sense of humor! All right, stay with me on this. Now one day, the big boss changes the name of the company and tells everybody it's time to make nice-nice with the competition. Has anything really changed?"

"In other words," Christian replied, "you see no difference. Even if the Communists are booted out, which seems likely, it will remain business as usual."

"We'd be damn foolish if we did. The same guys will be running the show. The main difference, as I see it, is that now the Russian mafia can branch out of the KGB and make some real money, that's all. They'll be selling suitcase nukes on the open market before you know it."

Seaver shrugged and glanced back at his table, where Philips was engaged in what appeared to be incredibly boring small talk from the glazed look of the two Americans. He continued, "Musical chairs. Don't forget that Yeltsin was Communist Party head in Moscow. He got where he is by being a good Communist. It's the same game — new names and new titles. That's all."

"So you view this as a further enhancement of your job security." Christian laughed.

Seaver's eyes grew small. "It's a dangerous world, and somebody's got to protect it."

Christian's father had often worked in conjunction with the old OSS, the CIA's precursor during World War II, and had told his son that when it came to intelligence work, the Americans were naive and simplistic. It had been Christian's observations since unexpectedly assuming the reigns of the family company, that those managing the CIA these days were primarily skilled bureaucrats following the way that most of Washington, D.C. operated and additionally were personal empire builders, but not much else. Subject to the whims of change with each new president and the changes of direction charted by each new director, the Americans did not enjoy the solid continuity of the British Civil Service and its permanent secretaries, who ran the country irrespective of the government in day-to-day control. That, his father had opined, was the reason that the British Empire lasted so long—continuity of political power. The CIA's misjudgments were legendary. Until this very month, the CIA had consistently grossly overestimated the not-so-great Soviet Union's economic base and military power.

"I don't see anyone else from International Trading Partners," Christian said, changing the subject.

"You're the only security company here, to my knowledge. And anyway, my job is to represent the American government and not get involved with such matters." Seaver smiled with his mouth while his eyes did not change expression. "You take care, Chris. Everything changes. It's the only constant in this world. You'll excuse me? I could eat a cow."

CHAPTER FOUR

1991
Day Three
London

Christian had requested a window seat and sat comfortably in first class on the British Airways 747 as it passed over the Mediterranean. He had a great deal to consider, none of it pleasant.

Once the airplane cleared Saudi airspace, a strange transformation had taken place. It was as if a great weight had been lifted from the majority of the passengers who were Saudis. The volume of speech rose several notches, and the occasion became something of a spontaneous party. The women disappeared one after another into the bathrooms in their robes, only to emerge moments later in Parisian frocks, wafting expensive perfumes across the cabin. The men emerged wearing expensive tailored suits and custom-made shoes. The airplane was now filled with Westernized people.

Christian smiled inwardly at the show. What had happened to the traditionally garbed, culturally arrogant Arabs that had boarded the plane in Riyadh?

Philips had stayed behind in Kuwait to finalize this first contract since the end of the Gulf War. Philips's report on Evvy had been depressing. He wondered, yet again, whether it might have turned out differently if they'd had children. Probably not. There'd just have been a young life or two thoroughly screwed up by unhappy parents.

Christian wasn't surprised that she was having another affair. That each of them would go their separate ways had been agreed years before. For a relationship that had begun with such passion, the flames had dwindled to ashes with surprising speed. No, what surprised him was her selection of lovers and the indiscreet manner in which she behaved with them. For a lady who relished her birthright and title, she was undemanding of lovers. Muscular bodies and small brains, thought Christian. Over the years, some had even been bar pick-ups, but none lasted longer than a few months.

Until now, she'd always demonstrated the ability to avoid any relationship that would cause him, and them, trouble. This time was different, and Christian wondered if she'd dropped her guard because of unfolding events. Things were clearly changing in the East. An opposing nationalist party had been launched the previous fall, and both Russia and Ukraine, the essential components of the Soviet Union, were declaring their own state laws superior to those of the Communist state. It was a direct attack on the Soviet Union, and a result of both glasnost and perestroika, Gorbachev policies that had liberalized speech and the marketplace. Since the beginning of the year, the Baltic States had been flexing their muscles. It all appeared to be the beginning of the end.

In the meanwhile, KGB officers of every ilk were exploiting their ability to travel, and many made their way to Britain seeking employment by trading their knowledge and contacts. A number had approached IMSS, and several specialists had been brought onboard. It had been a good time. The family company had been one of less than a handful that had conducted business behind the Iron Curtain since the beginning of the Cold War, and such operatives with detailed local knowledge were going to be very useful in this Brave New World.

Still, the KGB was still just that, the KGB. Most of its senior officers were no doubt planning how to turn the clock back, and given Russia's long history of despots, you had to think they'd find a way to pull it off. This Alexei Zakusov fellow his wife was bedding could be looking for job opportunities with any intelligence-gathering organization that would take him, or he could just as easily be a member of the Russian mafia, or yet even be a loyal Communist. Such intimate access to Evvy held the promise of a bounty of intelligence information. How often did a hostile foreign power get the chance to place an agent so close to the head of one of its adversary's best intelligence sources? Christian cringed at the thought.

Worse, once they learned Evvy could tell them little since he purposely told her nothing, the only real use of the relationship would be to use her indiscretion to discredit him and IMSS and there lay the real threat. The Russians were very good at destruction, very good, indeed. What if Hawkins had been wrong? What if someone in the British corridors of power *was* out to get him, and the pending article would not be quashed? He wondered for a moment how the headline would read, the one that could bring him down.

Not that his father, Julian, hadn't warned him. "She doesn't know it yet," he said, "but at heart she's a hundred-pound whore. Educated and well spoken, but a whore nonetheless."

At the time, the words had angered Christian, but now he wished his father were still alive. He'd like to tell him that not only had he been right, but Evvy knew what she was and relished her role.

At this moment, he suddenly understood when it had truly come to an end, when her destructive binge had begun. They hadn't been married very long before he grasped the two things that most motivated Evvy—social status and money. In marrying Christian, the only son of the earl of Carlisle, and eventual heir to the title, she had felt certain she acquired both. Though low key, it was no secret that Julian Hardaway was building IMSS into a very important and lucrative organization, so there'd always be money to spend on pretty things. Evvy understood genteel poverty and the loss of social standing. She'd thought her marriage to a future earl would end all that.

No, the beginning of the end had been the evening that Christian informed her that his father Julian was preparing to renounce the family title. The look on her face had been indescribable. Disbelief, rage, and finally hate, all within a span of a single second. Yes, that was it. It was the night she'd learned she'd become a commoner, neither birthright nor marriage had preserved her right to aristocracy. She'd vented her anger that very night, got more than a little drunk, then simply vanished for a week. Funny how he had never put it all together before.

Christian felt the plane ease into its descent. What had happened to him? And more to the point, what was going to happen to him in the days to come? He felt increasingly that matters were spiraling out of his control.

CHAPTER FIVE

1991
Day Three
London

It was dusk, and London's streets were slick from a steady drizzle that was in sharp contrast to the humidity, heat, and suffocating smoke of the Gulf desert. For all Christian knew, it had rained without a break since he'd left eight days earlier. The Rolls Royce worked its way through the traffic as Christian tried to reach Martin Hawkins at SIS to be reassured that *The Times* story had been successfully killed. The man's private line simply rang through to a most unhelpful secretary who stonewalled his every question. Christian tried Hawkins's car telephone and was surprised when he had to leave a message. It was unlike the man to be unavailable.

Someone, perhaps Churchill, had once said there are no real allies, only nations with common interests, or something like that. So it was in his world, Christian occasionally reflected. Who was his real friend? On whom could he absolutely depend? The disappointing answer was "no one. "Perhaps his girlfriend Hannah, but he wasn't even certain about that. And if a time ever came when he couldn't deliver the goods? What then? Where would his friends in the JIC be?

It was a dismal thought and the reason that so much of his personal fortune lay in a British Virgin Islands bank well out of harm's way. Christian sighed and then punched Hannah's number into his car phone. "Yes?" she answered. Just the sound of her voice lifted his spirits and excited him.

"It's me. I'm back. Shall I pick up something, or do you want to cook?"

"I've got food. I missed you. Just hurry."

Hannah Rossetti's parents had come to Britain from Naples in the late fifties to work at the Italian embassy, then had stayed on and become citizens. Hannah was a classic Italian beauty, just turned thirty-six years of age. A slender 5' 6", she had incredible legs leading to an incredible everything else. Her hips sway when she walked, not in a sluttish way, but rather like a hula dancer, sending out a message of promise. Her eyes were dark pools of passion astride an aquiline nose and above a full-lipped mouth, with naturally perfect white teeth and an inviting smile. Her olive complexion gave the impression of a light suntan, while her long black hair, usually tied severely back in a bun, was thick and shiny. When she let her hair down, she was transformed into a portrait worthy of the cover of *Vogue*.

Hannah's very obvious intelligence shone through, and her sexuality all but vanished under her business-like demeanor, but like a volcano, her workday looks covered a core of molten fire, capable of consuming any man she touched. Few realized the strength beneath that delicate look, a strength that allowed her former drunken beast of a husband to slap her around until there was no love left in her, a strength that allowed her to fight back by ripping his clothes to shreds and taking them to his dental office, where she threw the shreds around his waiting room full of patients, before walking out on him and demanding nothing more in the divorce settlement than that he leave her alone.

She had been content—happy would not be the word—living alone without a boyfriend and rarely dating until she met Christian Hardaway. This was the first man she had ever physically ached for.

The state of the Hardaway marriage was common knowledge within her social circle. She'd even had occasion to meet Lady Hardaway at a Foreign Office reception. It was not much of a secret as to how Evvy behaved. She was taking nothing from Evvy; she was taking something for herself. And it felt damn good. Christian was the perfect man for her—sexy, good looking, educated, well spoken, well mannered, and not interested in the handcuffs of marriage.

Educated in London, at the best schools that the Italian embassy could afford for its diplomats' children, Hannah had graduated with honors from Cambridge. Having worked for a time in the Foreign Office where her talents—not to mention her innate intelligence and good looks, or perhaps it was the other way around — led to a rapid rise through the ranks, seemingly without making a single enemy on the way up.

Hannah was now senior assistant to Douglas Hurd, the foreign secretary, tasked with liaison to the Joint Intelligence Committee, primarily with the coordinator of defense, intelligence, and security. Anyone thinking her relationship with Christian was created to allow the exchange of information missed the point entirely. Christian had worked through several lovers in his life, but none even approached the intensity and passion of this one. When it came to work, each respected the other's position and simply didn't talk about it except in the general way two adults will who work or come in contact with the same people.

Hannah lived on Upper Brook Street, Mayfair, just a few steps from Hyde Park and Marble Arch. Hannah had bought a fifty-year lease on the entire building, situated between the American embassy and Park Lane, which she sublet to two diplomats who wanted to live in Mayfair close to their Canadian embassy. Her first-and second-floor apartment had its own entrance; one of the Canadian families lived in the basement apartment, while the other lived on the third and fourth floors, accessed from a side door. She blessed her frugal parents and their insurance policy in her favor when they were killed in an airplane crash in Milan, which allowed her to invest in the property and have enough left over to make life easy. The area was a mix of offices and private apartments, most of which were occupied by Americans employed at the nearby American embassy.

Christian parked in the vast Marble Arch underground car park, close to the ramp up to Park Lane near Hyde Park. He noted the Rolls, Mercedes, and Jaguars parked along the wall as he strolled through the underpass, then went up the ramp on the far side of the road from where he ambled down Park Lane before turning right into Upper Street. Within a few minutes, he was ringing Hannah's doorbell.

The front door opened; no one was in sight. Christian curled his hand around the front door and ruffled Hannah's unseen hair. She laughed, then closed the door and stood on her toes for a kiss. Christian felt her warmth and pressed her to him, realizing that she was dressed only in a long t-shirt and nothing else. He stepped back to take a good look at her.

"Did you start without me?" he asked, laughing.

"No," she replied, "but it's been a long time!" She took his hand and led him upstairs to the bedroom. As he followed her up the stairs, Christian enjoyed the view that the t-shirt did nothing to hide, feeling a hardening in his loins.

Damn! he thought. Just like a teenager. They barely made it into her bedroom before Hannah had removed Christian's jacket, tie, and shirt, and her hands were fast at work on his belt.

Because of their work demands, they met only every week or so, and the time they spent together was precious to them both. They seldom went out, as Hannah enjoyed cooking for him and he enjoyed home-cooked food after the restaurant meals he had for business lunches and dinners. "Eating in" had become a standard joke between them, but often they had dessert before they even considered dinner. Tonight's "dessert" was followed by an excellent veal cordon bleu in the kitchen, Christian relishing the meal as he did all those Hannah prepared for him.

Afterwards, Christian showered as Hannah put the dishes way. He toweled then dressed in the flannel pajamas and robe he kept at her apartment. In the living room, he poured a cognac, turned out some lights, stoked the fire to a pleasant size, and then stretched on the Persian carpet, his back to the couch.

Moments later, Hannah entered the room wearing a kimono. She drew a Cuban Cohiba Perfecto cigar from the humidor. He watched as she cut then lit it without comment. She took three short puffs, creating a cloud of rich smoke, then placed the cigar into his mouth. He could taste her as he took his first puff. When he leisurely exhaled, the smoke was drawn through the air towards the fire, vanishing up the chimney.

"Tough trip?" she asked.

"Not bad. We'll get the business, and that's what counts."

"But something's bothering you. I can always tell."

Christian grunted. "Mitch Seaver was there."

Hannah straightened, took a sip of her drink, and asked, "What on earth moved his backside from behind his desk in D.C.?"

"The Company will have security issues. It's only to be expected."

She paused. "They don't need anyone that senior in the field."

"Maybe. I think he was primarily shilling for ITP." International Trading Partners was essentially an extension of the CIA, manned as it was by former Company agents, and tasked with making U.S. government-supported sales around the world.

Hannah rose, took a cigarette from a pack on the mantle, and lit it. She stood near the fire, the light playing on her body. "Darling, I need to break our rule a bit here."

Immediately he was alert. "Yes?"

"As I'm sure you already know, Her Majesty's government and the Company aren't getting on these days."

"That's nothing new."

"No, but this is different. I've not seen it before. The Company wants something, and I think HMG is being forced to give it."

"What?"

"I don't know, and that's why I'm talking to you."

Christian sipped his drink, the cognac hot against his throat. "I don't understand."

Hannah threw the cigarette into the fire and then sat next to him. "*I* should know, you understand? I'm liaison with the intelligence coordinator, and there's precious little that takes place that I don't hear about one way or the other. I don't have to ask, I don't have to be nosey, I'm just there and at one point or another it flows across my desk, or Mr. Hurd mentions it to me directly or in passing. I know everything he knows and then some, unless he wants to keep it from me, and that's never happened before. Let me see if I can explain this better so you'll understand.

"Three weeks ago, Mr. Hurd was talking to the prime minister on the telephone while his door was open and he seemed very upset. He told the PM that he wasn't going to let the boys from Langley push him around. He was quite adamant. I was busy at the time and gave it no thought. They all have too much testosterone anyway, if you ask me, and the older they get the more they like to bluster. Then two weeks ago, the CIA reps suddenly stopped attending the weekly meetings, you know the ones."

Christian did. It was a custom dating back to World War II. The Americans were allowed to sit in on the first half of the weekly intelligence meetings and information was freely exchanged between the parties. The last time they'd stopped attending had been following the defection of the "Cambridge Three" in the early sixties, when it was clear how badly the Russians had penetrated the

British Secret Intelligence Service. Hannah had his undivided attention. "Go on."

"Finally, Mr. Hurd got his marching orders from the PM, and he was pretty pissed off, I can tell you. When he came out of the meeting with the committee, he wouldn't look me in the eye, Christian."

"This can't possibly be about you."

"Of course not, silly. And you think you're so bloody clever. They *know* we're lovers." She returned to the mantle, lit another cigarette, and then said, "It has to be about *you*." For the first time in his life, Christian understood the expression "blood ran cold."

"How did Mitch behave in Kuwait?" she asked.

Christian replayed his minutes with Seaver. "His usual self. A bit more patronizing, maybe. I put that down as due to his promotion."

"Christian, I think you and IMSS are the target, and it's not going to be good. . . I can sense it. "

Christian finished his cognac and smoked a bit as he composed himself. "It's more likely about the Company insisting on having greater access in the Middle East; I cannot believe that I may have lost some of the British government's support."

Hannah shook her head. "You have no idea the number of enemies you've made. There are people who envy you plus those who hate you. Martin Hawkins left this morning quite abruptly.   A vacation, I'm told officially. But he had a terrible row in the director's office before leaving. His staff could hear the shouting, and he had several appointments this week—all of which had to be cancelled by his PA. No. It's much bigger than that."

"Maybe. There's something else going on." Christian told her about Evvy's affair. She took the information without revealing the slightest surprise. "Do you know this Alexei Zakusov?" he asked.

"No. I meet embassy types fairly often but not him. Why would she do something like this? She may act like a tramp, but until now she's always been a discreet one."

"I don't know. It makes no sense. I thought I could rely on her desire to maintain appearances. Clearly, I was wrong. But there's more." Christian told her about *The Times* article. "I haven't been able to get confirmation from Martin that it was killed. I tried on the way over earlier. His leaving like that is strange, I have to say … I'll make that a priority tomorrow, even if I have to track the coordinator down in person."

Hannah looked as if she was about to burst into tears. "If the article runs, then you'll know.   Oh, Christian! It's so unfair!"

"Fair's got nothing to do with it." And neither does faithful service, Christian thought.

A bit later, as he prepared for bed, Christian decided he had overreacted. Both he and his father had faithfully served the Crown for nearly forty years. How many times had information developed by IMSS been found to be of great value? How many scandals had the government been spared? How many national security leaks had been plugged? Had they listened to his father, much of the widespread damage done by the "Cambridge Four" would have been mitigated and the harm brought to British intelligence would have been greatly reduced. That was just one example. If Christian put his mind to it, he could have listed a dozen more. It wasn't too much to say that Britain enjoyed a measure of her security in large part to the Hardaway father and son, not to mention the influence of IMSS across the world.

Christian appreciated Hannah's concern, and especially her willingness to break her code of silence, but as he reached for her, he was more confused by events than concerned.

CHAPTER SIX

1991
Day Four
London

If he could say anything about Evvy, and Christian suspected that at one time or another he had, it was that she'd held her looks. She was at her last birthday forty-four years old yet looked not a day over thirty-five. She avoided heaving drinking, had stopped smoking years before because it was hard on her complexion, worked out at least four times a week, and devoted a minimum of two hours every day to her appearance. Not to mention the enormous sums she spent on a custom-crafted wardrobe. Yes, she looked great, while about as inviting to Christian as a viper.

"Where was it this time?" she asked as she sipped her morning cup of tea.

Christian had risen before dawn at Hannah's, showered, and dressed. This was Monday, and he would be putting in a full day at the office. But first, he had gone to his home. He almost never informed his wife of his travel plans, and she only rarely knew when he actually returned. Since he showed up obviously rested and ready for the day, he was certain she knew he'd come in the previous night, but it was understood that neither asked the other such questions.

He and Evelyn had bought their home the year after their marriage, and Christian considered it the best part of the bargain. The residence was some fifty-five miles outside of London and five miles from the nearest village. It was pleasantly situated on ten acres of land that had once been the vegetable garden of Lord Craven's estate. The house itself was atop a hill with a view of the rolling hills and river valley.

The house was approached off a meandering country road presenting the scene in the traditionally English fashion. Once on the premises, however, state-of-the-art surveillance was everywhere. Fifteen-foot-high electric gates flanked by television monitors surveyed the approaches and grounds, while ground sensors indicated when anything larger than a small dog was in the area. It was simply not possible for any living person to be on the grounds without his or her presence being detected.

Beside the garage was a stable for five horses, while above it were the quarters for the chauffeur who served also as valet and gardener. An indoor swimming pool with exercise room was used almost exclusively by Evvy, although Christian did enjoy the sauna from time to time.

The house was a mix of English traditional with the modern kept largely out of sight. Chinese silk carpets covered the entrance floor. At the end of the hallway was the kitchen to the left with the maid's room just off it. Christian's office was to the right of the hall, along with the formal sitting room, which held his collection of Russian icons, most gathered by his father, along with expensive drapes, carpets, and crystal chandeliers.

His office was accessed only through an electronic combination lock. It was constructed of cherry wood and held first-edition books and a grandfather clock he loved. There were three telephones with separate lines. The safe was built into the wall. In all their years of marriage, Christian could count on the fingers of a single hand the number of times Evvy had been in the office, but even so, he never kept any papers of importance there for more than a day or two.

Christian loved his home, and although a divorce would not likely cause its loss, Evelyn knew how he felt about it and would extract a prohibitive price elsewhere to allow him to keep it. Better all around to come to an accommodation, and, of course, Evelyn preferred to be the wife of an ersatz earl than a divorcee and daughter of a disgraced duke.

Breakfast was served by the housekeeper, Mrs. Jeffries, in the dining room. She lived in the maid's room, while Herbert the valet-come-chauffeur lived over the garage. The other two maids lived in the village and cycled in every day. The assistant gardener, who barely spoke a word to anyone, was in his seventies, but could still outwork almost anyone half his age. He had once worked for Lord Craven and lived in a cottage about a mile away.

The stoic silences between the husband and wife had attracted comment among the servants. They noted that the couple barely spoke to one another unless necessary, and then it was generally something to do with the running of the house and grounds. They seldom argued, but when they did, Evvy could be heard shouting from every corner of the property while Christian never raised his voice—no matter what the provocation. His calmness was remarkable, and the servants dearly loved Christian while tolerating his wife for his sake. Her constant criticisms were greeted with silence by the servants, who were well paid and knew that finding another job in that area was almost impossible.

Christian glanced through *The Times*, saw that it made no mention of him or IMSS, so tossed it aside and joined Evelyn at the breakfast table. Dismissing Mrs. Jeffries with a wave of the hand, Christian said, "We're going to have to talk."

"Whatever about?"

"Alexei, for starters."

If she was surprised, there was no hint in her face or manner. "My, you do go right to it, don't you? And what about dear Alexei? He's quite charming, in a sort of macho way."

"No doubt. He's also a Russian."

Evelyn smiled with condescension. "You really must keep up with the times, my dear. The Cold War is all but over. The Russians are now good capitalists or trying very hard to become so. Really. I read it in *The Times*, so it must be true."

"I wouldn't believe everything I read in *The Times* if I were you. The memories are quite vivid, and the jury is out as to how much real change is taking place over there. Regardless, they are still our adversary until long-term events indicate otherwise. Surely you can see that."

"I see no such thing. You and your crowd are a bunch of paranoids, if you ask me."

"It isn't just that he's a Russian. You've also been very indiscreet."

She laughed. "Indiscretion is the spice of life."

"Your indiscretion could ruin my business and the lifestyle you are accustomed to."

Her eyes narrowed. "Christian, what the hell do you care? Would you like to tell me about that Wop whore you keep on the side?"

"And when have we ever been seen in public together?"

"I'm sure I could come up with a time or two."

"And if you did, we would have been in a part of town neither you nor I frequent, and in some out-of-the-way place. These flukes will happen, and you and I both understand that. You've gone well beyond browsing an antique store with your Ivan. And you know it."

"Are you looking for a row? I just might be in the mood to give you one."

"You've placed me in a most awkward position. But that isn't the worst of it." Christian explained that he feared a very negative article about him and IMSS was about to run in The Times. The JIC, prodded by the CIA, was up to something. "They might very well be out to destroy me. You know how it's done. We've all seen it happen to others in the past."

"Not that it really matters, but how did you find out about Alexei and me?"

"A little bird told me."

Evelyn laughed out loud. "A little bird from Sicily who works in the Foreign Office, no doubt."

"She comes from Naples, not Sicily."

"Oh! I took her for one of those Cosa Nostra types."

Evelyn was in full bore now. "What is this all about Christian? It can't be about your country, certainly not the world. It's about Christian Hardaway, Lord of the bloody Realm if he were man enough, but for now just head of daddy's little company, selling joy buzzers and pocket radios to the Bedouins or Cossacks or some such, and now he's afraid he will lose his little company because his wife is indiscreet?"

Christian looked straight into Evelyn's eyes and asked, "Are you going to help me or not?"

Evelyn was suddenly still, and for the first time in years appeared sobered by something he'd said. Well, he thought, that's understandable. Destroying me means an end to this comfortable life I've given her. "What have you done?" she asked.

Now that was more like her. "Nothing of which I'm aware."

"Oh, come on," she said with venom. "These things don't just happen."

"You're right there. But it isn't because of any misstep on my part that I can see. It will take me time to learn who's behind this. But if what I suspect is true, by then it won't matter because the wheels of destruction will be well in motion. Nothing will be the same, even if I find a way to stop it midstream."

"I don't understand why you can't stop it. Surely you know where enough bodies are buried, literally as well as figuratively. You should. You've put enough of them there personally."

"That's what I've always thought. But indications are I'm mistaken."

Evelyn sat frozen. It was so quiet he could hear the grandfather clock counting seconds even through the door to his office. "You're a shit, you know that? Everyone says so. You've gone astray and haven't the balls to own up to it, have you?"

"You're mistaken."

She eyed him steadily. "Not on your life, Christian. Never about you."

"I need you to drop your Ivan."

"Go to hell!"

"It may be that the attack will initially be against something the company's done. I don't know everything we do. Or it might be against me personally. Regardless, we've both seen how these things are done. It *will* turn to our private lives; you can depend on it. And an excellent morsel for our salivating press would be the affair my wife is having with a Soviet spy."

"Who gives a damn? It's nothing, Christian. You make too much of it."

"It may be too late already, but at least break it off now, for at least a while. We must appear to be the perfectly settled couple, without hint of scandal of any kind." If Evvy really was going to help, and it certainly was in her interest to do so, perhaps that would do the trick. "I'm going to the office now. Perhaps I'm in a pessimistic mood, and it's not too late."

As Christian left and Evelyn watched his car race off, she picked up the telephone. After a moment, she said, "Just confirming two o'clock then. I'm positively gushing." She listened and then laughed in her deep throaty way. "Why not? You know I'm game for almost anything. I've got some perfectly delicious news for you."

* * *

Pauline Miller, Christian's personal secretary, was already at the office when he arrived, which came as no surprise. Of his eight-hundred-odd employees, perhaps a hundred were scattered through the building at this early hour. Bright, well educated, and stunning, Pauline was in her early thirties and had come to him from the Ministry of Defense, highly recommended by a member of Parliament well known to Christian. She was usually one of the first at her desk in the morning and one of the last to leave at night.

Though her dedication to the job was without question, as she worked most Saturdays and usually took work home on top of it, she was unhappily married to a real estate agent and, Christian believed, used work to escape the marriage. She was so good at her job he had never once even considered making a pass, though she had in her discreet way sent signals she was available to him. Tempted though he was, a lover he could always find, a devoted, competent assistant, especially one nice to look at, was a rare gem.

Pauline brought him coffee, and they discussed the projects on which she was working, but she understood at once that he was distracted. "I'll stay out of your way today," she said as she left his office. "If you need anything, just let me know."

Christian worked the telephone himself, but the day proved fruitless. No one who could be of any possible help could be reached, neither at work nor on their car phones. By noon, Christian knew what was coming. He made his way to a pub on the East End he frequented when slumming as a university student and drank methodically all afternoon and well into the night.

After midnight, the first editions of *The Times* appeared on the street. Glancing at the article on the front page, below the fold, Christian felt as if he'd been kicked in the stomach.

A taxi driver found Hannah's apartment for him. He staggered up the steps from the street and was still leaning on the doorbell when she opened the door in a nightgown. "My God, Christian! You look a mess. Come in, come in."

"Look what they wrote," he slurred, trying to thrust the newspaper into her hands.

"I've read it. It was faxed to me last night. Come on. Lay down." She helped him as far as the sofa, where he collapsed and was soon snoring lightly. She pulled off his shoes and loosened his belt. She took a pillow and blanket, placed the pillow gently under his head, then covered him. "Poor baby," she said softly and then lay down beside him, smelling the scotch and sweat. Towards dawn, she fell asleep.

CHAPTER SEVEN

1991
Day Five
London

It was almost noon when Christian stirred, and by then, Hannah had been up for some time. She'd never acquired the English habit of morning tea and preferred her coffee very strong. Her copy of *The Times* had arrived earlier, and she spread it on her kitchen table as she drank coffee and ate toast. She took the time to reread the article and consider it as so many others would.

Christian showered at length, forcing himself to stand under cold water at the finish. Hannah was ready with the coffee as he stepped out of the shower. He dressed, then joined her in the kitchen, where he managed one piece of toast. His stomach churned but he held it down and had another.

"Did you leave any scotch for the rest of us?" she asked lightly.

"I don't think so. Not in the East End, at least." He suppressed another heave.

"It's there if you want to read it sober. I almost lost my breakfast, too, so I'm cautioning you." Christian looked down and read.

BRITISH EXPORT FIRM ACCUSED
By Tim Barclay

H.M. Customs and Excise investigators have uncovered evidence that a leading British export firm, International Military Support Services Ltd., has systematically violated export laws and jeopardized national security for a period of some years.

"This is the most egregious abuse of the public trust in my memory," said Home Secretary Peter Wright late Friday.

Reliable sources, which asked to remain unnamed, report that IMSS shipped classified electronic time clocks through its French subsidiary to Saudi Arabian business interests. Such clocks are commonly used as explosive switches. One of these devices was discovered in the wreckage of Pan Am Flight 103, which exploded midair over Lockerbie in December 1988, killing 270. More of the switches have turned up in several recent terrorist attacks, according to Israeli security sources.

CEO and managing director of IMSS is Christian Hardaway, son of company founder Julian Hardaway, formerly the earl of Carlisle, who made history by disclaiming his title. The senior Hardaway was a widely respected counter-intelligence agent with the Security Service during World War II.

His company was the first British export firm licensed to sell goods behind the Iron Curtain. The founder was murdered in Warsaw in 1973 under circumstances never fully explained.

"For many years, IMSS was a respected and reliable supplier to the British and other governments," the home secretary said. "But it seems that recently it has turned into a supplier for terrorists."

Investigators report uncovering evidence the company repeatedly violated British export law over the last 20 years by providing militarily sensitive devices to the Soviet Union and other proscribed countries.

There was more, much more, and all of it bad, the worse being that a criminal investigation was underway.

"What are you going to do?" Hannah asked gently once Christian lay the newspaper down.

"I don't know what I can do at this point. Find out what's happened, of course, not that it will put the genie back in the bottle. What I don't understand is how something like this can have caught me on the blindside."

"Yes, well, that's their preferred modus operandi, isn't it? Why should you be any different?"

"Because it's my business, dear. It's my bloody business to know."

"I've had all morning to consider this. What about Philips? Why didn't he know? He always seems to get wind of anything in the offing."

Christian's mind whirred. "I really don't know, Hannah," he said. "It's the sort of thing I would expect him to have a good handle on. Shit! Now the SIS will have something to celebrate."

"The SIS? Really?"

"Indirectly. Put it this way. Certain persons at SIS have wanted us out of the picture for decades."

"What are you going to do?" she asked again quietly.

"First, I'm going to reread the article. Then, when I feel a little better, I'm going to see if I can find who is behind this and I'm going to settle scores if that's all that's left to me. It will never do to let the parties' primarily responsible get away with it. And if it comes to charges, my position will be considerably improved for bargaining. They may get me—we'll have to see just how 'got' I am—but I'm not going down solo. The people behind this have forgotten I know so much."

"The man who knew *too* much," whispered Hannah. "Be careful, Christian, be careful. This would be a very convenient time for you to drop dead."

A few minutes later, Christian lifted the telephone and tried Philips's number again. Voicemail. He's in the Far East, somewhere, Christian recalled. Odd he hadn't learned of this; odder still he wasn't in town. Hannah was right. Philips should have known. And what a very inconvenient time to be in Asia instead of London putting out the fire.

Bangkok, Thailand

Raymond Philips, dressed in tan slacks and a crisp, long-sleeved white cotton shirt, sat in the bar of the Green Parrot just off Soi 33. Thailand. Before him perhaps thirty Western men were pawing Thai prostitutes, laughing uproariously at their own ribald jokes and downing chilled bottles of beer.

Philips raised his glass to his lips and took a sip of gin and tonic as he eyed the spectacle. He found it amazing how so many otherwise normal Brits and Aussies could conduct themselves like boorish teenage boys set free for the first time once they stepped off the plane in Bangkok. There was no doubt this was an exotic location. On his first trip here, a Brit he'd had a drink with had called it Venus compared to the West, which was, of course, Mars. But still...

In Philips's view, there were beautiful and available women in most every country. The fact that Thailand had turned their prostitutes and lower-class women into a national industry was no excuse for losing one's composure.

The Green Parrot was one of two dozen or more bars in this part of Bangkok. More upscale than the ones to be found on Soi Cowboy or Nana Plaza, they were still just meeting places where young women cajoled drinks out of men or persuaded them into paying their "bar fine," as the fee to take them off premises for sex was known. After that, there was any number of short-time hotels in the immediate vicinity.

The Green Parrot was loud, the laughter all but overwhelming the relentless throb of music coming from enormous speakers placed, it seemed to Philips, everywhere. He glanced at his wristwatch and was relieved to see it was nearly midnight. He wouldn't have to wait much longer.

Initially, several of the young women had approached him for company, but he had sternly turned them away and now was left alone. The women assumed he was a watcher, too embarrassed to join in the nightly debauchery. Given enough drinks and/or time, they were certain that would change. They'd seen it before. For now, there was plenty of other game on the dance floor. It was hot even though the Green Parrot was air-conditioned. Philips removed a clean handkerchief from his pocket and wiped his brow again. He finished his drink and gestured the boy behind the bar for another. The slender young Thai grinned as he presented the drink, and Philips considered it no accident when their fingers touched as he took the cold glass, a mist already forming on it.

"Am I interrupting?" Moussa Khaldun said, suddenly appearing beside Philips.

"Not at all. Just a bit of play. Let's take a seat at a table. Care for a drink?"

Khaldun ordered a scotch, and then the pair took one of the small open tables in the far corner. "Did you read the story?" Philips asked.

"What story?"

"The one in *The Times* about my company. I brought a copy." Philips handed it over.

Khaldun scanned it quickly as he sipped his drink. "I'd say he is ruined. He'll be lucky not to end up in prison. Are you behind this?"

How much to say? "Hardly. My plans were yet to be formed, though I do now see the opportunity of which we've spoken before. Are you in a position to help?"

"I admit I heard a bit about this from our American friends. I can make a few discreet calls. But don't assume this will be easy or that Christian will roll over and play dead," the Arab said. "This is the opening shot, not the ending broadside. This affair will continue for some weeks at the very least. Your 'boy,' as you call him, will put up a good fight. While it's true he has many enemies, he also has many, many friends, as well as those who are in debt to him." Khaldun leaned forward. "And he knows a lot of secrets. He's in as good a position to hurt others in power as anyone on earth. But you could be correct; this just might be the opportunity about which we have spoken previously. Now is the time for you to position yourself, I would think."

Major General Raymond Philips had not wanted to retire from the army five years previously, but having been passed over for further promotion, he had no alternative. In the dreary months leading up to the end of his military career, he had contemplated finding a similar position in the army or police forces of some tin pot dictator. Perhaps even a place within the security apparatus of any number of Middle Eastern or Asian nations. Men such as him were always in demand in the Crown colonies.

But he'd found the very thought of permanently leaving Britain to be more than he could bear. He still carried his dreams of eventual knighthood, perhaps even a place in the House of Lords, and there would be no chance for any of that in some dreadful, mosquito-infested backwater. The chief of staff had suggested a lunch with one of the senior officers at SIS, and there Philips had been approached about accepting an administrative position with IMSS. "We need good men there," he'd said. "Men loyal to queen and country, you understand?"

Philips had thought initially that the pay was excellent with enough travel to allow him the opportunity to "wet his stick," as he liked to put it, without repercussions. And as the true nature of IMSS became clear to him, he came to believe that, given time, a knighthood might yet be his.

Philips had never considered that he would so deeply resent taking orders from Christian Hardaway, from any civilian, for that matter. Unlike himself, "the boy"—as he thought of Christian—had been born to privilege and been handed his station in life on a silver platter. So a year earlier, when the emir's right-hand man had first approached him about meeting in far-off Bangkok for a personal friendly chat, Philips had done so.

He'd been surprised to learn how much he and Khaldun had in common. The Arab's taste was eclectic, running from young women to even younger boys. The women were readily available in Europe, but boys there were risky, while in Thailand they were a stock in trade. Philips had found himself in a form of carnal heaven during his first trip to meet with Khaldun. After a night of debauchery, they talked for hours.

"The emir is old and frail. When he dies, the new emir will throw me out with the trash," the Arab had told him. "I must make mine while I can."

"You're doing all right, it seems to me."

"Yes, all right, but I want to do much better than 'all right.'"

In time, Philips mentioned that he had aspirations of removing Christian from the helm of IMSS and taking it over for himself.

"Why would I assist you in that?" Khaldun had asked.

"Because you will be well taken care of. I'm prepared to be far more generous than the boy."

Removing Christian appealed enormously to Philips, who envisioned himself assuming command of a revitalized IMSS. With such an influential company, he would be in a position to perform the services and spread the wealth needed to earn his knighthood. Indeed, all things would be possible. And so, every scheme he'd pondered had been devised to undo Christian without destroying IMSS. In the end, though, he'd had no choice, and now the cat was out of the bag; there was a great possibility of both happening.

In the Green Parrot, Philips gestured for two more drinks. "You must try and influence events if at all possible. I still want the company. It is in both our interests for IMSS to survive. You and I will do very well indeed when I take over."

"I will do what I can, my friend. The Americans are so lacking in class. I don't like them one little bit and will be pleased to deal with an officer and a British gentleman like yourself—who understands the needs and requirements of his trading partners." Khaldun smiled.

CHAPTER EIGHT

1991
Day Five
London

Christian felt as if he had been beaten with lead-filled rubber hoses. He filled a cup with coffee, took a fresh packet of cigarettes, then walked slowly into Hannah's garden, where he sat on a stone bench smoking one cigarette after another.

Today his long family history weighed heavily on him. Christian recalled vividly that day at university when the senior Hardaway had come to recruit his only son into the family's secret world.

The year 1964 had been a watershed for Britain, for Christian, and, ultimately, for his father, Julian. Among other things, it was the year Concord Trading Company was transformed from a small export company, whose founder occasionally slipped nuggets of foreign intelligence to MI6, into a fully operational intelligence organization with the specific approval and support of key people in the government.

In Christian's case, the meeting and the change in the family company was pivotal because it was the end of his childhood, late as that was in coming, and the true beginning of his adult life. It was for him, personally, as significant a demarcation as the one historians once used for BC and AD.

Christian was twenty-three years old that day twenty-eight years ago, when his father had walked across the lawn at Lincoln Inns Fields and gestured for his son to join him at a park bench. Christian was attending the nearby London School of Economics, completing his graduate work, and often came here on Saturday afternoons to play a pick-up game of rugby. He left the rugby scrimmage and jogged casually over, quite surprised to see his father. He'd heard he was in Hungary and was expected to be gone the rest of the month. Julian Hardaway was forty-nine years old that day, just one year younger than Christian was now as he chain-smoked his way through the cigarettes, his thoughts buried deeply in the past.

The previous year, 1963, had represented a major change for Britain. War Minister John Profumo had resigned following a sex scandal and national security concerns, a disgraceful matter Christian and his classmates had followed with prurient interest, agreeing that both Christine Keeler and Mandy Rice-Davies were dishes. How they would have loved to join the girls in an orgy. Then Labour leader Hugh Gaitskell had died suddenly and unexpectedly, elevating the obscure and very left-leaning Harold Wilson to party leadership and to all but certain election as prime minister.

Not as publicized, but at the same time, Guy Burgess, one of the first three of the "Cambridge Three" to defect, had died in Moscow, reportedly of alcoholism. There had been an article in *The Daily Express* but little official notice of his passing until, shockingly, Kim Philby, once one of the most trusted operatives in British intelligence and the head of counter espionage operations for MI6, the spy-catcher department, had defected to the Soviet Union. While his wife waited for him at a dinner party, he'd simply walked in a heavy downpour to the dock in Beirut Harbor, Lebanon, and boarded a Polish cargo ship that immediately set sail for Odessa in Russia. The last of the three British intelligence traitors, Philby's defection had sent shock waves through the British government.

The "Cambridge Three" had conducted one of the most successful penetrations of any national intelligence service in history, betraying their nation for decades to the Soviet Union. Their crimes were all the worse because they came from the very best of families and had attended the finest schools. Their pedigree alone had protected them despite rising suspicion over the years; they were part of what the British like to call "The Establishment"—the ruling class—and were part of the famous "old boys" network of school chums that ran Whitehall and the British government.

What the CIA and others had claimed for years had become common knowledge. Russian penetration of the British elements of national security, as demonstrated by the "Cambridge Three", had been absolute. The CIA had been unwilling to fully share intelligence for some years because of this conviction, and the British could no longer plausibly deny it. Indeed, the British government was well aware that the Secret Intelligence Service still had Russian sympathizers in it and could not be trusted.

The nagging question, one that thankfully remained largely off the pages of the nation's newspapers, was just how far that Soviet penetration extended into British politics. Clearly, the Russian effort to subvert Britain had been massive. Why should it have stopped with intelligence agents? Hadn't Philby also been a respected reporter? How many others in the press were tainted? More importantly, how many *politicians* were secretly Soviet operatives? There were those in MI5 who believed that Harold Wilson himself was a Russian agent. Now he stood poised to grasp the pinnacle of British political power.

It was in such a climate that Christian's father came to visit. Julian Hardaway was not a handsome man by traditional standards, and a quite-distinctive scar slashed across his right cheek, giving him a swashbuckling look. There was, however, a powerful magnetism about him that people found all but irresistible. He possessed a sardonic sense of humor and had a way of cocking an eyebrow when poking fun. He was self-possessed and reflective in his actions almost to a fault. Just over six feet tall, he had remained fit though not obsessively so. As viscount, he was at that time still heir to the title Earl of Carlisle and would someday sit in the House of Lords, if events were permitted to take their natural course. But there was no knowing it from his manner, and he chaffed at the slightest hint of deference from anyone. His decision to relinquish the title was not yet made, but the path of his life that led to that decision had long been set.

Julian smoked a pipe and could often be seen cleaning it, refilling it, or endlessly relighting it. As father and son sat on a wooden bench, he dug his pipe from a pocket, scooped a special blend of tobacco into it, then puffed away as he lit the thing. He slipped the tobacco pouch into the pocket of his jacket and took in the landscape around them with obvious pleasure as the immediate air filled with the sweet aroma of the pipe smoke.

"This brings back memories," he mused.

"I didn't know you ever scrummed here," Christian said.

"A time or two. I hope you've enjoyed LSE."

"I suppose. Much of it's a bore, but I enjoy the atmosphere here far more than I would have Oxford or Cambridge."

"Much of life's a bore, Christian, if you let it be. Have you been following current events?"

By "events," there was no doubt what his father meant. Though Christian was not part of his world, Julian had made it a point to routinely discuss with him the politics and economics of the family business. Christian had never considered otherwise than that he was being groomed to join the company, or take it over in time, as both his formal and informal education had been pointed that way.

"It's time I discussed certain matters in confidence with you, Christian. You know the saying, 'Two men can keep a secret if one of them is dead'?"

"Yes, sir."

"There's another. If a father can't trust his son, whom can he trust? What do you think of our soon-to-be prime minister, Harold Wilson?"

Christian shrugged. "I don't know much about him. He seems to have come out of nowhere. A little too far to the left for my liking, though."

Julian grunted, and then said, "Hugh Gaitskell was party leader and should have been in line to be PM right now. Do you have an opinion about his death?"

"I don't know any more than what was in the papers. Sudden, very sudden."

"If I told you Wilson was a Communist, or so close that the difference is meaningless, what would you then think of Gaitskell's 'sudden' death'?"

"Extraordinarily convenient for the Communists and the Soviets, I'd say. *Are* you saying there's something there?"

Julian didn't answer, saying instead, "Our Russian friends had one of their men very near the top in British intelligence; they could exclude or feed information into the intelligence chain as they wished. Then that fool Profumo forced an election and made a Labour victory certain. Whoever led the Labour Party was going to be the next prime minister. It was more than they could resist. Poor old Hugh."

"They killed him? The Russians did?"

His father nodded his head. "Oh, yes. It will never be public knowledge. Our new PM will see to that."

"Do you know who did it?"

Julian puffed at his pipe, but it had already gone out. As he reached for a lighter, he said, "I believe so, and I must say, I'm shocked to think I might be right. When are you due to finish your studies here?"

"The autumn term has just begun. I'll be done by Christmas, sir."

"I need you to join the company, Christian. I can't wait until then. Events are moving very rapidly."

Christian avoided his father's eyes before speaking. "I don't know what to say."

"Say nothing. Listen for a few moments." In the distance, Christian's friends called out to him, and he shouted back that he wouldn't be rejoining the game.

"Richard Butler has asked that I reconstitute Concord Trading Company to perform an ad hoc intelligence function." Butler was the outgoing foreign secretary. "It must be accomplished before the election."

"What about British intelligence? Why would you be asked to do their job?"

"Penetrated through and through."

"Won't the new government do the same to Concord, or undo what Butler does?"

Julian paused before saying, very quietly, "It won't know."

Christian wrinkled his brow. "I don't see how that's possible."

"Anything in this world is possible, and at some point, probable. There are patriots within the Civil Service, even men I can trust in MI6. I'll report to one of them, most likely to the coordinator of defense intelligence and security. There's enough dirt on Wilson and the ministers he will appoint to keep the coordinator on. He will, of course, not pass anything up the chain to the Foreign Office and will use the information in such a way as to mask from where it has come."

"I don't see how much different that is from what you've been doing, as I understand it."

Julian smiled thinly. "The coordinator will see to it that certain trusted retiring military officers find their way into my employ and the business receives some decent-sized contracts, located, naturally, in countries from where they most critically require intelligence. Still, the number of people who can be trusted with the complete picture is extremely limited." He paused. "And it includes you. Which is why you must drop your studies and join the company at once." Christian was more puzzled then opposed to the idea and didn't respond. "Son, just as the Civil Service sees that the government runs day to day no matter what idiot is PM, there has always existed a core of British patriots who have, in their way, seen to our nation's security. This is nothing more than a continuation of that tradition, one to which you and I are duty bound.

"The company will prosper as never before. You'll be well compensated, both financially and spiritually. You'll find that being truly on the inside, knowing what is really what, can be very intoxicating. Most of all, I need you. You mustn't turn me down."

"No, sir, I wouldn't think of it. When do I start?"

Julian smiled broadly. "Monday, nine sharp. I've already bought you a coming onboard present. Take a taxi to work. You'll find it in your new parking place next to mine. Please try not to wreck it, at least not in the first week."

And so it had begun.

The next nine years had been, unquestionably, the most exhilarating Christian could have imagined, marred only by the single misstep of his marriage to Evelyn.

"Are you all right, dear?" Hannah asked, joining him outside and breaking his reverie.

"You're looking very preoccupied."

"Just lost in thought. Anything to keep my mind off how terrible I feel. I've managed to hold down some coffee. A fresh cup of coffee would be very nice." Hannah rose, filled his cup, placed it on the table, then turned to the kitchen to make more toast and to leave Christian to his thoughts again.

Julian Hardaway had been a remarkable man, and perhaps the greatest gift he had given his talented son was personal confidence. "We are all strong in one way, less so in another," he would say. "Despite what the world thinks, no son walks in his father's footsteps except by choice. You're your own man. First and always. I'd have it no other way."

Julian, the accomplished Cold War warrior, vanished for weeks at a time behind the Iron Curtain, doing business, courting the money-grubbing Communists he'd identified, doing favors, gathering information as he went. Others in the CTC performed very similar work at various levels with different people. It was a dangerous world in which he moved. He excelled so incredibly at it that it seemed to Christian he could never fail. Over the years, Christian, too, traveled increasingly, not as an operative, which in effect was the role his father served, but as a businessman. Still, certain close and personal contacts with the underbelly of espionage were inevitable.

So it was that in 1973, on the eve of his son's unexpectedly early birth, Christian was committed to a trip to Warsaw to sign a long-term supply contract for transistors and other electronic components. Evelyn had not wanted to be pregnant, and it had taken substantial bribes by Christian to persuade her not to have an abortion. With the hour of birth so near, she was insistent that Christian remain with her. He had told his father of his problem.

"I'm taking the trip," Julian had said. "You should be here in any case. The happiest day of my life was when you were born. Bombs falling, your mother screaming like a banshee, then you popped out, wet, pink, and ugly. What a glorious night! I'll go."

"It's my trip. I'll be back before the baby comes."

"No point in pressing it. And anyway, Mishka called and asked for me to make it."

"He has? When was that?"

"Last night, by telephone. I'm going. He said it's urgent. He says there is something coming up that will require our attention. You see to your wife and child. I'll see to Mishka. It's been a while."

Four days later, just a few hours after he watched in horror as his stillborn son emerged from Evelyn, Christian received word his father had been murdered in a Warsaw brothel. All he could think then, all he could think now, as Hannah placed a plate of eggs in front of him, was the thought that it was him they really wanted to kill, and his father had taken his place. Over the years, as he gained no understanding of what had actually happened and why, his guilt was slowly replaced by a need for revenge. Someday, he would have his answers, and when he did, those responsible would die.

CHAPTER NINE

1940
London

Boom! A bomb landed on the street not far away. Julian felt the ground shake under his feet as East Enders died.

He had listened to the steady drone of the German bombers closing on the city; the nearly steady distant thud, thud, thud of the anti-aircraft ack-ack could be heard. This night was to be a one, two punch. The Blitz, as the newspapers called this slaughter of civilians by the German Luftwaffe, had begun the previous September, just as the Battle of Britain came to an end. At this point in the war, the only original thinking was in the catch phrases streaming almost daily out of the Ministry of Information. Former Prime Minister Neville Chamberlain had had nothing to offer his country and spent his final days at Number 10 Downing Street chain smoking, wondering why "Herr Hitler," as he called the Nazi dictator, had lied to him at their meeting in Munich.

More than 300 German bombers joined by some 600 Luftwaffe fighters made the regular night flight across the Channel from bases in occupied France. The darkened city was nothing like its pre-war self, with sand bags piled high at some point on nearly every block and barrage balloons floating overhead, keeping the island from sinking beneath its weight of war material, it was joked.

On many nights, Julian had gone to the roof of his London house to witness the spectacle. First, there was the sound of the air raid sirens, directing everyone to take cover. Then the whistles of the Home Guard and air raid wardens directing Londoners into shelters. Nearly 200,000 Londoners alone were temporarily housed in the miles of underground railway tunnels during the air raids.

Next came the drone of the bombers, distant at first, then growing louder. Almost at once, powerful searchlights played across the night sky, searching for the enemy planes. From high above came the sound of exploding ack-ack followed soon by tracers arcing up gracefully. When the lights found a bomber, others fixed it in their glare and both ack-ack and fighters were drawn to the doomed craft and crew. Then the night was filled with sounds of exploding bombs, usually along the Thames near the docks, but not always.

As the last of a relentless string of German bombs exploded, Julian quickly crossed the street to the hospital's maternity ward. He'd been taken away from his vigil briefly and didn't want to miss the moment. He heard the glass shattering and falling from a nearby window and then the loud clatter as it struck the street all about him. He instinctively pulled away, covering himself as best he could with his arms and hands. Charing Cross Hospital trembled, as if struck by an enormous blow, although the nurses and doctor on the other side of the pane of glass behaved as if nothing out of the ordinary had occurred.

Julian straightened, the air suddenly calm. He entered the hospital and went straight to the maternity ward, but was stopped at once by a nurse. "Sir, you've been injured."

Only then did he realize that something wet was dripping from his face. When he touched his cheek, his fingers came away red with blood. "My son is being born just now," he said.

"I see. At least let me bandage it for now. A doctor can check it for stitches later." She smiled and sat him down as she quickly tended to the gash.

Julian had asked to be present in the delivery room, but hospital rules flatly prohibited his presence. They'd turned the simple delivery of a baby into a major medical procedure, Julian considered, as if women haven't given birth for thousands of years without their ministrations. After all, in the rice paddies of China, women gave birth in the morning and were picking rice again by teatime. Julian almost caught himself smiling at the mental image of his wife Sarah in a rice field. Most of what was called "modern medicine" was, in his opinion, so much hocus-pocus.

As he neared the maternity ward, he heard another string of bombs strike the city. He thought of the people who were dying while he was waiting for a child to be born. His child. A child entering the world in the midst of the horrors of war.

He stood watching through a glass partition as nurses and the doctor dressed in white fussed around the five or six newborn babies behind the panel, which had crisscrosses of adhesive tape in case of breakage. Sarah had already been wheeled into one of the delivery rooms off to the side. A team effort, he mused; it took two of us to create a baby and it takes four to deliver it.

Sarah had been in labor for more than twenty-four hours and had been exhausted even before they'd wheeled her into the delivery room. The birth of the future Earl of Carlisle was of sufficient note that Lord Hardaway himself, Julian's father, had dropped by twice, asking if it was to be a boy or a girl, unwilling to accept the reality that no one would know until the moment of birth.

"Think positive, old boy," his father had said to Julian.

Julian had been quite surprised at the unexpected emotions he experienced during these interminable hours. He had thought about the love between himself and Sarah. Close as they were, he'd assumed that the heat of passion was behind them.

There had, in his opinion, been nothing maternal about his wife in any way, yet from the moment she'd learned she was pregnant she had taken on a new persona. She'd stopped smoking, given up alcohol save for an infrequent glass of sherry, and in the last few months, had stopped riding with the hounds, and now had shown as much courage and tenacity in this most difficult delivery as any soldier in the field.

Julian didn't care one jot about carrying on the family title, considering it an anachronism in the modern world, something well done with, but he felt a surprisingly powerful stir within him for continuity, to know that some portion of him would remain once he was gone. For the first time in many years, Julian felt he understood his father just a bit. Not the cold aloof aristocrat, but the head of the household—any household—looking down the line of succession and wanting to see his seed continue to flourish. Nothing wrong with that, he thought, in fact quite admirable.

On that day, Julian Hardaway was twenty-six years old, and as the wet, pink infant was revealed to him by a nurse, he felt for the first time as if he was truly a man. How primitive, he thought wryly.

"It's an 'ealthy boy, m'lord," the nurse said in a bright Cockney accent with obvious delight before hurrying back into the delivery ward. Julian sometimes wondered who needed the aristocracy more: the lords themselves with all their airs and pretenses, or the commoners, eager to curry favor, dip their heads, and have someone to look up to.

A son! Julian was thrilled. The other fathers gathered around to congratulate him, forgetting for a moment that they were in the presence of nobility while they clapped him on the back and shook his hand with their work-worn hands.

A series of distant explosions, like dull thuds, resounded through the corridors of the hospital. The docks are taking a real beating tonight, he thought. He wondered idly just how long the Germans were prepared to keep this up, how long they were willing to sustain the losses in aircraft that this pounding of London was costing them.

Prime Minister Winston Churchill, a politician with a gift for elegantly crafted phrases, periodically ordered the bombing of Berlin and other German cities to keep Hitler in an agitated state. The Nazi leader had tossed away his chance to subdue Britain when he'd abandoned his battle against the RAF and switched to bombing the cities, most especially London. In Julian's opinion, Churchill was a wily old goat who understood Hitler better than anyone in government. Much as Churchill had hated to order the bombing of civilian targets, he had realized that the British would not respond well if retribution was not visited upon the German people. The attacks had the bonus of turning the Luftwaffe away from its campaign against the RAF to these attacks on cities, which would not win them the war.

Julian went to the nearest telephone to advise Lord Hardaway that a son and heir had been born. Lord Hardaway sat in his usual overstuffed armchair at the Athenaeum Gentleman's Club where he spent most of his evenings. They spoke briefly, but the approval in Lord Hardaway's voice could not have been more apparent, as the earl who had never whispered in his life proclaimed in full voice, "Wonderful news, dear boy! A boy! The dynasty is safe!"

He and Sarah had already decided that if a son were born, he would be named after Julian's grandfather. He had fond memories of the old rascal and his almost treasonous views of British society. A lieutenant general in the Coldstream Guards, ferocious in battle during the First World War, he was one of the few British generals who actually tried to avoid casualties to his men.

God preserve anyone who used the expression "cannon fodder" in his presence. It was a shame that the old scoundrel could not be around for the birth of his great grandson.

A hand touched his shoulder. It was a doctor. "Let me look at that." He removed the bandage, glanced at the wound, then replaced it. "No stitches, I think. You will have a deep scar, however. Better than I can say for some tonight." With that, he left.

For all Julian's love and respect for his wife on that night, little actually changed in the marriage once Sarah and the baby Christian were home. She was occupied with the running of the estate as well as with supervising nanny and her helpers taking care of the baby. There was always plenty to do.

Lord Hardaway had insisted they reside at the family estate in Newbury Berkshire, in part to escape the dangers of central London and Nazi bombs, but primarily to allow him the opportunity to beam down at his infant grandson several times a day when the House of Lords was not in session.

Julian took the train home on most weekends, but until recently spent his weekdays in the city at his flat in Dolphin Square. It was a flat that happily Sarah hated, as it was a remnant of Julian's rambunctious bachelor days, too small and too cramped, yet located a stroll from the House of Lords where one day Julian was expected to sit in place of his father. Easy access to the City of London as well as the City of Westminster made this the perfect London residence.

The family home in Chelsea stood unoccupied due to the war. Servants were increasingly hard to find, and that house required at least six to be comfortable. In Dolphin Square, Julian could manage with Mrs. Kench, his housekeeper and cook. The discreet Mrs. Kench had known Julian since he was a toddler and had assisted in the kitchens of Lord Hardaway's estate. Her devotion to the "young lord," as she called Julian, was absolute. With his most recent mistress gone, Julian was lonely in his flat. Mrs. Kench had never approved of Julian's infidelities but had also always kept her knowledge of his various mistresses to herself.

Julian Hardaway, as the future Earl of Carlisle, was viewed in social circles as something of a genius stricken with a certain archaic, though now quite fashionable, streak of patriotism. His formal education, first at Harrow Public School and later at Trinity College Cambridge, where he studied Russian literature and German, taken with his extensive family ties, brought him into contact, and friendship, with the finest of British society.

Long before attending Trinity College, however, Julian found himself at odds with his social equals. The airs and graces of the inherited and often titled class disturbed him deeply. He had watched his classmate's abuse servants and mock workers. He had come to share the view that Britain would be better off without class distinctions, to the extent human nature made that possible.

At the same time, he felt a powerful stir within himself for continuity, for the knowledge that some portion of him would remain after he was gone. This stir persisted into adulthood and was stronger than ever in the present day. It overwhelmed the misgivings he had about his father's stubborn class snobbery and made him feel deeply bonded to the man. So Julian had posed the question to himself: Will I renounce the title when my father dies? He admitted that even he did not know the answer to that question yet.

While at Trinity College, Julian had met a charming young man named Roger Hollis at a College Sherry evening. Though ten years his senior, the pair soon became fast friends, with Hollis serving the role of mentor and Julian often acting as his research assistant. As the clouds of war had gathered over Europe, then finally rolled across Poland, Julian considered joining his father's old regiment, where he would be destined for staff work. But in October 1939, before he had acted, he received a short note from Hollis asking him to meet for lunch at his club, The Carlton.

The taxi dropped Julian off outside The Carlton in St. James's Street, a stone's throw from Piccadilly at one end and Kensington Palace at the other end. He skipped up the four stone steps but before he could touch the door, one of the uniformed porters opened it.

"Hello, I'm here to meet Mr. Hollis," said Julian.

The porter looked him up and down somewhat in the manner of a sergeant major addressing an officer cadet, then said, "I don't believe he is here, sir."

"That's odd. I have a lunch appointment with him."

The porter's manner changed entirely. "Oh, in that case, I will look for him, sir."

In a few moments, the porter returned and ushered Julian to Hollis. As they climbed the elegant curved staircase, Julian glanced at the oil paintings of former prime ministers of Great Britain adorning the walls, and felt himself sinking into the deep plush carpet. The porter opened the double doors leading to the sitting room and led the way to the large armchair in which Roger Hollis was just putting down *The Times*.

"A visitor for you, sir." The porter bowed, then almost floated out of the room, leaving Julian standing in front of Hollis.

"Good of you to come," Hollis said as he shook Julian's hand with a warm smile. Julian joined Hollis in the comfort of a leather armchair just beyond the circle of similar ones near a fireplace.

Julian ordered a glass of port and accepted the Cuban cigar extended by his friend. Once he was well lit and comfortable, Hollis, as was his nature, got right to the point. "Well, old boy, what will you be doing this fine war?" he asked with a roguish smile.

"I haven't decided, Roger. The army, I suppose. Diggs—you remember him, don't you?—is a half-colonel in the Coldstream and has offered me a place on the general staff. It sounds very boring, but father wants me to take his place with the regiment. What I'd really like is something a bit more glamorous, perhaps the commandos, or something like that."

Hollis regarded his cigar tip momentarily, then said, "I'd hardly call it glamorous, dear boy. Running around with bayonets, slashing throats and so on..."

Julian smiled, and before he could stop himself, found himself saying, "I would love to do what you do."

"Oh? And what is it I do?" smiled Hollis, exhaling as he spoke.

Julian hesitated and replied, "You know, old chap."

"Yes, *I* certainly know. What I'm asking is what *you* think you know."

Julian looked around to be certain no one was listening, leaned forward, and said, "Hush-hush work."

The British Security Service existed more as rumor than as fact. It had begun thirty years earlier, charged with determining the extent of German espionage and Fifth Column penetration of British naval ports. During the Great War, it effectively identified some thirty German spies and became part of the new Directorate of Military Intelligence, where it received the name by which it was best known, MI5. Since then, its role had been expanded to include the coordination of government policy with aliens and security measures at munitions plants. It also oversaw counter-espionage throughout the empire through its offspring, MI6. In short, Hollis was a spy, or to be more precise, a catcher of spies.

Hollis grunted and took a sip of port. "I suppose that's no great secret, but I appreciate your discretion in not having previously mentioned it. So you'd like to come aboard, would you? A bit more attractive than leading a bayonet charge?"

"Yes, very much." From the first, Julian had been filled with excitement at the life his older friend led. Hollis had quit Oxford to take a position with the British-American Tobacco Company and been dispatched to Shanghai. Julian found the mere thought of it exhilarating. Hollis's stories of the exotic city, of the spies hanging about in smoke-filled nightclubs, had been fascinating. Unfortunately, Hollis had contracted tuberculosis and was ordered to Switzerland for a cure. Instead of taking a long sea cruise, as might be expected, he'd elected to cross the Soviet Union by train, to see the "workers' paradise" firsthand. He was obviously impressed by the experience, though he was quick to point out the shortcomings he'd witnessed. He'd been invited to join the Intelligence Service not long after leaving the sanitarium. A born bureaucrat, Hollis had risen quickly as the small operation, just ten men at the start of the war, had been rapidly expanded.

It had been Hollis, who had recruited Julian into the Freemasons two years earlier, and Julian had patiently waited, he felt, these past weeks for the invitation to join the Security Service. He had felt that, similar to the Masons, one did not ask to join, one was invited. Asking to join was tantamount to being blackballed. But here he was, all but soliciting for the job.

"I suppose the chief could always use another good hand, especially one who speaks German and Russian as well as you do."

"I'd be very pleased at the opportunity. What exactly is it you do, if I may ask?"

"Of course you may ask, dear boy... but exactly what I do is something that I cannot tell you. I've the Russian desk, of course. Now, I've heard that there is a position coming up in the Russian section for which you're qualified, but I doubt you'll stay there long. We've few German speakers, you see. Our threat is the fascists, not our Communist allies."

"That's great! I'm your man. I won't let you down."

Hollis's lips curled in the faintest of smiles. "I've no doubt. No doubt at all, in that regard."

With such high expectations, it was somewhat of a letdown that Julian found the job anything but glamorous. His office at Wormwood Scrubs Prison was cramped and windowless. Because nearly everyone smoked, the air was filled with cigarette, pipe, and cigar smoke. Fortunately, as the Blitz began, most of the still-small staff had been relocated to Blenheim Palace outside London. Just weeks before the birth of his son, David Petrie was appointed director general and granted enough of a budget to allow the rapid expansion of the Intelligence Service.

The worst part of the job was that Julian wore the uniform of an army lieutenant, hardly the rank he would have enjoyed in his father's regiment, and was unable to say just what he was doing in the war effort, beyond that he worked in the Ministry of Defense library. There were those who opined that the lord's son had got a safe and cushy number at home, while the workers of the British Isles died overseas. He accepted that as the price he must pay.

With Sarah and Christian safe at the estate in Hertfordshire, Julian began staying at his London flat in Dolphin Square. The city had been transformed by the near-nightly German bombing, though the first casualties had been caused by the blackout. The tail and headlights of cars were all but extinguished, and for reasons that escaped Julian, drivers raced through the black streets as if no one else was about. Many pedestrians had been struck, and there had been horrific accidents at intersections. Now speed restrictions were rigorously enforced, and lines of lorries, each with its nose pressed nearly against the rear of the other, traversed the city like long twisting snakes.

Hollis had been correct, as he usually seemed to be. Julian spent very little time on Russian matters. The director of MI5 had seen his talents almost at once and assigned him to interview shot-down German aircrew to gather intelligence information. Some weeks later, Julian filed a report with the director advising him that the morale of the German pilots and crew was being severely tested by the extended bombing campaign against Britain. Prisoners reported the German air force was suffering heavy losses to no effect that they could see. German aircrews were experiencing battle fatigue after more than six months of nearly daily action.

Petrie had been delighted at the report, since it confirmed what the Air Ministry wanted to hear. While the RAF pilots—with help from the free Poles, free French, plus a smattering of Canadian and American pilots—were likewise exhausted, their morale was at an all-time high. Against all odds, they'd stemmed the tide of invasion and were inflicting disproportionate losses on the enemy. And when they bailed out of a plane, they were more often than not greeted by a grateful farmer and a cuppa, while the Germans found themselves prisoners facing the wrong end of a pitchfork.

At about this time, Hollis invited Julian to join him for dinner at his club. "There's a chap you should meet," he said through the thick cloud of smoke that perpetually hung in his office like a low cloud.

The club had not yet been reduced to serving Spam, that strange American invention that had quickly become an unfortunate staple in every London home, but the nightly supper was noticeably diminished in variety. When Julian arrived, he was shown to a discreet table in the corner where Hollis sat with two men.

"Dear boy," Hollis said with a warm smile as he rose, "allow me to introduce Guy Burgess and Kim Philby. I don't believe you've met previously."

Julian smiled at the pair and shook hands. He knew both of the men by reputation and was not surprised in the least that they were acquaintances of Hollis, who always seemed to know everyone. Burgess was, as they say, well into his cups, though that wasn't readily apparent until he spoke. He was about thirty and unusually handsome. He had been four years ahead of Julian at Trinity College, but even so, he had heard reports of the man's intellect and charm. One professor had referred to Burgess as "the most brilliant young talent of the day." Philby was the same age, definitely not as handsome but considerably more sober, or perhaps holding his liquor better as a good journalist indeed should.

"I've read Mr. Philby's byline, of course. Those were wonderful reports from Spain. It must have been very exciting."

Philby nodded politely and said, "Those days seem quite naive now, don't they?"

Burgess leaned forward on the table, screwed a cigarette into his lips, and said, "Perhaps you heard my interview with Kim on the BBC?" He lit the cigarette with a lighter that seemed closer to a flamethrower than a device for lighting cigarettes; he then leaned back in his chair as if to await an answer.

"I'm sorry, but if I did I don't recall."

Burgess shrugged the matter off as one of no concern. Julian knew that Philby was now working with MI6, the Secret Intelligence Service. He'd instructed agents in black propaganda and was now moving into counter-espionage with some success, it was said.

Burgess, meanwhile, was one of the senior agents in MI5, whose job was to acquire intelligence. In his present drunken state, it seemed as if it would be impossible for Burgess to acquire the time of day, and Julian asked if his job was onerous.

Burgess dismissed the matter with a casual wave of his hand, then spoke in precise though slurred words. "My job is to save this country, old boy—nothing more, nothing less. Why is my glass suddenly dry?"

As dinner arrived, Burgess rose and made his excuses. "Must leave. Sorry about that." He slid around the small room towards Julian, took his hand possessively, and said, "A delight to meet you. We must spend some time together. Give me a call, won't you?" He met Julian's eye and held his gaze for far too long, in what he could only take as a sexual invitation, then slowly released his hand and with a wave to the others left.

As dinner progressed—it was some sort of shepherd's pie, Julian noticed—Hollis said, "Kim and I've been working together a bit lately. Tell him, won't you?"

Philby shrugged and lit a cigarette between bites. "Nothing special. I've been putting our people in touch with the Sandor Rado group in Switzerland. You've heard of them?"

Julian had in passing and was surprised Philby would mention the subject in public, but then from the first he'd been shocked at the casual manner in which matters of national importance were discussed in MI5. Why should MI6 be any different? Sandor Rado was a Russian spy operation that, rumor held, was in a position to pass along important information about the Germans.

"It's really not all that different from civilian life," Philby said, continuing. "It's all a question of knowing the right people and introducing those who should be introduced." He picked at his pie, stirred it a bit, then devoted his attention to his string of cigarettes and drink.

The rest of the evening passed mostly with talk between Hollis and Philby, talk Julian thought should have taken place in a secure office. It was, nonetheless, fascinating. Philby was clearly brilliant and had an excellent memory for past conversation and detail. Julian felt honored to be in the same company and service as such men.

* * *

With the end of the Blitz that spring, as Hitler prepared to invade Russia, though they didn't know that yet, Julian was given a new assignment. Since before the war, MI5 had been compiling a list of suspected German agents. These had been arrested with the start of hostilities. Rumor had it that while some had been hanged, many had been convinced to turn against the Nazis, their arrest kept secret, and that they were now sending false information back to Germany under the promise of their lives being spared.

Only when he was recruited to work in Operation Double Cross did Julian know for a fact of its existence. The Germans continued parachuting agents into Britain throughout the war, and Julian was now one of those responsible for catching and turning them. He enjoyed the cat and mouse game of the interrogations, though he understood that once a German agent was faced with the choice of a noose or cooperation, the outcome was usually pretty well predetermined. Few seemed excited at the prospect of a posthumous Iron Cross.

In the meantime, young Christian thrived in Hertfordshire; with its vast expanse of carpeted lawn and cultivated trees, Julian considered this as the best home for a very young child, one not yet aware of the nature of the world into which he'd been born. Julian's increasingly responsible work kept him in London, though at least twice a month he joined his son for a weekend, and he came to relish these trips greatly.

By this time, Hitler had launched his new terror weapon against London, the V1 rocket. The flying bomb would appear over the city, then plunge to the earth when it ran out of fuel, destroying whatever it struck.

"How arbitrary it's all been," Julian had mused, lighting his pipe as he'd witnessed the first such devastation. "A puff of wind and the flying bomb would have gone a bit further, a headwind and it would not have gone as far, a pint more or less of fuel and the bomb would have dropped somewhere else, and it would have been someone else's time to die."

It was the very capriciousness of the unmanned flying bomb, the Doodlebug as it was unofficially known, which made them such a devastating weapon in Hitler's arsenal. No predefined target, just fly until their fuel ran out and drop down onto whatever, or whoever, had the misfortune to be below.

One day, out of the blue, Julian was summoned to a private meeting with Anthony Eden, secretary of state for the Foreign and Commonwealth Office in Churchill's cabinet. At forty-six, Eden was the most influential member of the war cabinet. A veteran of the Great War, he'd attended Oxford, where he'd studied Persian and Arabic. Afterwards, he'd pursued a career in politics and been elected a Conservative MP. On the fast track, he'd been appointed foreign secretary while not yet forty but had resigned in 1938 in protest of Chamberlain's appeasement policies, an act that had caught Churchill's eye. He'd held his current post since Churchill had become PM and, it was said, Churchill so valued his advice he'd asked the king to appoint him prime minister in the event of his sudden death.

Julian had risen to the head of his section by this time and was now one of three coordinators providing misleading and false information to the Germans through Britain's supply of turned spies. Their most successful operation had been convincing Hitler that the allied landings at Normandy were feints, that the true landing would take place at the Paix de Calais days later, exactly where Hitler had been encouraged to believe it would come. It had been a master intelligence coup, providing the German's with key information just hours after it did them no good but convincing them that what they were hearing was absolutely reliable. In its own way, it had been as responsible for the success of the landings as all the planes, ships, and brave boys had been.

In response to his summons, Julian walked from his office to the Foreign Office, which was just across from 10 Downing Street. A polite bobby stopped him and asked for identification. The two uniformed military police guards at the door simply saluted. Even at the height of a war, security was so casual Julian was appalled. After a very short delay, the foreign secretary met with him in private, something Julian was certain was quite unusual. No permanent secretary, no assistant, not even a note-taking clerk.

Eden looked tired, his face drawn, his eyes puffy from lack of sleep. He was a handsome man with a neatly trimmed mustache and an air of quiet confidence. He indicated a heavy leather chair before a fireplace holding a bed of dying embers. "You are to be commended on the outstanding job you've been doing," he said after they exchanged greetings and had taken their places.

"Thank you, sir, but I'm just a small part of a very talented team. They deserve the credit."

"Quite." Eden stared at Julian a long moment, as if taking his measure. "I must get straight to the point. I really have so little time. I've already spoken to the director general, and he has approved your new assignment. In fact, he recommended you for it."

"What assignment is that, sir?"

"The one the prime minister, through me, is giving you. Let me ask you first, just what is your opinion of our Russian allies?"

Julian thought a moment and said, "Tough, secretive. The leadership is dedicated through and through."

"Dedicated Communists, you mean?"

"Yes, that too."

"I suppose during the Spanish Civil War, your sympathies were with the Republicans?"

"I never gave it much thought. The whole affair was a tragedy. It was never the cause for me that it was for others."

"The leftist leanings of many students at British universities is well known."

"Yes. Most seem to grow out of it, though."

"Most. Yes." Eden smiled. "What about the workers' paradise?"

"Ask the Ukrainians that have starved to death or any of the millions slowly dying in the gulags, or if you could, the former members of the Politburo with a bullet in the back of their heads."

Eden lit a cigarette and leaned back in his chair. "You studied Russian literature, I understand. How's your Russian?"

"Rusty, sir, but I could bring it up to scratch pretty quickly if required."

"Good. What I'm about to tell you is strictly confidential. It is on a need-to-know basis, and no one else needs to know. Right?" Julian nodded. "It is not to be shared with anyone. Not anyone, clear? I know how casually you intelligence types chat about your work with one another. That is not to happen in this instance."

Eden took a moment to smoke then continued. "Winnie is concerned with what he fears is a growing penetration of Britain by Soviet agents and fellow travelers. In this war, the enemy of my enemy is my friend, so we and the Americans have become quite cozy with the Russians. With the defeat of Hitler not far off, that will likely no longer remain the situation. At that time, we will not only find ourselves face to face with Mr. Stalin and his armies, but our instruments of national defense could well be saturated with British subjects holding loyalty to the same Mr. Stalin and his thugs. Today, no one questions their loyalties because we fight a common enemy, but that will change."

"You mean that Russia will become our new enemy?"

"Inevitably. Stalin's gobbling up every bit of Central Europe he can, even diverting his armies from the assault on Germany to ensure they fall within his power at war's end. At that time, we will face each other across an uneasy border. The Americans will consider their job done and will go home, as they did last time. It will be us and them."

"I see."

"Your assignment is to discreetly assess the extent of Soviet penetration into our government and news outlets. The PM and I will expect regular reports. They are for our eyes only, and we rely on your absolute candor. You must pull no punches."

"I understand."

Eden took a moment to light another cigarette. "Do you know Kim Philby?"

The question caught Julian by surprise. He'd not seen the debonair spy catcher in some months. "We've met a time or two. He was ahead of me at university and is in the SIS."

"Quite. That's the lad. You should know that Mr. Philby has established an anti-Communist desk inside SIS, called section five. The PM had indicated he wanted the Russians monitored, and that was the responsibility of MI6. His office is on Ryder Street, you know the building, I'm sure. He's on the floor just beneath the American OSS. He's making reports on reputed Russian spies among us."

"That seems reasonable, sir."

"I want you to keep in touch with him and feed him any information that you get. He is destined for great things, that one, maybe even head of SIS one day. He is being groomed, indeed, as you are. Do you understand, my boy?"

"I do, sir."

Eden eyed Julian for a long moment, then smiled and finally said, "We're depending on you.

Do a good job." There was a long pause, then Eden added, "Don't get dazzled by the bright lights. We want you to see what is behind the lights, hidden in the darkness."

Julian left the meeting a bit dazed and very soon felt overwhelmed by what was expected. The new duties brought with them an adjunct office and orders to wear the uniform of an army major. Four days after he'd settled in, Kim Philby dropped by, urbane, smiling, just to say hello and give Julian a brief run-down on his operations and how the two might be able to cooperate.

CHAPTER TEN

1991
Day Five
London

After assuring Hannah yet again that he was perfectly all right, although he was still miserable with a hangover, Christian re-read the damning *Times* article a final time, searching for the slightest hint of the source. He came up blank once again. He wondered for a moment how many at the newspaper would have been required to approve such an article.

On leaving Hanna's apartment, he drove through the rain to his office. Wednesday was generally quite busy at the IMSS office, which was nearly a twenty-four-hour-a-day operation. A score of employees could be counted on overnight to work the telephones to the Far East, where it was already tomorrow. As he drove up, he saw the parking lot to be more than half empty. Executives by the droves had obviously not come in.

Christian let himself through the secure side door and went quickly to his office, the building sounding oddly lifeless. Even the ever-trusty Pauline was absent. Christian brewed a pot of Earl Grey and carried it on a tray to his desk with several biscuits, hoping to settle his stomach. Outside the sky was stubbornly overcast, and a steady drizzle had resumed.

Irritated, he punched in the home phone number for Oliver Scarborough, the company's public relations man. "Hullo?"

"Oliver, why aren't you here at the office? Don't you have work to do?" It might be to no avail, but the company needed to issue a denial.

"Sorry, sir, but I'm terribly under the weather. I took the liberty of drafting a reply the moment I read the article and have sent it to *The Times* and all of the other major news outlets. You'll find a copy in your personal fax machine there in the office."

"All right. What else?"

"I recommend that at this point we not speak out publicly; let the news release speak for itself. This is just the opening shot, in my opinion. We don't want a face going on record until we know more. And you most certainly should be unreachable for the time being."

"Fair enough. That last won't be difficult. Let's meet at seven o'clock tomorrow morning, and I'll want your ideas on a proper campaign to take this on."

"Yes, sir, and I'm sorry about this, sir. I could come into the office for a few hours if you like."

"No, I'll be out of here very shortly. I'll see you in the morning."

Christian considered that. He agreed that it was best to keep their head low for the time being. The public eye was simply not their venue. IMSS did best in the dark, or at least in the shadows. No, what he needed were a few friends, if there were any to be found. He began calling everyone who, in other times of crisis, had been of help or at least sympathetic. It was an educational experience. He could not get past the stonewalling secretaries or PAs. It seemed that he was very much alone.

Christian sipped tea and watched the rain outside. Who's behind this? He asked himself for the hundredth time. The problem he'd realized pretty quickly was that there were so many possibilities.   A personal enemy could be the culprit. The world was petty enough for it to be that simple. God knew he'd made enough enemies in his life. A corporate competitor struck him as more likely. The CIA's front, International Trading Partners, came first to mind, but there were French companies, as well, one in Germany, a Czech state-owned company, even a Russian one now emerging from behind the crumbling Iron Curtain, not to mention China, South Korea, or Taiwan. The choices were endless.

Christian took a bite of biscuit then smiled inwardly. The potential enemies could even stretch back to the years of his father's tenure as head of the company. This was, after all, a family company.

Whoever was behind it was in a position to neutralize MI6 because it would otherwise have stopped the story. A "D" or Defense Notice would have been hand delivered to the newspaper editors and radio producers, forbidding them to mention this topic. This brought the American CIA to mind again, though the Company's favorite commercial enterprise was not popular there. Why would the British Secret Intelligence Service bend its knee to the American CIA so that the American company could displace the existing British one? Christian could think of no reason. Not that one might not exist; he just didn't know enough to have an opinion.

But the more Christian considered it, the more he found himself actually agreeing with Mitch Seaver, as distasteful as that was. Seaver had said that nothing in Russia was really changing. The old Soviet Union was simply shedding its skin, like an aging snake, but would remain unchanged beneath. But they certainly had no reason to ruin him, or at least no reason above that of anyone else. Yet he was certainly becoming more convinced that only the Russians could have somehow managed the right combination of events to bring this about. His gut told him that, and his mind concurred.

For the fourth time that day, Christian called Philips's number.

"Philips," crackled that familiar voice in the telephone earpiece.

"Where are you?" Christian asked.

"Just back from Bangkok, sir. I was meeting with a Japanese vendor. You know how the Japs are about mixing business and pleasure. I feel like a brothel madam. I returned just a few hours ago. Saw the article and I'm damned sorry."

"I thought it was to be quashed."

"So I was told."

"Get to the office as quickly as you can. I need you to trace those timers. I must have a full report immediately."

"Of course. I'll be there within the hour. This isn't over by a long shot."

* * *

The apartment was in Paddington, not far from Hyde Park, in Sussex Square. Evelyn Hardaway entered from the garden in the rear. It was discreet and quiet, in its way an island within the City of Westminster. She tossed her purse onto a chair, hung her coat, then drew out a cigarette and lit it. She stood smoking as she felt herself growing more and more excited. In another room, she could hear a shower, and she considered, for a moment, stripping off her clothes and joining in. But she'd just had her hair done.

It had begun with that bastard of a father-in-law. In all her life, the most crushing moment had been when she'd learned he was giving up the family title. If she wasn't to share in the title, then what had been the point of the marriage? Her rampant teenage promiscuity had brought with it one advantage when it came to landing a titled husband—and that had been her goal. She knew she was fantastic in the sack; and if she could keep a virile young man stirred up long enough, she'd been quite certain to get the job done.

Christian had been a snap, as it was. Julian had been tougher, seeing through her as he did; but she'd kept his son so deep within his own sexual juices that he hadn't had a clear thought until long months after the wedding. She'd even done her part to give them an heir. She wasn't to be blamed, after all, if the damn thing had been stillborn. She would have been willing to give it another go, if the old man hadn't thrown the title away. After that, what was the point?

Having slept with whomever she'd liked and spent all she could manage, what was really left? They could not divorce, so she could only try to hurt him in every conceivable way.

Then there was his Italian whore. Evelyn had no idea why the woman angered her so greatly. Both she and Christian had taken various lovers, years before; yet none of Christian's paramours had ever enraged her as did this one. She suspected that Christian was in love with the bitch.

Evelyn stabbed her cigarette into a crystal ashtray she'd given as a gift to the occupant and then began to disrobe as she made her way to the bedroom. She stopped in front of a full-length mirror as the shower was turned off. "Old," she murmured under her breath. "I'm getting old and I look like shit." She turned away from the mirror and slipped quickly between the cold sheets.

And then, there was the news that morning. Christian's many sins were coming home to roost. This was going to be a delicious ride, as first she played the loyal wife, then in time became the tragic victim. She wondered if there might be a book to write about this when it was all over. She wouldn't mind a bit of fame; and, of course, the money would be very handy.

From the bathroom stepped a well-muscled man in his mid-thirties. "You were quiet as a mouse, my dear," he said, his voice flavored with an accent.

"Come here, my dear Alexei," Evelyn commanded, tossing back the covers. "I need to taste you."

* * *

Before leaving his office, uncertain where he would go, Christian made a final telephone call. He wondered why he hadn't thought of Ian Cathcart from the first. Perhaps it was the man's age, or that he was now retired; but perhaps Ian, one of his father's oldest friends and most trusted allies, and a mainstay in British intelligence for decades, might be able to point him in a direction. At the moment, almost any direction would do.

The telephone rang until Christian was ready to hang up, then the familiar voice answered. "Cathcart."

"Ian, it's Christian."

"My dear boy! How very good to hear from you!"

"How's the boating?"

Ian had retired to one of the many narrow boats moored on England's extensive inland waterway system. He cruised about the English countryside on the canals, stopping where he fancied for as long as he fancied. His radio telephone was his only link to the outside world; and, sometimes, Ian even turned that off for days at a time. The canals were expensive to build, especially as so many locks were required to compensate for the changes in elevation. Once in place, however, they provided a reliable and economical means for moving coal, iron ore, and the like wherever needed. Though never entirely supplanted by the railroads, the canals had slowly fallen into disuse and disrepair—until they were re-discovered by vacationers in the early 1960s. The system was mostly restored, and many families even lived fulltime aboard the narrow boats.

The craft were also quite popular with certain retirees, like Ian. With a maximum width of seven feet to allow it to enter the locks on the canals, the boats made up for the lack of width by their length—fifty feet or sometimes more, the boats were outfitted to be a home. They moved with complete freedom about the extensive inland waterways. No one tracked them nor took any note as they quietly motored through the English canals and locks.

At last, Ian answered Christian's polite question. "Good, good. A world away, you know, a world away—and all the better for it. Opening and shutting those lock gates keeps me fit."

"I'm sorry to come so directly to the point, but I wondered if you might have some idea of what is going on?"

"Going on? Oh! *The Times* article, you mean. Why, they are out to destroy you, young man.

It's that simple."

"I understand that. I'm wondering just who 'they' are."

"Well, of course. That's always the question, isn't it? Who are 'they'?"

* * *

The weather improved as Christian drove northward to Northampton, where Ian Cathcart's narrow boat was moored. The leaden clouds became spotty with tarnished patches of blue between. A fine mist hovered over the green fields on each side of the road, and even the drone of traffic seemed muffled and respectful of the quiet countryside.

Christian spotted the sign for the Raynsway Marina and took the exit. As he approached the moorings, he spotted perhaps twenty narrow boats at anchor. Ian had said he was towards the far end. Christian parked and then walked the length of the bank, scanning the boats carefully for any sign of the old man.

"There you are, my boy!" Ian called out, waving at the approaching Christian. He was dressed in a gray Irish fisherman's sweater and heavy twill trousers of a dark brown. "Careful with your step. It can be a bit tricky for landlubbers." He laughed as he reached out to take Christian's forearm to steady him.

Christian had not seen Ian Cathcart in three years and was pleased to observe that the man had scarcely changed. Slender, as always, now in his mid-seventies, he'd retained his hair, though it had turned to silver. His eyebrows had become bushier and he wore glasses; but otherwise, the man was much as

Christian recalled him. If there were a single individual on earth his father had trusted without reservation, it was Ian.

"Nasty day, though improving," the man observed. "Let's go below." The pair ducked to enter the living area, and Ian indicated a chair for Christian to take at the kitchen table as he put a kettle on the gas hob to boil. "Ugly piece, that in *The Times*," he said as he laid out cups, saucers, canned milk, and sugar.

"Yes. I guess the fat's in the fire."

Ian eyed Christian above his glasses. "You should expect the worst, you know. A story like that doesn't make *The Times* unless the decision's already been made. You aren't trying to fight this, are you? You can't win, not now."

Christian had thought as much since first reading the article. Still, he was sorry to hear that summation from Ian. Christian realized he'd been hoping for another analysis, some plan of escape that would salvage his life and the family company. "I don't want to concede that you're right."

"I'm afraid I am, barring a miracle. I take no pleasure in saying it. Your family has served Britain very honorably, and this is despicable." The water came to boil, and Ian occupied himself filling their cups. He replaced the kettle and took his place in the chair across the table from Christian. "What do you need from me?"

"A heads up. I'd like to know who's behind this. It might be there is something I can do, after all."

"Someone powerful, obviously. Perhaps someone out to get you for revenge, or just to knock you off your perch. This might be a 'brave new world,' but the leopard doesn't change his spots—certainly not overnight. SIS is still penetrated, I regret to say. Any one of your old enemies in the East could be wagging the tail."

"I thought matters had improved there."

"I wish that were true, but we Brits seem to have this affinity for socialism, and some have a love affair with Comrade Marx. It would be better if the traitors did it for money; that, at least, we can detect. But, ideology is something else altogether." The man stirred his tea. "There's really nothing you can do at this point, I'm afraid. The possibilities are limitless, and, in the end, finding names won't be any help."

"You're probably right, but it might not be as hopeless as it seems. And, even in the worst case, I might be able to do some damage control, such as keeping out of prison, for example, and retaining my assets. I don't want to lose everything. And I'm not yet convinced that I can't win this."

"You might have a point there. I tend to see the dark side of things too often. All those years in the shadows, I suppose. The harm is done; but, yes, it can be limited."

"Who? Where? How?"

"I don't know and I doubt I can find out. The old guard at Joint Intelligence Committee is gone. Skinner's, in effect, running the show these days. Know him?"

"Lawrence Skinner? We've met at the club. Can't say I was impressed. He looked pretty shifty."

"You've got his number. He back stabbed his way to deputy director of SIS operations. As near as I can tell, his sole loyalty is to himself. He and Hawkins scarcely speak to one another. Skinner would have had to sign off on this, at the least. Any reason he'd be your enemy?" Ian queried.

"No direct reason that comes to mind. Which doesn't mean someone with a reason isn't going through him," Christian countered.

Ian sighed. "It never changes. And the old place is still riddled with lefties. Outside of JIC, who profits best from your demise?"

Christian scarcely had to consider his reply. "International Trading Partners, for one."

"The CIA front?"

"That's the one. They were quite active in Kuwait City last week, and a top-level CIA man, Mitchell Seaver, was there as well."

"That's to be expected. It doesn't necessarily mean there is a connection, though the CIA would clearly promote ITP. And, of course, the SIS has despised you and your firm since your father's days. He and you have embarrassed them too many times. And the old boys never forget. All of them would go along with this effort or, at least, look the other way. My guess is they're in on this."

Christian grunted in disgust. "On the one hand, this looks like a Russian operation; but, on the other, our best suspect is the CIA." He shook his head in disbelief. "What about the newspaper?"

"Just running a good story. Destroying reputations is at the heart of every great newspaper. It sells more copies than almost anything else that they could write about."

The men sat and reminisced for the better part of an hour as Ian told Christian of his life about the boat. Outside, a light rain returned and tapped against the windows. "I enjoy it so much more than I expected. There's a regular community of boaters out here, and the scenery is constantly changing. When I get tired of one place, I just move on to another." Ian paused, looking off into the far horizon for a few moments. "I cannot stay in one place since my wife died." Christian realized that this was the first time he had ever heard Cathcart say a single word about his own life.

Ian rose and refilled their cups. "If you believe there is any true value in knowing the who behind all this, you might concentrate on that aspect and see if you can come up with a name."

"My list is pretty long with possibilities."

Ian sat again. "One name comes to mind. Have you considered Nicholas Rashidov?"

CHAPTER ELEVEN

1949
London

Ian Cathcart had first met Christian's father, Julian, when Ian was in his thirties. Ian was usually seen with a cigarette in a shiny golden holder, the latter so often grasped in his fingers it seemed an added appendage. It was not unusual for him to have more than one cigarette going at a time, one in the holder and one smoldering on the edge of an ashtray. The intelligence community seemed to be in competition with each other over who smoked the most, and Ian Cathcart may have well been in the lead.

One day, years after that first meeting, Ian and Julian had each taken their pint and settled into a quiet corner of The Boar's Head, the pub where they usually met. The arrangement had seemed entirely natural to Julian when he'd first launched the Concord Trading Company. It was part of the reason why he believed Concord would succeed, though in retrospect, he'd given MI6 far more than he'd received in return. He'd worked with Ian towards the end of the war, the last of his days at chasing Red spies who were infiltrating Britain throughout that dark time.

After the war, Ian had moved up in the senior Civil Service ranks. He was a school chum of the chairman of the Joint Intelligence Committee, which oversaw both MI5 and MI6, and Ian and his friend were close. During those early days of the Cold War, the Joint Intelligence Committee reported to the chiefs of staff of the British Armed Services.

Julian was not the only source Ian had for informal intelligence. "Someone's got to keep the Reds at bay," he'd often remarked over lunch.

Julian was assured his information was purified in such a way so that, when it actually reached someone who might want to act on it, there was no way of knowing its source. In exchange for what he could provide Ian—and a friend or two elsewhere—Ian had assisted him in acquiring certain usually unobtainable export licenses. It was understood that nothing went East through Concord that might actually harm Britain. However, the rules were routinely bent for items that really no longer needed to be on the proscribed list, yet lingered there, trapped by Civil Service inertia.

"Anything new?" Ian asked before taking a pull of his beer.

"This and that."

"From your Russian bear?"

"Yes, of course. He can be a veritable gold mine, at times."

It was an irony Julian couldn't escape, that so much of his success in the years immediately following the war had depended on a Russian named Mishka. He, the product of Britain's finest education, a spy during the war, had to rely on a political ruffian, sent to Warsaw to run errands and keep the peace for Stalin. In some ways, the irony gave him a great pleasure, and made Mishka far dearer to him than the Russian could have imagined.

Christian had met Mishka at a Polish "event" in Warsaw in 1948; something the Poles had called a party because they obviously knew no better. The Poles were as skillful at throwing a celebration as were the Russians. Both groups drowned themselves in vodka, sentiments growing increasingly maudlin as their blood alcohol level rose. The primary difference between a Russian celebration and a Polish one, however, was that the Poles were quite genuine in their fun. With a Russian, during the post-war period, at least, one could never be sure.

Another difference was that the Poles divided into two groups early in the evening, and each bloc spent the night lambasting the other. No one seemed to know how they chose sides. There were no serious issues debated, no reasons for battle. Yet, it was impossible for a Pole to be neutral. The moment a new guest entered the reception hall at the Bristol Hotel, he moved to one side or the other of the vast room and took up arms against the other group.

Julian, standing away from the two gangs that opposed each other in the hall, had taken another sip of the Polish vodka. He assumed that the factions understood their own rules, but assumed as well that such a game could wind up hazardous for a foreigner, so he stood in the neutral ground a few steps away from either group.

The well-worn hall in which the party was held had been the only such gathering place to survive the German occupation and bombing. The carpet was threadbare, and the curtains had lost any semblance of elegance. Two of the five chandeliers overhead did not match. Beneath them perhaps one hundred of Poland's new elite were hobnobbing, served by a large force of stoic, slender young men in dinner jackets. The Poles believed the hall would be restored to its former grandeur in time, but Julian was not optimistic. Though the reconstruction of Warsaw had already begun by then, only three years after the end of the war, it was obvious that the new Warsaw would be a grim landscape of shoddy buildings, as bleak and devoid of humanity as any city in Soviet Russia. The Soviet architects and engineers managing the designs would see to that.

Julian had been in Poland for more than a week and was concluding negotiations with the state director of purchases, Kazimierz Kurek. Assuming all went as Julian expected, his company would soon be shipping machine tools, cement, steel, aluminum plate, telephone equipment, and telegraph sets, everything a largely destroyed nation needed to begin rebuilding.

Julian had been impressed with Kurek, in particular with his integrity. As Julian understood it, the thin, contemplative man had been a partisan throughout the German occupation, fighting out of the city sewers. He'd lost his wife, brothers, and most of his friends in the ferocious battle and emerged with a serious case of tuberculosis, now largely controlled. He was no Communist, but he'd worked closely with them during the war and did so now that they were in government. Julian hoped Kurek lasted long enough in office to finish the deals they'd negotiated.

Julian watched Kurek in the far corner standing awkwardly alone, holding what Julian suspected was a glass of mineral water. The older man finished the drink and left the hall. So not all Poles take sides, Julian thought—at least not politicians of a certain rank.

As Julian bemusedly eyed the Polish bureaucrats' ill-fitting, baggy suits and their overdressed wives, he became aware of a pair of eyes watching him with equal amusement. He recognized Micha Kirov, another man who seemed to avoid the Polish habit of taking sides. The man met Julian's eye with a quick wink and moved across the room to shake hands with Julian. His huge paw crushed Julian's as they shook. With scarcely a preamble, Micha Kirov began to discuss the details of the ambitious Polish plan to rebuild Warsaw as it had been before the Germans all but leveled it.

"You must call me Mishka. My good friends do," the man insisted after their third glass of vodka, a brand that he disdained as scarcely better than bath water. "Only Russians can make real vodka," he'd declared, though he'd shown no hesitation in downing the Polish variety.

Mishka was in his late thirties, tall for a Russian, with distinguished, finely chiseled features, high cheekbones, and piercing blue, eyes. He wore a suit of Western cut, the only Russian at the affair who did. He was bright, funny, and their conversation was working wonders for Julian's rusty Russian.

"See the one with big ass," Mishka said, pointing with his chin towards a Polish wife. "A peasant, dressed up for big city ball. Russia is filled with women like that." He muttered something darkly under his breath and then downed his drink.

The occasion was the celebration of the election "victory" of the Polish Workers' Party, and was a tribute to its chairman, Wladislaw Gomulka. The non-Communist parties had been routed through the ruthless application of wholesale fraud, select violence, and outright Russian intimidation. The following month, February, Julian understood Gomulka would declare a people's republic and move Poland officially into the Soviet sphere. The Polish Communists were, understandably, euphoric, if still drab and decidedly rural. That came as no surprise. The Germans had worked hard at liquidating the Polish intelligentsia who'd once occupied these buildings, and all that the country was left with in their stead was ill-educated and easily swayed bureaucrats.

The Russians, on the other hand, were depressingly overbearing. What had taken place these past weeks was a charade, really nothing more than a public show for the world press, ultimately intended to accomplish what Stalin had ordered. World War II, as it was being called in the West, or the Great Patriotic War, as it had come to be known in the East, had been over for nearly three years. A free and independent Polish state was supposed to come out of all the carnage of World War II, but, when the fighting stopped, Poland was occupied by Soviet armies. Stalin was shrewd enough to give his former allies the appearance of an election, which swept the Communists into power.

At the conclusion of the war, Julian had left British intelligence and established Concord Trading Company, Ltd. He had thought to trade on his widespread intelligence contacts and a post-war economic expansion to carve a lucrative niche for himself. His father, the earl, had been outraged that his only son should engage in common commerce. "Good God, boy! Seriously! A tradesman? In our family?" bellowed the earl. Weren't the family holdings enough for him? His title assured him that he'd never lack wealth.

And yet, after the war, it wasn't wealth Julian wanted. Perhaps what he craved was nothing more than to prove his worth, unlike the rest of Britain's flaccid aristocracy with their cricket and recitations of Keats. Julian had patiently explained his desire to make his own way. In the eyes of the old aristocrat, plain business was unacceptable for a future earl. His son had a station in society and was expected to take that place.

Julian had gone about his business regardless. He'd been vague about what exactly he'd intended to trade in when he'd opened his small office on the fourth floor of Walmar House, an office block on Regent Street, midway between Oxford Circus and the BBC building. He reasoned that people everywhere were sick to death of war and sacrifice. He was certain better times were coming. But, whereas the pre-war world had been divided into the mostly free West and the fascist states, the post-war world was divided into two hostile camps, this time with the Communists on the other side. The two sides had, indeed, become separated by an "Iron Curtain," a phrase recently coined by Winston Churchill, a barrier that divided Europe into two antagonists as evenly as were the Poles in the hall, and, perhaps, for just as incomprehensible a reason.

Even more ironic was that, in many ways, the war had yet to end. Rationing continued in Britain, and Stalin was determined to maintain an atmosphere of conflict with the West. Civil war was raging in China, and Julian would not have been surprised at all if the Communists won there, as well. The French were reoccupying Indo-China and more bloodshed in that arena was certain.

After a lackluster year searching for hopeful businesses, Julian had been on the verge of quitting. At the time, Admiral Mountbatten was moving to partition the Indian subcontinent into two states, one Hindu and one Muslim. Julian had no doubt at all that would mean war the moment it was accomplished, probably late that summer. But, before war became official, Ian Cathcart had called on Julian and assured him that he was free to arm both sides. Julian had hesitated only briefly, not certain he wanted to be known as an arms merchant, but he'd gone ahead and found it somewhat profitable, though, in reality, there was too little money in that part of the world to make serious profits.

That was why he was in Warsaw, drinking vodka with his strange new comrade, Mishka, joining in the triumph of Godless communism and the Stalin cult over the forces of freedom. Despite Churchill's Iron Curtain between East and West, Julian was finding it to be porous, indeed. Although the Russians already had all the weapons they required, there were still things they needed.

"She fucks like a peasant," Mishka said, still staring at the Polish wife with the ample posterior. Julian took a closer look. The woman was not yet thirty, and her flesh was still firm, if substantial. In a few years, he supposed, she'd have the stout, heavy frame common to so many Slavs and Russians; but that was still a few years away. "I mean that as a compliment. I have always found peasants to be the very best. They are animals when they fuck. That one screams loud enough to hear in Moscow! With that big ass, she has plenty to grab hold of. I passed some time with her last week, while her husband was picking out his new office." Mishka laughed. In the same breath, he summoned another vodka from one of the servers.

"Now there's a nice one, even if she has a skinny ass." He indicated a trim woman in her early twenties, with long dark hair and pouting lips. "Her father is the state director of purchases."

"Kurek?"

"Indeed; the same one you've been negotiating with for a week now. I don't know how she fucks—not yet."

"What would you say if Kurek found out what you were doing with his daughter? He would be furious," Christian opined.

"Nonsense!" laughed Mishka. "He could not risk being angry. I would tell him to go and have intercourse with himself, before telling him to hold my jacket while I fucked his brand-new wife, as well."

Mishka had been vague about his work, but Julian saw all the signs of NKVD, the Russian secret police, even in the way Mishka had initially sought him out. He was polished, multi-lingual, reserved where it counted, and supremely confident. More significantly, he could dress Western style and get away with it. But, it was the deference and fear Julian saw in the eyes of others that told him the jovial man was part of Stalin's terror apparatus. It seemed the Poles wanted to know him, but none of them wanted to be known by him. And Mishka had certainly done his homework on Julian.

"And what will your company be trading to our new ally?" Mishka asked and, without waiting for an answer, launched a second question. "Can you get, say, electronic components?" Suddenly the Russian seemed very sober.

"Resistors, electronic valves, radio technologies, and such. What do you have in mind?"

"Me? Nothing. I think electronics could be very lucrative for you. But not just any electronics, you understand. Can you get the right ones out?"

Julian knew what he meant. "I have friends. Within reason, I should be able to get the necessary export licenses."

"How is it you have such helpful friends?" Mishka asked with a broad smile.

Julian smiled. "You might say I was born with contacts. My father's an earl." He was surprised to hear himself say the words, and it was a measure of his quick affinity with this man that he did. He rarely shared information about himself, particularly in business, where it was usually counter-productive.

Mishka paused, as if he were about to say something, then laughed. "Me, too!" He laughed at the joke. "What did you do in the Great Patriotic War?"

"A bit of this, a bit of that," Julian answered, eyeing Kurek's oldest daughter. She moved with grace and had already met his eye.

"Me, too!!" the Russian exploded. "A bit of that, and a bit of this!" He gestured towards Julian's scar. "Perhaps a little more than you say? Tomorrow, we have lunch. There is someone you must meet. He can tell you what electronics will be especially profitable for a British trader in Warsaw. And," he added with a wink, "you won't forget your new old friend, Mishka, will you?"

"I wouldn't think of it."

"Good! I like you British! You are gentlemen. Come. I'll introduce you to Victoria—that is her name—and tomorrow, at lunch, you can tell me how she fucks. That is, if you are the man I think you are."

CHAPTER TWELVE

1917
Russia

Micha Vladimir Kirov was actually born in 1910 as Georgi Alexandrovich Romanov, nephew of the czar. But for as long as he could remember, people had called him Mishka.

He could not recall his father, the grand duke, who had the distinction of being czar for but a single day, when his brother, Nicholas, abdicated. But the day following the grand duke's ascension, the Bolsheviks had demanded he sign a document that was, in essence, an abdication. He was then transported to the city of Perm, near the Urals, and three months later was murdered by the Bolsheviks, placing the young Georgi Alexandrovich next in line to become czar of Russia.

Georgi, his mother Natalia, and the greater part of the Romanov family, including former Czar Nicholas, were imprisoned at the summer palace in St. Petersburg. It was at the palace turned prison where Georgi would have expected to meet his maker, if he had been old enough for such thoughts. His mother was certain of the Communist intentions to assassinate the Romanov clan. Imprisoning the Romanovs, even in such palatial surroundings, only meant they were kept close at hand for the inevitable moment of their murder. Georgi was too young at the time to understand the details, but his mother's distraction and distress unsettled him. He found he had no way to comfort her.

The Baroness Natalia had doted on her only son since his birth. Born a commoner, Natalia's marriage to the grand duke had swept her away from a mundane life as the wife of a Royal Guard captain into the fabled world of Russian royalty. The grandeur of wealth had faded quickly for Natalia, however, and with it, the infrequent charms of her husband, the grand duke. Surrounded by a world at her beck and call, entombed in a marriage based on the grand duke's royal whims and held together by circumstance more than love, she found herself an outsider—and very alone.

Georgi's birth had changed all that, had given her a companion, a purpose. Once imprisoned in the palace, Natalia was determined to see him survive—whatever the cost. The Red Army soldiers, who served as guards, treated them with a mixture of deference and contempt. Commoners themselves, their revolutionary ardor didn't shield them from the awe that peasants experienced in the presence of royalty; and with the exception of an occasional awkward show of authority, the guards left the Romanovs to themselves.

Czar Nicholas was a wreck. His empire ruined, forced to abdicate, he seemed happy to walk away from Mother Russia with nothing but his life. Natalia had always known him to be a coward at heart. What other kind of man would come to sleep with his dead brother's wife and end the night crying at his self-made predicament?

She wondered at herself as well. If not exactly happy with her guard captain, she had not been discontented. When her grace and beauty had caught the eye of the grand duke, and she'd found herself summoned to his chambers, she had been in a state of shock. But there was no denying the royal what he wanted; and when his lust had turned to a peculiar desire to marry her, she'd insisted her husband be treated with respect and promoted, if she was to leave him. And now, with her grand duke husband scarcely cold in his grave, his brother claimed her body as if by right. Sometimes, she felt like little more than a palace whore, to be used by the rulers of Russia.

In those moments, when the former czar of All Russia snored beside her, Natalia wondered if the Red Army would be foolish enough to let him live. The White Army, defeated, was not without resources, though they cared nothing for Nicholas as a man. They were only concerned with restoring a czar—any czar—to power. Unless the Red Army was saving the Romanovs for future negotiations, the obvious choice was to slaughter them all.

A few weeks after her husband was murdered, the Communists took away Nicholas and his immediate family. Initially, Natalia had no idea to where, but a kindly older guard assured her the royal family was safe. They had been taken to the Urals for safekeeping. That struck her as ominous. She'd received the same assurance when her husband, the grand duke, had been taken to the Urals.

So her situation remained for a year, until word arrived that Nicholas, too, was dead, with all his family. Though she had expected such news for months, it was still a shock. All but forgotten, she and her son, now the sole heir to the throne of All the Russias, remained prisoners in the palace, along with a gathering of distant members of the once—royal family. She'd wondered when some bureaucrat would finally realize that young Georgi was heir to the throne —and she lived in dread of that day.

St. Petersburg in summer was humid, hot. The prisoners slept most of the day or spent them in the drawing rooms. Natalia was determined to keep Georgi's education moving forward, stalwart in her faith that she would some-how find a way for her son to become czar. A better czar than Nicholas, for certain. A true monarch, perhaps the greatest Russia had ever known.

"Remember," she told him, speaking in a near whisper. "Always remember your heritage. You are now the true czar. Your uncle abdicated and passed the crown to your father, who was then murdered by the Bolsheviks. You have a place in history; you must take it, one day."

They were surrounded by the palace's beautiful paintings and ornate furni-ture, but the palace itself was falling into disrepair, having suffered a period absent servants or groundskeepers. The palace staff, which had numbered in the hundreds, had been dismissed. The prisoners tended to their own needs as best they could.

"You will rule this country one day, and you must be prepared. You must be ready, in every way, to lead the new Russia," Natalia told her son. She gripped his shoulders and held him through his thin summer suit, kneeling in front of him and staring deeply into his ice blue eyes. She knew she would have to hide him for at least a few years, until this insane revolution had exhausted itself and the Russian people realized their rightful place under the wise guidance of the Romanovs, under her son's brave, strong rule. She also knew that she would have to leave him in order to protect him. The thought brought tears to her eyes.

"Mother?"

Natalia shook away her sorrow and faced her son. "It's nothing." She kissed his forehead gently and held her lips against his warm skin, the strands of his sandy brown hair soft on her face as she stared out into the arctic summer sky.

* * *

The civil war that raged in Russia worked to their advantage, as did the confusion about the fate of the remaining Romanovs. The combination gave Natalia time to plan her course of action, and the general indifference of the Red Army guards made them negligent. She began sleeping days and keeping herself awake at night. At bedtime, they locked her and Georgi in a room and stationed a guard outside their door; but there was a window in the room, and only a single story drop to the garden below. It was as though the soldiers didn't believe the Romanovs would try and escape, that the Romanovs would prefer to bargain for clemency with the new regime rather than steal away into a life of anonymity. Or maybe the Bolsheviks simply assumed that people raised as royalty were incapable of fending for themselves. They had certainly been right about Nicholas, as well as Natalia's late husband.

Natalia plotted the escape carefully. She kept a letter opener she had once found beneath her pillow. If she could stab it directly into the guard's throat, then lock the door behind them, that would give them half the night and maybe until morning to make good their escape. She briefed Georgi Alexandrovich, nine years old, on her plan; he was to follow her and only to follow her. They would go directly to the stables. There, they would steal two horses. If they were separated, they would meet at her old home, where her parents had lived. Did he remember it? She briefed him on the directions until he could recite them flawlessly on demand.

Like most escapes, this one did not happen as Natalia planned. They were abruptly moved from the palace, taken off to travel east. And though their destination was never announced, the Romanovs all assumed they were en route to Moscow. None, however, could determine why. They traveled in carriages pulled by the royal horses, with mounted guards at the front and rear, as they crossed the wide plains, the pastoral landscape flooded with violets and daffodils.

The nights were warm, the road crowded with travelers to Moscow, curious what the Bolsheviks would mean for them, whether a new life would suddenly become available and what the workers' paradise would look like. It was the crowds that made escape possible, Natalia realized, and the excitement of the revolution would cover that escape.

At night, despite the vigorous efforts of the guards, people slept all around the royal party, under the carriages, cluttering the fields nearby with bodies. It was as if they still held some affinity for the Romanovs, perhaps memories of better times than these; but, more likely, it was the safety of having an armed contingent nearby.

When the moment arrived, Natalia and Mishka bundled themselves in as many layers of clothing as they could wear. Natalia waited until she heard the breathing of the guard immediately outside begin to slow. They were forced to sleep in the carriage, but she'd managed to leave the window open a slit. She slid it down behind her, blocking the guard's view with her body. She had observed the guards for many nights, timing their behavior. Georgi was already awake when she touched his shoulder.

As planned, Georgi filled his blanket with clothing, shaping it into the outline of a body, then slithered out the window first. He disappeared into the thick carpet of sleeping bodies, crawling along in the dirt. Natalia tried to follow, but her clothing proved too thick and made a loud rustling sound. The guard stirred, and she panicked; if he awoke to find Georgi gone, there would be an immediate search. Georgi would never have time to get away.

She pulled back into the carriage, slid the window closed, coughing to hide the noise. The guard outside stood and lit a cigarette. She lay down quickly and listened to him inhale, exhale, and pace the dirt road around the carriage for a few moments before settling back to his sentry post. She coughed again to make sure he heard her.

All the while, Georgi, at the edge of the field, pretended to sleep, making sure there was no one following him. Then he rolled away from the bodies and began to walk briskly towards the mountains. His mother hadn't followed, and he worried that she had been caught, that there would be a manhunt with guards fanning the fields searching for him. But he kept going, as she had ordered.

Georgi had promised his mother he wouldn't wait, and he kept that promise, tears streaming down his cheeks. He was too conspicuous, she had said, forcing the promise from his lips and reminding him that a czar should never break a solemn oath. She had promised him herself that they would meet in Kiev at her brother's home, where they would be safe.

Georgi was lucky the moon was nearly full, and he could see the stalks of summer grass that rose to his knees as he began the journey to Kiev. He had at least a two-week trek ahead of him, even if he made good time, though he had no idea of that then. By the light of the moon, he stripped off a layer of clothing, tearing away the royal livery. He soiled his face and hair with dirt, pushing his fingers beneath a patch of flowers and bringing the dark earth to his face, smearing himself.

After about two hours of walking, he began to lag in his determination, tired and worried. What if his mother were caught? Would they hurt her? Would they kill her? An image of his mother's body left by the side of the road haunted him. Despite his promise, he retraced his steps, breaking into a run to cover the distance back to the carriage.

He caught sight of the carriage in the distance, with the fire embers dying out, where the half-dozen Red Army guards had camped nearby. There was movement in the camp; the guards were awake, and he could hear their shouts, though he couldn't make out the words. He crawled closer until he could hear the words clearly and see the uniforms and the rifles strapped over the soldiers' backs.

"... enough to not hear? Idiot!" A shoulder lifted and an arm tore through the air. Georgi heard the crack of a fist against a jaw as the captain struck the guard who had been nearest to the carriage. Two other soldiers dragged a struggling body towards the captain. Georgi recognized his mother's long hair and her screams as they pulled her mercilessly along the dirt road and threw her at the captain's feet. The captain lifted Georgi's mother to her feet.

"Where are you to meet?"

"Nowhere," his mother answered. "I will never see my son again, and you will never find him! He is gone. I do not know where he went!"

The captain struck her brutally with the back of his hand, and she collapsed to the ground. The captain lifted her up again and held her face close to his. He growled something too low for Georgi to hear.

Georgi began to crawl closer, every ounce of his being drawing him to his mother's defense. He wanted to stand, to throw himself between her and the captain, but her voice in his ears stopped him. "You must survive to be the czar of Russia."

He watched as the captain struck her again, this time with a closed fist, and she crumpled to the ground, sobbing.

"Where is he going?"

"I don't know," she answered. He kicked her, the flash of his long black boot shining for an instant in the moonlight as his foot slammed into her ribs. He put his heel on her cheek.

"Where?"

She was sobbing loudly now, obviously terrified.

"I swear, I don't know. I only told him to run, to get to Moscow somehow and find the czarist supporters and defeat your horrible revolution!"

The captain raised his boot, and she shrieked, burying her head in the road, protecting it with her hands. One of the guards standing closest to him barked a plea for care and he shifted his weight, bringing his boot down in the dirt just beside her head. The other two guards lifted her limp body like that of a rag doll and all but threw her back into the carriage. They secured the windows, locked the door, and sat beside it, one leaning against each wheel, both lighting cigarettes. The captain untied a horse and began to ride slowly back in the direction of St. Petersburg, scouting the sides of the road in the waning moonlight, searching for the escaped young boy.

Georgi crawled back through the sleeping bodies laid out across the field like pieces of a jigsaw puzzle, back into the rocks. He found a cave, wriggled five feet into the pitch black, and slept.

It took three weeks for the boy to reach Kiev, repeating to himself the directions his mother had him memorize. At times, he traveled with some of the many strangers on the roads, at other times by himself, eating whatever vegetable he could still find in the fields, and at night curled up into a scared ball under a tree or bush.

Finally, one afternoon, he reached the outskirts of Kiev and soon found his uncle's house. He hid under an overgrown hedge until darkness fell, then went up to the door in what was, by then, total darkness, save for candles glowing in the kitchen of the house.

Georgi didn't recognize his uncle, but the large, graying man, practically lifted the boy off the front step and carried him inside. Though it was night, the man seemed in fear for both their lives. Georgi could barely keep his eyes open, but his uncle carried him into the basement and locked the door. The first bath in what seemed like an eternity was followed by hot soup with potatoes and some bread. Then a bed—a real bed—to sleep in for almost a day and a half.

The next evening, his uncle spoke to him of important matters. "We were prepared for the possibility of you coming to us—but I am surprised your mother is not with you, I cannot image how you made the journey on your own, your mother contacted us long ago. These are now your papers," he said, pulling a packet of documents from behind a barrel of wine standing in the corner. "You will need to understand and remember everything that is in them. Your name is no longer Georgi—you are now Micha Kirov. You are my wife's cousin's son, from the countryside, and you are staying with us following the death of your mother. Your father is in Moscow, triumphant with the Red Army."

The newly rechristened Mishka said nothing, but he knew that this was the start of a new life for him.

CHAPTER THIRTEEN

1949

Warsaw

Julian did not disappoint Mishka; and despite Victoria's constant harping for expensive jewelry, she was to be his Warsaw mistress until her father was ousted from political office and accused of corruption by the new party chairman, Boleslaw Bierut, some months later. Bierut launched a full-fledged Stalinist dictatorship, along with a massive program of industrialization. Kurek was a victim of the new regime, as were his two daughters and others of his family.

Julian's first meeting with Mishka had proven providential, even if not coincidental. As he came to know his new friend better, he was more certain than ever that their friendship had not been accidental. The Russians, employing Polish front companies, were in the market for a wide range of electronics and had identified Concord Trading Company as a possible source. Mishka, Julian learned from friends at MI5, was the Soviet head of the NKVD in Poland. It was he who engineered Bierut's installation, along with the reign of terror. And it was Mishka who personally saw to it that a lion's share of business went to Concord, rather than the other British export firms trying to do business behind the new and still shiny Iron Curtain.

Officially, trade with the Soviet Union was prohibited, but Poland was considered acceptable. To move his goods from Britain to Russia, Julian routed them through Warsaw. Mishka proved essential, first in seeing to it that Julian learned what was desired, then in assuring that the Polish government issued the necessary paperwork, and finally in making certain that Julian received payment. All too often, companies supplied goods and could not collect what was due; this never happened to Concord Trading Company.

What they wanted, what Russia desperately needed, was electronics of almost any sort. World War II had proven that Russia could compete in industrial output with the West, but the technological developments of the Allies, especially at the end of the war, had been sobering to Stalin. Soviet agents were stealing the design plans for anything electronic they could lay their hands on. But theft, while vital for quality items, was impractical for quantity. Britain's left-leaning government encouraged trade with the East, especially with Poland, for whom they had gone to war—provided the items were non-military in nature.

All things considered, matters had gone as well as could be expected since Julian had met Mishka. Though a number of his friends had expressed concern when he had gone into business, even his father had eventually come around, particularly as his own assets were taxed ruthlessly by the new British government. An earl he might be, but the enormous inheritance taxes imposed by the Labour government would make it nearly impossible to maintain the family holdings upon his death. Even before the war, his father had been compelled to sell pieces of land here and there to keep up appearances. After the war, the entire hereditary class of lords entered steep decline. Labour was merely driving the nails into the coffin.

As Concord had begun to enjoy a reassuring cash flow, Julian had been glad to help with expenses at the estate—much to his father's pleasure—though he harbored no illusion about the eventuality of what was to occur.

Mishka was increasingly pleased with the ever-growing Concord presence, and demonstrated it with bottles of Russian vodka and jars of caviar. Julian, on the other hand, was doing very well indeed with his door to the East. His first gifts to Mishka, one a Longines wristwatch, the next a cashmere sweater, were well received. But when he slid a sealed envelope of pounds across their dinner table, Mishka had shaken his head and pushed it back.

"You are generous, my friend, and your Swiss watch is a wonder. The sweater I can only wear in my modest apartment, but if it were a woman, I would marry her. As for that," he indicated the envelope, "it does me no good here. You understand?"

Julian did not. He had never met anyone in Poland who did not want American dollars or British pounds. "I don't."

Mishka lowered his voice. "This is dangerous for me, my good friend. Open an account for me in Switzerland. Put it there, and say no more about it to me until I mention it to you again."

Now that, Julian had thought, was interesting. A devoted Communist operative who wanted a Swiss bank account. Dangerous was an understatement. Three months later, Mishka handed Julian a thick envelope. "Add this to my Swiss collection," he said. Strange, thought Julian. Mishka had never even asked him for proof that he opened the account, had never asked for a bank statement or other documentation. All he had was the account number, password, and bank details that Julian had scribbled on the inside flap of a packet of cigarettes.

Inside the envelope was an incredible ten thousand pounds in large, white ten-pound notes. Julian had never heard of anyone smuggling currency from behind the Iron Curtain; the traffic always went the other way. And once Julian grasped what the wily Russian was up to, he was awed by it. Mishka was embezzling NKVD funds and having him—Julian—smuggle them into his— Mishka's—Swiss bank account. If the arrangement were found out, it would mean an unpleasant death for Mishka. But then, Julian laughed to himself, what death was pleasant?

For all the success of Concord, all the pride Julian took in it, it was the development of his only son that caused Julian's heart to swell. Christian was a precocious child, and, though Julian knew it to be very un-British to take such pleasure in the boy, Julian really couldn't help himself. The only regret his long weeks spent traveling imparted to him was the absence from his son.

* * *

"And how is our Russian bear?" Ian Cathcart asked Julian in one of the obscure London pubs they used for such meetings.

"Mishka's been transferred back to Moscow." Julian lit a cigarette of his own and glanced at the customer who'd just entered. With a copy of *The Times* tucked under his arm and a harried expression, he appeared to be a businessman from around the corner, come in for a quick pint or two.

"Did he say for what?"

"He's to assume head of the NKVD intelligence unit concentrating on the UK. His mission is to make us the next member of the glorious international Communist community."

Ian smiled bleakly. "With Labour in power, we just might do the job ourselves."

Julian took a sip of his beer then said, "We should talk about the replacement valves for the communications sets I shipped. They've learned that the entire consignment was defective and are squawking. I explained they were likely damaged in transit, and they seemed to buy it. Transportation in Russia is notoriously harsh. But they want replacements."

"Well, they'll have to squawk. We can't give them operational ones. What can you offer in exchange?"

Julian thought a moment, then said, "I understand that a batch have been made that did not meet specifications and were about to be ditched. I plan on supplying those. They will work after a fashion, but burn out quite quickly. The Russians will blame their own equipment for that. They are also very keen on getting radar gear."

Ian nodded his assent. Radar technology was advancing so rapidly, the older models posed no security problems. He said, "This news on your Russian is interesting. Can we use him?"

Though Julian was pleased to cooperate with JIC and see to it that Russia never actually received anything that would hurt the West, and though he gladly passed along those bits of information he picked up from time to time, he'd never divulged to Ian that he was funneling money for Mishka into a numbered Swiss bank account. There was already over £150,000 in the account. The Russian had very sticky hands, indeed.

"I don't see how. I have no way to communicate with him. Even on those occasions when I go to Moscow, I only see him at functions where everyone is watched closely. You know how paranoid it is there. All we do is shake hands and exchange greetings, then move on."

"I was under the impression that Mishka is one of the watchers."

"Still, there are those who watch the watchers, Ian."

"I get your point—unfortunately. Anything else this time?" Ian asked. Julian briefed him on the Stalin deathwatch. No one openly spoke of it, but it was obvious that the Soviet nation, as a body, and nearly to a soul, couldn't wait for the despot to die.

Ian snorted. "Nothing new there. I don't think your Russian friend will be so happy to see the Man of Steel go. He's built his career doing the man's bidding. I say, do you know Lazar Kaganovich?"

Just hearing the name sent a shiver down Julian's spine. "Of course I do." Kaganovich had been Stalin's architect of terror for nearly twenty years. He'd conducted purge after purge, murdering tens of thousands, overseeing the deportation to Siberia and the eventual death of hundreds of thousands, merely to keep terror and fear foremost in the minds of every Russian. Very few of those he'd helped murder were guilty of any crime.

"Your Russian, we hear, was Kaganovich's right-hand man. That's how he has risen." Among his many titles, Kaganovich was also a member of the Politburo. "You like the man; just don't like him too much." Ian finished his pint and rose to retrieve his umbrella and bowler hat. "Very helpful, as always. Don't let the Ruskies get to you, now."

"Not if I can help it." Julian watched Ian leave the pub while he himself sat for a while, musing about their conversation.

CHAPTER FOURTEEN

1950
Istanbul

The Times proclaimed that Turkish President İsmet İnönü was about to lose the next election. Julian sipped his sweet, thick coffee and puffed on his cigar. Serves the old boy right, he thought, for holding free elections.

The bright Istanbul sun radiated warmth that permeated his body, and Julian was relaxed as he glanced at his watch, then took in the scene once again. Below, to the right, sitting in the open-air café, he saw students from the nearby university, passing their lunch hours with *caj* and small snacks, huddling in conversation around the tables.

This afternoon it was reasonably quiet in the cramped market streets of Ortokoy, streets leading down to the riverside. In addition to the ever-present students, there was the bustle of bargain hunters and the odd adventurous tourist who had ventured away from the Blue Mosque and St. Sofia, seeking the "real" Istanbul. Julian could just make out the Bosporus, which, from his vantage point, appeared blue and clean in the sparkling sunlight, resembling not at all the open sewer that it really was.

Julian gestured for another coffee and placed his newspaper on the open chair to his right. Ahmet Yuksek was late. Julian pulled out his dead pipe and lit up with an expensive gold lighter, a gift from his most recent mistress. He eased back in his chair and enjoyed the smoke.

He'd only met the Turk the night before, at one of the endless informal gatherings Kim Philby hosted wherever he was stationed. With a hint of humor in his voice, Philby had suggested Julian might want to spend some time with the Turkish armaments minister, who'd be in attendance. Officially, Philby was first secretary of the British embassy in Istanbul, but, of course, it went without saying that he was the MI6 representative. To describe the charming and clearly brilliant Philby as a friend would have been taking the matter too far; but Philby went quite a bit out of his way to introduce Julian to the minister, going so far as to say that Julian's company was one of the most trustworthy companies with which to do business.

The reason for this trip was that Turkey was looking for special equipment to aid in its ceaseless internal war against the Kurdish minority. The minister, with his heavily oiled hair and smelling of violets, had quickly proven to be totally corrupt, eager to make deals before President İnönü was ousted in the pending election. They had an appointment in the minister's office that afternoon, but first was this meeting with Yuksek.

Julian had initially seen the little man standing off by himself at Philby's party, a cigarette in one hand and a glass of something clutched in the other. In time, Julian had realized the Turk was studying him. When the approach came, it was just as he was leaving the party. Yuksek stepped from the shadow of a doorway as Julian was searching for a taxi and asked to meet for coffee at this café.

"I believe we should know one another. We have much in common. I could be very valuable to you and your company," Yuksek had advanced in heavily accented English, as if that explained everything. So here Julian sat, wondering if this would be a waste of time, trying to make the most of his wait by eyeing the pretty female students not far away.

Julian's mind returned to Philby and the suspicions Julian held about him, suspicions Julian had never uttered. There was just something too good, too slick about Philby. It was as if everything came to him with ease. As far as Julian could see, his real line seemed to be collecting friends. Julian wondered why. No one, in the normal scheme of things, could possibly want or even need to know everyone.

Take the introduction last night. Julian had no idea how Philby had known he was in the country, let alone that he was there to meet the minister, but Philby had reached him at his hotel and invited him to the gathering. He had, it seemed to Julian, been too solicitous, too eager to be of service.

Philby reminded Julian a bit of himself, the way he operated behind the Iron Curtain, making connections, doing favors, gathering "friends," all so he could learn as much as possible. Such information was good as gold, either for business or to be passed along to Ian Cathcart.

It had been the same during the war. Philby either knew, or was in the process of knowing, just about everyone. He dazzled with the attention he lavished on each new conquest, was restrained with heterosexual men, flirtatious with homosexuals. And he was always witty and brilliant but especially when it was a woman, he was devastatingly charming.

What troubled Julian most of all was how little of that so-called great mind actually showed itself in the reports Philby had filed during the war. Though they'd cooperated on gathering information on Reds in Britain, they had filed separate reports. As detailed as Philby's had seemed, Julian had been troubled by certain omissions. Granted, those Julian suspected of Communist tendencies had shown such predilections primarily at university, but it struck him that any Brit serving as a Russian agent would have cut off obvious connections with the Communists. The idea was to seem to be a patriotic British subject.

In his own reports, Julian had made passing references to these men of questionable politics only because they held positions where, if they were, in fact, traitors, they could do harm. Philby omitted their names altogether. When Julian had questioned him on this, Philby's reply was always along the lines of, "He's one of us, old boy! No way that he's a spy; no point in blackening his name."

Yuksek came from behind Julian, then gestured at a chair and said, "May I?"

"Please."

The Turk was a spare man with one of those pencil mustaches common to pimps and certain movie idols. He smelled of ouzo and harsh Turkish tobacco. His suit looked as if he'd found it at a flea market and had slept in it for several days. He'd identified himself as working for *TASS*, which was as good as showing Julian his Communist party papers. The man was a spy, and Julian wondered why the fellow had wanted to meet quietly with him.

The Turk ordered coffee and made to light a nasty cigarette but could not find matches. Julian handed him his lighter, which the man took with a gracious nod. He lit, then inhaled deeply as he leaned back in his chair. When he straightened, he handed the lighter to Julian, who said, "Keep it. A gift." He'd learned that such gestures often brought enormous rewards. The Turk looked surprised, then smiled, fingering the lighter lightly.

Julian waited. Yuksek began with general comments about the weather, the city, a few of its landmarks, and the agreeable local climate for business, all quite friendly and innocuous. The conversation rambled, with the Turk seeming to have nothing to say. Finally, he referenced the gathering the night before and commented seemingly innocently about some who had been in attendance. He asked—as if out of the blue—how long Julian had known Philby, the first actual direct question.

"Since the war."

"I see. You are good friends, then." Yuksek indirectly eyed one of the students at a nearby table, who had just stretched himself out and was reading a textbook.

"'Friendly,' I would say. We don't usually move in the same circles."

Yuksek seemed not to have heard him. "You are a lord in your country, yes?"

Julian wondered where he'd heard that. "My father is an earl. I am scarcely a lord. And none of it means much, these days."

"I was born in Ankara. You know Ankara?"

"No. I've just been to Istanbul."

"Very cold there in winter. Very cold. My father died fighting you British in the other war. Life was very hard for my mother."

"It's been difficult for many people, these last years." The slender young man Yuksek had been watching rose, gathered his books, then left, laughing, making no eye contact with the Turk. Yuksek turned his attention to Julian. "What did you do in the last war?"

"Pushed papers, mostly."

"Pushed papers? Oh, yes! I see. A good job in war. To push around papers." The Turk laughed and rambled on while Julian drifted a bit in his thoughts, then came sharply alert. There was a pattern here, and Julian suddenly realized how seriously he'd underestimated this little man. "You have been to Russia?" Yuksek asked, answering his own question, saying, "Yes, so I heard. Things are very bad there, very bad, indeed. I think if they did not guard the border with the guns pointing inward, there would be many defections. Yes, many defections, indeed. It is all a question of opportunity. I have a question for you, Mr. Harda-way."

"Yes?"

"Can you be discreet?"

"Certainly." Here it came, the approach.

"You are here to do some business with the government. I am here to tell you that you have friends in the government, and they would like to conclude contracts with you. It is required that you have a local agent to assist you in this transaction, a local agent who will receive twenty percent commission."

Yuksek handed over a grimy business card that looked as if it had resided in his crumpled suit since the day that he had acquired the garment. The card had the name and address of a rather elegant-sounding company, located in the best part of Ankara. On the back was the name and address of a bank in Liechtenstein, with the account number and password required to make deposits. "This is your agent."

"How do I know that you are not just muscling in on a contract that is pretty obvious, given my company's activities?" asked Julian

"Then, very discreetly, look over my shoulder." The Turk's English had suddenly improved. Julian looked. "Do you see the family sitting in the corner, having lunch? Do you recognize the man?"

Julian answered, "Yes." He was surprised to see the minister at lunch with his whole and rather large family.

"When he leaves, he will put a copy of the English *Daily Telegraph* on the table. You are not to speak to him, under any circumstances, but that newspaper is proof of my request. You have been most charming and generous with your fine lighter. I must be on my way." He finished his third coffee and made his good-byes.

Julian remained where he was. Then, from the corner of his eye, Julian saw the minister gather up his family to leave, dropping a copy of the *Daily Telegraph* on the table as he did so.

CHAPTER FIFTEEN

1950
London

On the celebration of Christian's tenth birthday, Julian had occasion to reflect on the life he was carving out for himself. He had no complaints with Sarah, though he could scarcely say they were close. Lately, she'd served as the local magistrate and also busied herself at the church with jumble sales. Each Wednesday, she volunteered at the army hospital, within view of Julian's office. Twice a week, she shopped in London with friends. Sarah maintained a busy social calendar, mingling routinely with the wives of other lords, disdaining politics—except to comment on the Labour Party and its outrageous policies. All very proper.

His father, the earl, railed bitterly against the Labour government and the loss of empire. The more he complained, the more full of life he became. His girth had continued to swell, and, while he limited himself to a single cigar a day, he was otherwise as full of vigor as Julian could ever remember.

When it came to business, again, there was little about which to complain. Julian was making money at an unlordly rate, with his contracts in Poland lining his pockets without requiring much of him. In fact, he spent much of his time in London dealing with his money managers and government suppliers, ensuring that he had access to ample surplus goods and that his money would go to the right investments.

Christian laughed and ran about playfully with the other children at the party. He was a strong, happy child, full of charm, possessed of a quick wit.

Work, for Julian, meant using his company as an intelligence-gathering front. He had found that he had not just an aptitude for private enterprise of this sort, but, in fact, a real passion for it. He offered small electronic items, communication equipment and components, plus various military surplus goods to a few of the Soviet Bloc countries, with Poland his best client. The Bloc countries were all desperate for his merchandise and, not the least adept at bargaining, were fairly easy marks. The game was part cat-and-mouse, and Julian learned a lot about that. Another part was just helping people out. Julian particularly enjoyed that, as the people whom he helped reciprocated, and his business grew.

For zest and to satisfy his patriotic instincts, Julian did not mind serving his country as an intelligence operative, the word "spy" having such unpleasant connotations. He gleaned all that his government needed in terms of technical information, volunteered by his clients for the goods they required. This data told the assessors at the SIS precisely what the Soviet Bloc already had, what they required, and, even more, what they intended to do with the goods they obtained. Julian was not allowed to sell to the East any of the very latest technologies; he could only provide items that were, technologically speaking, a generation or two back. This was not a problem as, in large part, his clients could not tell the difference. In fact, what he provided was so superior to what they had, they were happy to obtain whatever he sold. Their need for technology was great and urgent.

Beyond the rewards of good salesmanship and above the pride of doing patriotic work, Julian took great satisfaction in staking his one claim in the world. He was taking real strides towards freeing himself from the seductive embrace of family title and wealth. He was gaining strength to resist the temptation to merely float through a comfortable existence.

For all this, Julian's ultimate goal was still a long way off. Concord Trading Company was growing but was not immune to setbacks and potential ruin, should his markets dry up. The truth was, Julian's professional and personal hopes could collapse at any moment.

As the years passed, Poland and the Soviet Union were becoming more lucrative for Julian, resulting in increasingly lengthy business trips. The Stalin terror apparatus was driven by paranoia, and there was no escape from it. Julian could imagine no greater evil in the world. The stories coming out of recently Communist China were of millions liquidated in the name of the revolution. Everywhere communism stretched its hand, misery and death were to be found, crushing the human spirit.

More than one of his sources in Poland had disappeared. Julian had learned not to inquire after them. No one wanted to talk about them. It was as if these vanished persons had never existed.

Julian, of course, never told anyone he was, in reality, a secret agent, although he felt instinctively that Mishka had guessed this before the Russian had returned to Moscow. The crafty Russian gathered information like a maiden collecting flowers in a field, a bit here, a little there.

Still, it seemed to Julian that if the disappeared were properly debriefed, his own name might be mentioned repeatedly; and once his name was found too frequently listed in a dossier, he would attract the attention of the NKVD. While he felt relatively safe as a foreigner behind the Iron Curtain, it was always possible that he would inadvertently find himself mixed up in something of which he was unaware. This would be followed by a traffic accident, notable only in the fact that it would take his life.

Julian had always assumed the use that he was to the Communists in Poland and Russia gave him a measure of safety, but he was not so foolish to assume that this alone entitled him to immunity. Others with smaller businesses had already disappeared. More than luck was keeping Julian safe, and he knew that Mishka's presence remained in Poland, watching him. Julian was, in his own way, part of the apparatus, a fringe player who offered a bridge to Western supplies that the Soviets could not afford to lose.

The most troubling aspect of his life was the disrepute in which he was held in his own home country. While he was seen as a "merchant of death" for the little arms dealing that he actually did do, others in London high society considered him a traitor for dealing with the Communists at all, all the worse because he had been born to a noble title. Treason was inexcusable for a commoner, but for a lord it was incomprehensible. He had soiled not only himself but his family name, as his father had told him on more than one occasion—though his father continued to accept Julian's money to support the family estate. That portion of society that welcomed Julian as a compatriot was the left, the very people who were destroying Britain's nobility. His competitors left a great deal to be desired, as well, and did nothing for the image of his profession. The image meant nothing to him, but he worried about the legacy he was preparing for Christian.

Julian emerged from his musings, glanced at his watch. "Leaving?" Sarah asked.

"I'm afraid I must. Meeting in the city. Couldn't be put off."

"You might wait for the cake cutting. I'd like a photograph, so the boy at least remembers that you existed during his childhood."

"Yes, I planned to. But perhaps we could get on with it?"

Sarah summoned a servant straightening utensils on the long table that held the elaborate birthday cake. They huddled momentarily, then Sarah turned towards the shouting children and clapped her hands to bring them. The herd stormed towards the table of goodies like an invading army.

Christian smiled broadly, then caught his father's eye with a look of absolute adulation. Julian returned it, swept away by his love for his son and by his son's adoration of him; it was a feeling he'd never shared with anyone but the boy, and he treasured it beyond words. But then, the clamor of the celebration returned, their moment was over. Sarah intervened, as did the other children. Julian helped the boy cut the cake, kissed him on the cheek, and left quickly afterwards, feeling something moist in the corner of his eye.

* * *

Julian handed his car over to the doorman at the Colony Restaurant at Berkley Square and made his way inside. He spotted Tommy Harris through the thick cloud of smoke and walked towards the man. The restaurant was crowded, waiters weaving their way among chairs and tables, carrying trays of steaming food, the steady din of diners broken from time to time by a loud peal of laughter.

Across the room, a small Big Band was playing, as couples shuffled across the modest dance floor.

The first word that came to mind to describe Tommy was thick. Julian was always amazed by how thickset the man was—biceps, thighs, neck, even head. The former OSS operative seemed forged in some fabled kiln, hardly born to a normal mother, and it was as if the man's entire body exuded a mythical strength.

Seated at the tablecloth-covered dinner table with Tommy were two women, both good looking and a little on the young side. Julian had no doubt one was meant for him. One looked scarcely old enough to be here—she, no doubt, would be for Tommy, who liked blondes, the younger the better.

"Julian!" Tommy exclaimed as he looked up from the cleavage of the woman sitting closest to him. She wore a button-down shirt and a bra that pushed her small breasts together into something worth looking at; these professionals had a way of knowing what a client would find irresistible.

She looked up at Julian invitingly as Tommy inserted his cigarette between his lips and rose, extending his hand. Ah, the refreshing Americans, Julian thought, pleased to have his hand engulfed in Tommy's massive palm, and pleased with the company.

After introductions, Julian took his seat. The brunette to his right—Betty—greeted him with a hand on his thigh. She smiled warmly, flashing straight, bright teeth, uncharacteristic for a Brit.

If he hadn't known better, he might even have thought the smile genuine. She appeared the older of the two, old enough to be fresh out of college, maybe. The two girls could have been sisters. Perhaps they were. That would have been very much Tommy's style.

Julian had first met Tommy when they'd both been at the Ryder Street offices of the OSS during the last year of the war. Tommy had been one of Wild Bill Donovan's favorite operators. Donovan had earned the Congressional Medal of Honor in World War I and, following a highly successful business career, had spent much of his own fortune creating an overseas intelligence operation as the threat of a new European war loomed. In 1941, with America's entry into the war, Donovan had created the Office of Strategic Services, or OSS, also known as Department II.

Tommy had run agents into occupied France and been dropped into France several times himself, each time returning with war stories so incredible Julian had found them nearly unbelievable. They matched the man's extraordinary physique, making him seem like something torn from the pages of a comic strip.

After surviving what was to have been a suicide mission into Germany, reportedly an attempt to assassinate SS Reichsführer Heinrich Himmler, he miraculously made his way to Switzerland and, from there, to London, where he spent the final months of the war recuperating from injuries, manning a desk all the while. On that desk, he displayed a Nazi helmet with two bullet holes, one entry, one exit, the inside coated a suspicious brown color. He claimed to have fired the round that penetrated the helmet and a German soldier's brain. His cigarette lighter was made from an American .50 caliber shell casing, though he'd never claimed it had once held the very bullet that had slain the Nazi.

Tommy had no great love of the British, or of England itself. Many of the Americans stationed in Britain had affected a British accent, or at the very least liberally laced British expressions into their speech. Tommy did the same, tossing in the odd English expression now and then, but always with a mocking voice. He described English gentlemen as being effete and frequently referred to them as "pooftahs."

It might have seemed surprising that he and Julian had hit it off. Tommy, however, was an admirer of class, which he'd said more than once, and he felt that Julian possessed class in abundance. And Tommy admired courage, which he attributed to Julian, earned for Julian's willingness to work undercover behind the Iron Curtain for so many years. Like Mishka, Tommy simply assumed that Julian was a spy, though the subject was never discussed. Their friendship held the added advantage that they shared an appetite for high-class ladies of the night.

"Good to have you back, Tommy," Julian declared as Betty delivered his genitals a probing squeeze, resting her hand again on his inside thigh. She smiled at Julian again, approvingly. If she were working on her tip, she was off to a good start, Julian thought, as he shifted in his seat to accommodate the sudden bulge between his legs.

"I can't believe I'm here again," Tommy enthused, lighting another cigarette. The American spoke with a Southwestern American accent. Julian remembered that Tommy came from Arizona or New Mexico, one of those American desert states, maybe even the one with a big canyon. Since his return from Washington, Julian had grown concerned that Tommy's drinking and drug use had escalated. He'd been part of the new American Central Intelligence Agency, the direct descendent of the OSS, but had chafed at returning to desk work. Files had accumulated in his office at an alarming rate. Because he was now in his fifties, his repeated requests for a field assignment had been refused. Why he was back in the London he disliked, surrounded by pooftahs, was a question to which Julian had yet to learn an answer. Tommy had, however, been quite insistent that they meet.

Tommy leaned closer to Julian and spoke quietly. "Have you heard about our old friend Kim?" During the war, Tommy had despised Philby and had warned Julian more than once that the man was Pink, if not an outright Red.

"Nothing since he was in Turkey." *Not* strictly true, but close enough, Julian thought.

"You heard about his buddy Donnie MacLean and that homo Burgess?"

Who had not? Burgess had been dismissed from his job with the British embassy in Washington—on account of his excessive drinking—and been returned to Britain. Within weeks, MacLean and Burgess had defected to the Soviet Union, outright admission that the pair were spies. "Of course."

"Of course, our friend Kim tipped them off, I'm certain. The CIA has known for a while that Kim was Red, but your people wouldn't believe it. He wore the right school tie and was so damned glib. Hell, Burgess even lived with Kim in Washington for a time, while he was posted there. Besides picking up the soap for one another, they weren't discussing old times there. I hear Kim's back in London, selling real estate or something."

"So I understand."

"I've got a message for you, old boy." Tommy's dark eyes twinkled. "I was asked to deliver it. You remember a Turk named Ahmet Yuksek?"

Julian immediately recalled the so-called reporter for *TASS* he'd met in Istanbul. The memory was so vivid, Julian could almost smell the fellow's Turkish tobacco and ouzo. Julian nodded.

"My last official duty was to debrief him. He's come over to us. He's been picked clean and someone wanted my impressions before they cut him loose and gave him the soft life he was promised. He knew I knew you, which disturbed me no end. He said to tell you that Comrade Kim is making a laugh-ingstock of you all on this jolly little isle."

"So he made it?"

"Oh, yes. He's the real deal. He's why we know Kim is dirty. The CIA was working with you boys on an invasion of Albania, the only field assignment I ever wrangled from that bunch, but each goddamned detail was passed through Kim's trusted hands. The Ruskies knew our every step. I wanted to have a shooting accident, but the boss had a fit when I suggested it. So instead, I ended up pushing paper and Albania is Red as fresh blood. He said he'd tried to contact you as well, claimed Philby and the others had you marked as a Red in waiting."

"That's ridiculous," Julian told Tommy, laughing. "I only met the Turk once. And Philby—well, I thought Philby was trying to arrange something like that, but he wouldn't cop to it, and Yuksek didn't mention anything. I'm as far from a Red as they come, Tommy. I'm a capitalist, for God's sake. No one believes it, do they?"

"How do I know? I'm just an American."

Tommy laughed, his eyes closing into slits as he leaned back again in the booth.

After the claret, when it became clear that Tommy could not decide which of the girls to take home with him and so had decided to take both, Betty feigned disappointment, hoping that Julian would remember her fondly and no doubt call upon her services again sometime. Tommy's in for a very busy night, Julian thought as the three went off together, one of the American's great hands planted squarely on the buttocks of each woman.

Back at his London townhouse, Julian considered what he'd learned tonight. Tommy had insisted they get together, and, though he'd hinted he was getting into the arms business himself, for Julian the really tangible event had been Tommy's information on Philby and Yuksek. He was surprised that he'd been implicated as a possible turncoat.

Julian was between mistresses, but Mrs. Kench, the faithful nanny of his childhood, had waited up, despite his instructions that she should not, and set out hot cocoa. "Go to bed now," he instructed before taking a comfortable seat by the fireplace. He lit a Havana Perfecto Robusto and contemplated his good friend and mentor, Roger Hollis, one of Britain's most trusted and senior spy catchers at MI5. Seeing Tommy again had brought it all back. Julian had tried to lay all of his wartime suspicions to rest, but recent events had proven many of them correct.

In recent years, Julian had ceased passing along any meaningful information to Hollis. It wasn't only that Julian had become less interested in his alliance with MI5 and more concerned about maintaining his good relations on both sides of the Iron Curtain, although this was certainly good for business. There was something else. Since the end of the war, nothing tangible had ever come from the really juicy items he'd given exclusively to the man. Cathcart had been far more effective, and Julian continued to deliver gems of intelligence to Ian and his team. Julian couldn't remember Hollis ever acting on a single piece of intelligence. If Philby was Red, the odds were that Hollis was as well. Only a few years after the end of the war, and the Communists were well penetrated into Britain and its security services, perhaps enough to make a difference in the country's future.

The recent defections of Burgess and MacLean, two very close friends of Roger Hollis, had disturbed Julian. But then, many of them at university in the thirties had Communist associates. It was fashionable to be a Communist at that time. Tommy had informed him of the suspicions directed towards him as a friend of the defectors and, hence, making him worthy of being suspect. That was the news Yuksek had carried, and Julian was certain that the information could come from nowhere else but Philby's mouth.

Julian knew from experience that such suspicion could be every bit as corrosive to a career as a public accusation. It put him in the terrible position of defending himself. His past—particularly his connections in Warsaw and Moscow—made him a conspicuous target. He thought bleakly of what had happened during the McCarthy witch-hunts in America. If anything similar swept England, he realized that he might be one of the first to be sacrificed, innocent or not. He had already profited from the Cold War, and, while he still had friends in government, they would be no help against a hungry public and an even hungrier press searching for scapegoats for Britain's steady decline on the world stage.

If what Tommy said were true about Philby, how could there really, any longer, be doubt about Hollis? Julian had heard that Hollis was staunchly defending his old friend, Philby, arguing it was unfair and even un-British to judge a man because of the treachery of his associates and old school chums. On one hand, that was quite noble. But there was another way of looking at it. Julian could see that all too plainly now. At this point, a fervent patriotism on Julian's part could be taken the wrong way, and he might jeopardize not only his future, but his life.

Julian puffed on his pipe and grimaced. What a mess Britain had become. With Churchill back as PM and Anthony Eden again foreign secretary, he had luxuriated in a bit of hope. However, it was soon clear that neither Churchill nor Eden could undo the socialist programs Labour had set in place. The economy had never properly recovered from the Depression before the war. With the United States rebuilding the shattered German and Japanese industrial bases, how could poor Britain, with its antiquated factories and punitive taxation, ever hope to compete? No. Difficult times remained ahead.

But what most disturbed Julian was the unwillingness of those in power to doubt the loyalty of anyone who'd gone to the right school, come from a respected family, no matter how damning the evidence. The smooth, genial, hard-working Hollis would see that Philby went unscathed as his own stock continued to rise. Possibly, he might even bring Philby back into the fold at MI6.

Julian was deeply troubled by his own situation. If Philby was out to use Julian as a scapegoat, where could he turn for protection? He'd always thought Hollis would back him if suspicions ever arose. But if Philby and Hollis were in league together…

As his pipe died, Julian sighed. It was beyond him. He was just a small a cog in a very big wheel.

CHAPTER SIXTEEN

1954
Warsaw

If anyone had thought the death of the mass murderer Stalin in 1953 would turn on the lights in Eastern Europe and the Soviet Union, they were sadly mistaken. Warsaw remained in perpetual night, and as the drunken Mishka careened his lime-green Pobieda through the all but black streets, Julian wondered if he'd live through the night. Mishka may have kept him safe from certain dangers, but the Russian seemed to risk their lives whenever they were in a car.

Though Mishka mocked the change in his fortunes, there was no doubt he'd had a close call in Moscow. Rumors abounded on just exactly how Stalin died. Julian suspected it would be years before the truth finally emerged, if ever. The story he liked best, and which seemed to most closely match the Kremlin's account, as Julian had come to know it, was that the seventy-three-year-old Stalin had suffered a stroke. His corps of doctors, which were kept on hand since the war, labored mightily to save his life. They succeeded, but Stalin experienced lingering effects from the stroke in his speech and his movement. Stalin blamed his doctors and ordered them shot.

Several months later, in March 1953, Stalin suffered another, even more debilitating stroke and was found sprawled on his office floor. At the time, he had been actively purging the Politburo, the members of which gathered to see for themselves if the butcher were going to die. A new corps of doctors was summoned. Certain of the fate in store for them if they revived the dictator, they elected instead to oversee his death. In the adjoining room, the complicit Politburo drafted the text of the official announcement and plotted the power succession.

Yes, Julian thought, that was the mad world the Man of Steel had created.

Julian's money was on Khrushchev to assume total power. Khrushchev was ruthless enough for it but presented a non-threatening demeanor. Beria the Butcher had been put against the wall in Lubyanka prison the previous December and shot. And here was Mishka, back in Warsaw, vague about his duties, obviously happy to still be alive. Almost everyone who'd been close to Stalin was dead or awaiting death. It was said that Mishka's mentor, Lazar Kaganovich, was running the Urals potash works in Perm Oblast, his life only spared because he'd once defended Nikita Khrushchev when Stalin had wanted to execute him during the war.

Through the night, Julian could just make out sights of the construction that consumed central Warsaw. Drab brick buildings were rising everywhere, seeming to lift themselves from the rubble like leviathans. Russian trucks and cars could be seen throughout the day, transporting building materials and workers with the sterile energy of the Communists everywhere.

"How close was it for you in Moscow?" Julian asked, trading on what was becoming a close friendship with the Russian. Mishka could talk freely while traveling in the car—if he wanted to.

"Close? I don't even want to think about how close it was, my friend. I felt the cold wind of the wings of the Angel of Death, I can tell you that. Thank God, Nikita, bastard that he is, is not the bloodthirsty murderer Stalin was, and that I still had a few secrets to offer."

That was as much as he'd ever likely learn, Julian thought. "And what are you supposed to do, now that you're back in Warsaw?"

"I am the new director general of Polymot," he slurred. Mishka had consumed at least a bottle of vodka already. "Now, I become a Communist capitalist, if there is such a thing. We can finally be partners in business, officially!"

Julian had not heard of the company, so assumed it was a new creation of the Polish government for trade dealings with the West. He smiled and said, "Will you be satisfied being 'just' a businessman?"

Mishka laughed and declaimed, "I am a businessman now! I am anything that I have to be, at any time."

In the four years Mishka had been stationed in Moscow, he and Julian had seen one another fewer than half a dozen times, usually at an official function. Twice they had managed to meet in private, and each time Mishka had slipped Julian a package for Switzerland. One contained just over £120,000, the other almost £80,000. In return, Julian had received substantial contracts, contracts he knew he would never have earned without Mishka's help, though the two men never discussed them.

Mishka pulled the ugly car to the front of the Fukier restaurant, one of Warsaw's few surviving. High class restaurants As Mishka entered, he was treated with all the deference he'd received when he'd been head of the Russian secret police in the Polish capital. The main dining room was hued in gold by the soft light that bathed the vaulted ceilings. Candles abounded everywhere. A deep red velvet curtain was draped across the expansive, arched front window. Flowers and bowls of fresh fruit were scattered throughout the room. The average Pole outside might be sucking on a bowl of warm cabbage soup for dinner, but here, the party elite enjoyed the pleasures of power and success.

The patrons were primarily Polish members of the Communist Party, plus a scattering of former nobility, intermixed with Russians and East Germans. Julian and Mishka were shown a prominent table, then fed some of the finest food Poland offered, washed down with excellent pre-war bottles of French wine. If Mishka's new job was a demotion, there was certainly no sign of it.

Towards midnight, the Russian led Julian out, then wheeled the green car with even greater abandon, taking them to Warsaw's sole nightclub, the Krododil, located close by in the old city.

There, they joined a group of businessmen, along with a number of good-looking women whose eyes seemed to have seen a little too much over their short adult years.

Mishka was greeted like a conquering hero. The men took their places at a long table and joined in the well-established festivities. Night might have descended on Poland for a time, but the Poles still maintained their customs, even splitting into two camps at the Krododil. Here, they drank vodka to the Polish toast of "*Nazdrowie!*" which meant "here's to your health" and required everyone to drain his glass in a single shot. To ensure that no one switched to water, from time to time, Mishka had everyone pass his drink to the person on his right.

"You see, I am good news for them," Mishka whispered sloppily to Julian. "If Mishka can make money legally, then soon they know they, too, will make money—and not get shot for it." He roared with laughter, as though that was a great joke.

Two hours later, so wobbly that Julian and Mishka leaned on one another for support, they made their way to the car. Mishka fumbled with his keys to both open the door and find the ignition. Finally, he fired the car up and roared off like a Cossack leading a charge, wheeling his way dangerously through the city's winding streets. He came to a stop outside one of the new high-rise apartment buildings. There he killed the engine, reached behind the seat, and produced a bottle of Russian vodka.

"*Za vas!*" he said as he took a long hit, then passed it over to Julian, who said, "*Spasiba,*" then poured the vodka down his throat. It fell like chilled water. Outside, it was below freezing. A single pedestrian, wrapped in a bundle of rags, made her tentative way along the street, mist forming in front of her face as if she were a draft horse laboring with a heavy wagon. In a darkened doorway, a match flashed, flickered, then was extinguished.

Mishka stared in that direction a moment, then said, "He watches."

"You?"

"Me, you, everyone, and everything here. But he likes dollars, so we can sit and talk a bit." Mishka had never before wanted to sit privately and talk. In fact, he seemed to be a man who demanded constant stimuli. Business turned into pleasure at five o'clock daily with an inaugural drink, followed by dinner, more drinks, various entertainments, and—invariably—women.

This was new. "Talk about what?"

"In Moscow," Mishka said in a nearly sober voice, "I was closer to death than I ever was in the Great Patriotic War. The new Politburo was settling long-remembered scores, like old hags, and they call themselves men. But Khrushchev put a stop to it, before anyone got to me."

"Why would they want to kill you?" Julian knew an answer to that question; he wanted to hear Mishka's.

"You cannot have power in Russia without making many enemies. When you have the power, you must use it to destroy them before they destroy you. I did not kill all my enemies, though I assure you I tried. But tovarishch Nikita says the days of murder are finished; so, for now, I am here, ready to serve the revolution in a new way." Mishka drank, but this time did not pass the bottle. He paused for a long, contemplative moment. "Someday, you will be an earl in your country. Is that not true?"

Julian was so drunk, he leaned heavily against the door, his eyes thick with sleep. "I suppose I will, when my father dies."

"That was the way of things in Russia before. The elite decided matters for the masses. Then came the revolution. The elite were killed or driven into exile, and men who were lowborn, from the masses, peasants, tried to do the same thing. Imagine peasants ruling Mother Russia! Look what it has done to us. Millions slaughtered, economic ruin, rampant poverty, and lies everywhere. How many more must die before it ends?"

Julian's mind snapped to alert. There it was: treason. If anyone was standing close enough to hear, if some agency had planted a listening device in this car, Mishka would be as good as dead.

"You take risks, Mishka," Julian whispered as he reached for the bottle.

"What we need is a czar," Mishka said with a low slur.

Julian lowered the bottle and handed it back. "You had a Red czar in Stalin and have a new one now in Khrushchev, although I'm not certain what color this one is."

Mishka spat on the floor of the new car. "I mean a *real* czar, not a selected one nor one who crowned himself! I mean the man born to rule."

"The czar is dead, and there is no heir. You would have to find someone, somewhere."

Mishka cast his eyes towards the hidden guard. "I would think you of all people would know better. With nobility, there is always an heir. The bloodline always survives."

He turned towards Julian, and some peculiarity in what little light there was in darkened Warsaw caused a flash to cross Mishka's face for an instant. In that moment, Julian saw a look on the Russian he had never seen, nor ever expected to see. "I would be a great czar," Mishka said in a low voice.

Julian almost laughed out loud at the mere thought of Mishka as czar, but he held back, sensing that would not be welcome. Instead, he said, "I don't believe that you would be the czar. You are, after all, as you said, now a businessman."

Mishka answered almost gently, "You can believe whatever you choose, Julian. I choose to believe in what I know."

Julian said nothing. The vodka was talking; that was for certain. What did he mean? Was he dreaming of being czar? Or was he trying to tell Julian something? Was there a plan here, or just a drunken fantasy?

They sat without speaking for a very long time. Outside, Warsaw was still as a cemetery. Finally, Mishka's voice came from the darkness. "I am the heir to the czar."

Then Mishka laughed the hearty roar that made him the life of the party. "Come. I have a surprise for you." He climbed out of the car awkwardly and let them into the building. The all-but-new elevator creaked and groaned as it slowly rose to the top floor. Mishka leered as he extracted a large key, typical of those in use in Poland, and opened the door to an apartment.

Across the well-furnished living room, on a comfortable overstuffed sofa, sat two very beautiful women. Julian recognized Victoria, his former mistress, immediately, but he had to be introduced to the other girl before he realized that she was Victoria's younger sister.

Mishka nudged Julian in the ribs. "Victoria is with me; Monika is for you. She is my gift to you. I think she, too, fucks like an actress. I tell the sister you will take her to England. Now she do anything for you." His eyes turned as the women rose, postured to the best advantage for their figures, and glided towards them. Mishka laughed, then shouted, "Why is there no music?"

Victoria said a pleasant hello to Julian, giving him her hand as she flashed a slight smile, her once-bright teeth slightly yellowed by cigarettes. She had aged a little too quickly. Life in Poland without her father's political cache had been difficult, he was sure, but she remained good to look at. She put a Benny Goodman album on the turntable.

Monika stood, her breathtaking features fixed directly on Julian, her long, blonde hair cascading down her back, her large lips pressed in a barely visible smile as she moved towards him, slowly, her eyes telling him that she was his for the taking. Her body was remarkably thin to be carrying such large breasts. Julian, drunk, felt the saliva rushing into his mouth. He had not dined on so exquisite a morsel in ages—possibly never. She was perfect. She eased out of her dress as she reached him, revealing black lace lingerie, garters, and stockings to match her black heels. So the girl had a taste for the West. "You like?" she whispered into his ear, rocking to the music, taking his hands and putting them on her body.

Mishka dizzily circled the room, dancing with himself. He knocked over a tall porcelain vase before falling onto the sofa beside Victoria. He continued to speak, though the words were unintelligible. His eyes grew bleary, then closed for the night.

Mishka had underestimated the younger girl. She did things Julian wouldn't have dared to ask, things that made him hard again, even after he had fucked both her and her sister. She did things that seemed even to slightly embarrass her older sister, though Victoria remained quiet and compliant. Monika fucked like a porn star, not an actress.

CHAPTER SEVENTEEN

1937
Russia

The Bolshevik authorities, such as they were in those turbulent times, proved too confused and elsewhere focused to ask about the son of the czar-for-a-day. They were overwhelmed with changing the regime and maintaining contact with Moscow. Fortunately, and as Mishka's mother had surmised, they knew little about Natalia's family of commoners. Outside of her marriage to the czar's brother, her family had never earned distinction.

The Red Army had plenty of work in keeping the White Army at bay, reorganizing the capital, and imposing some sort of order to fulfill Lenin's proletariat promises before the population grew restless and turned on them. It was the first moment since Russia's inception, hundreds of years before that the czars had not ruled. The first rush of excitement for the peasants had been replaced with a pervasive unease. Later that year, the Romanovs were declared dead—all of them. And, as Uncle Oleg hypothesized, it was very possible that the guards assigned to the Romanovs had reported them all dead rather than admit to an escape and face the consequences. In those times, anything was possible.

Mishka attended a local elementary school. The curriculum was quickly changed to reflect the new order. Communist philosophy, with the works of Marx and Engels, was taught beginning at age ten. The evils of the czars were expounded upon at great length. Mishka was instructed to write essays on the subject, to stand in front of the class and denounce his ancestors, the former rulers, as well as all bourgeois influences.

Over the years, Mishka made no close friends at school, and no one besides his uncle and aunt knew his true identity. By the age of nineteen, it seemed to him as though that identity belonged, like so much else, to another era, to history. But he remembered, and that was what really mattered.

Mishka excelled in every class, achieving well beyond his peers in both academics and athletics, with a fierce competitiveness that more than once earned him a reputation as a less-than-model proletarian. Uncle Oleg, a schoolteacher who had studied in England as a young man, helped Mishka appear to be a prodigy rather than a noble. By his teenage years, there was already talk of the great service Mishka would do as a leader for the revolution. He was more than simply talented; his efforts to prove his patriotism and his true passion for Russia made him appear as one of the new Soviet Union's strongly loyal citizens.

Neither this recognition nor the early honors he received gave him pleasure. He was driven only by hatred, hatred of the people who had taken his title, killed his mother and father, and soiled the name his ancestors had struggled for centuries to make noble.

Mishka was accelerated into Kiev's most advanced secondary school, an institution once used for education of the nobility, that the revolution had seen transformed into a facility to teach politics. The top students from this school were sent to Moscow, to the central government's university for political study, a school established by Lenin to train a generation of enlightened political leaders. Early in Mishka's last year, his uncle, who taught languages at the Kiev secondary school, informed Mishka that he was to attend the university in Moscow.

His uncle, though once committed to seeing Mishka returned to the throne, had been silent on the subject these last years. Mishka could see in the man's eyes that his aspirations for Mishka had changed. If Mishka could become a Communist leader of the Soviet Union, was this not another way, a way easier than forcing the overthrow of the entire system to become its single ruler? Uncle Oleg believed that the age of monarchy had come to an end.

Mishka, however, did not.

Afternoons were reserved for soccer, his only other passion besides Russia. On the field, he was a hero, a leader; when he scored both goals in a 2-0 victory, he was, for a moment, elevated above the group in glory. He was, at that instant, reclaiming his birthright. These were the only moments he allowed himself to imagine someday standing in Red Square, triumphant as czar.

It was after one of these afternoons, raised above his teammates on their shoulders after they captured the Kiev football championship, that he found her waiting for him at home. She was sitting beside his uncle, at the kitchen table, sipping a tall glass of hot tea. He didn't recognize her for the first minute, and the way she stared at him made him uncomfortable.

"We saw the game," Uncle Oleg said.

"You play brilliantly," she said. She looked remarkably like someone he felt that he had once known; strangely, her voice was familiar, yet, at the same time, strange. She wore the same clothing as the other women in Kiev, the dull grays and browns of earth and factory.

Mishka watched her carefully, as he had learned to watch strangers carefully as a child, to detect their strengths, their weaknesses, their intentions. He watched her, also, with the caution he had learned in Kiev, where any stranger might know he was a Romanov, where his execution might be a moment away.

"Do you recognize me?" she asked.

"I—I—" Mishka stuttered and looked to his uncle for support. Uncle Oleg kept his head down and stared at his thumbs.

"I am your mother."

Mishka stared at the woman, remembering the night on the road. "My mother is dead," he said without inflection.

"I thought it best that you believe that. For your sake," she said. "I didn't know if I would ever be back. I shouldn't be back now."

"My mother is dead," Mishka repeated, still staring at her. Suddenly, he remembered her, clearly, as though she had left for a trip and only just returned, as though she were still the czar's sister-in-law and the revolution had never happened. He fell to his knees at her feet and, for the first time since he had arrived in Kiev so many years before, he wept large salty tears that he felt would never stop...

She continued, recounting how she had lived in Paris in fear, existing comfortably on the generosity of czarist loyalists. Though she was in exile, she no longer believed her life to be in danger. The Soviets seemed content to allow her to live.

"I'm taking a terrible risk coming here, but I had to see you and make sure you are safe, so it is all worthwhile," she insisted, holding Mishka's hands and turning his chin up to face her. His eyes were swollen, the stone face that he had kept for years suddenly broke, once again becoming the face of a boy. From beneath her wool shirt, she removed a ring, a gold signet ring with a large ruby in the center.

"This belonged to your uncle, Czar Nicholas. He feared the worst and gave it to his brother, my husband and your father, before he was taken prisoner. *This* is the ring of the czar. You, Georgi, will become the czar one day." She ran her fingers through his hair. He took the ring, slid it slowly onto his finger, and held his hand out to see what it looked like, then removed it and clutched it in his fist.

"I will be the czar," he swore, both to himself and his mother. It was the last time in his life that he would see her, except in his dreams.

CHAPTER EIGHTEEN

1954
London

"And there," Julian noted, nodding briefly to a former school chum passing in the opposite direction with his own son, "is where I broke my leg. I'd been matched against older boys because of my speed. The earl was furious. He came storming over from The House of Lords cane in hand. He was finally persuaded it was on account of my talent, as it were, that I'd been matched with the older lads."

Julian smiled at the recollection. His father's face had turned a beet red, and Julian had really feared the master was about to be beaten as the earl waved his cane over his head in a continuous circle, as if searching for a target. It had been one of the most gratifying moments of Julian's life, despite the pain of the broken leg, the surest sign he'd ever had that his father loved him.

It was Old Boys Day at Eton, and the traditional cricket match between fathers and sons would begin shortly. Julian had never liked this enforced distance from his son while the lad was at boarding school, but it was the English way. So it had been for his grandfather, father, for himself—and now for his son. It was essential to attend the right schools, make the proper friendships, the necessary connections. Christian, in fact, had been placed on the House List the day after his birth. He was boarded in the same house where both the earl and, later, Julian had resided.

"I miss you, dear boy," Julian said as he took a seat on a bench overlooking the gently flowing river. Insects buzzed in the warm sun. A dozen dragonflies hovered, then skimmed about the surface of the water. The scene brought to mind many memories of his years here. While not all of them were happy ones, still, by and large, he'd enjoyed Eton.

A boat containing father and son drifted past, the father in obvious ecstasy, the teenage son seemingly confused. "I regret that this is necessary, but public school gives you so much—things that you will not appreciate until you are much older. Local schools are not for the likes of us. We have a different course to chart, and these schools, the important half-dozen, are for the future leaders of Britain and, indeed, the world."

Christian, looking sober as always, so adult in his manner, said, "I understand, sir. I miss you, as well, but I quite like it here."

"I'm getting good reports on your work. Your marks are satisfactory, except for mathematics. You'll want to bear down a bit, there."

"Yes, sir."

It was, Julian thought, remarkable that he could feel such love for this young man. He wondered, for a moment, if his father had ever felt the same for him. No—despite the display of rage at the master, not like this. Julian was his father's heir, someone about whom his father could brag. His father had never felt this way for Julian. It just wasn't in the man's nature. "There's a matter I want to discuss with you. It's personal and must remain between us. You understand?"

"Yes, sir." Christian looked at his father keenly.

"What are your thoughts on becoming earl?"

The boy shrugged. "I have never really thought about it much. I suppose it will happen when it's time for it to happen."

"Matters are a bit easier for you here because of it, aren't they? In British society, life is simpler if you are a lord. No doubt about it. But the system, at heart, is not a good one. Have you ever heard how the earldom for our family began?" Christian shook his head. Though he recalled his grandfather's glowing sagas of the first Earl Hardaway, he declined to admit it. "Not long after William the Conqueror took control of England, he faced a rebellion of the Saxons to his north. He dispatched one of his more ruthless knights, Sir John de Troye, to quell it. Sir John did just that, in the typical Norman way. He burned and slaughtered, destroying the region until the remaining Saxons were more concerned with avoiding starvation than rebellion. Then, he had erected a great stone tower and, ensconced there, commanded absolute obedience.

"After that first year, Sir John even managed to send taxes to William, gold and silver he managed to extract somehow. The king was so delighted, he gave this savage knight the farmlands and estates that we have today—and even more. The earldom was born. That savage knight is our ancestor. Your grandfather has a painting of John de Troye in the parlor of the great house, where you spend your summers. Now I am sure that you have seen it, even if you did not know the history of the man.

"My point is there was nothing noble about Sir John, nothing noble in how he became an earl, no great deed behind our land and estates. It's nothing about which we should feel proud, and it's not only us. It's the same for all the lords. Look candidly at their ancestors and you'll find the same slaughter and rot. It's no different than what the Communists are doing now. Whoever has the power and is a party member considers himself above all others. There is a strict pecking order in the party itself, so everyone knows very clearly who is above them and who is below them. But beneath it all, they are rotten to the core. Corrupt and greedy and out for everything that they can get for themselves, with no other considerations. Remember it."

"I've read the history, sir." Still, Christian liked his grandfather's romanticized version far more and preferred to think of Sir John as at least a tiny bit noble.

Julian looked back at his son. "I believe it was Churchill who said that history is the version of events written by the victors. The point I am working around to, Christian, is to ask how you would feel if you never became earl?"

The boy shrugged. "I don't know. I don't really care that much, I suppose. I know you don't want the title, sir."

"You do?"

"Yes, sir. I've heard you talk about it to Mother. I know you don't want it. I don't know if I quite know why, but I'm beginning to understand your reasoning a little—I think."

"Well, that's an excellent start. I wouldn't just be doing it for myself. It would be for you as well, and your children, and their children, too." The boy looked stunned. "Yes, Christian, your children will eventually have children. Once done, it can never be undone. The line of John de Troye will be finished as it now stands in British nobility. We will be commoners from that moment onwards. Enough for now. You have years left before you have to worry about these things. So, who's going to win today's game?"

Christian grinned his winning smile and jumped to his feet. "We shall be most honored to thrash the fathers soundly, sir!"

Julian rose, laughed, then set off preparing to be thrashed.

* * *

A few weeks later, Julian met once again with Ian Cathcart. The bureaucrat arrived late, apologizing. "I should have remained in the army," he said as he took his seat. "At least I'd have breathed fresh air from time to time." His heather coat reeked of stale smoke.

Ian, Julian noted, was aging well. Since they'd first met during the war, the only change Julian could detect, beyond the usual hair thinning, was a spider's web of faint wrinkles at the corner of each eye. Julian wondered if the same could be said for him. He watched as Ian inserted an American cigarette into his holder, this one ebony as a lump of anthracite. Julian sipped his beer while they chatted about nothing in particular before getting down to business.

"I've been hoping that my bits of information over these years have been found to be useful," Julian began.

"Quite, from time to time. So I'm told."

This was a matter Julian dreaded raising, but the last few years had been increasingly difficult for him financially. "Things are very tough in the East right now, and competition in the West is unbelievably keen, especially from the Americans. These extra trips for you and your friends often come at some cost for me. Plus, there are your technical specialists whom you asked me to hire who seem to do little but consume my payroll. I'm sure you can see that. I'm hoping British intelligence could see its way clear to render a bit of assistance; otherwise, I'll have to limit myself. I'll be glad to forward anything of interest I stumble across, but I won't be able to make special efforts, as I have previously."

Ian pursed his lips. "You're not asking for actual money, I take it?"

"For assistance, in any form that it may take."

"I'll see what I can do, old boy. You've managed to get some very difficult export licenses, but I know what you mean. Perhaps we have not provided enough profit for your company to handle the tasking we have given it. Maybe it will help you overseas if you become a supplier to Her Majesty. We should be able to place a decent contract or two on behalf of the armed forces with you. I'm surprised no one has done it before now. How would that be?"

"Depending, it might be just the ticket."

"Fair enough then! Consider it done."

Ian was true to his word. That year and those following were pivotal to Julian and his company. The British military placed several large contracts with the firm, one especially for the design and development of advanced bomb-disposal equipment, which proved most profitable. The company grew at a solid pace and became a major contractor to the British government, which never failed to pay in advance for development projects and, even better, always directed Julian towards the small two- or three-person company that possessed the specialist skills needed for that development. Concord Trading Company quickly purchased such companies, or offered the owners or staff excellent packages to work with CTC. As a result, the company grew exponentially and became well known for its specialist skills and staff.

CHAPTER NINETEEN

1963
London

Against his better judgment, or perhaps thinking more with his loins than his brain, Julian had brought Monika to England two years after he'd met her. It transpired that the girl was only nineteen and that proved a minor complication in registering her with the British government. He kept the girl in the London flat he stayed at once or twice a week and arranged for her education, pleased that he could make up for his betrayal of her older sister by giving the younger one the best that Britain had to offer, while she, of course, continued to give him the best that Poland could offer. He'd been searching for the right mistress, one he could control, one who would be pleased with the spoils of the mistress life, not wanting marriage or legitimization. Most of all, one that gave him everything, to his exacting wishes.

One sunny day, Julian received more disturbing information about Kim Philby. Since the defections of his friends, Burgess and MacLean, some eleven years before, Philby had maintained a discreet life, though Julian had heard about, and more than once witnessed, Philby's excessive drinking and rather outrageous homosexual escapades. Percy Sillitoe, head of MI5, Julian understood, had pursued Philby for some time, attempting to show that Philby was a Communist infiltrator. SIS Chief Graham Menzies remained Philby's staunch supporter, and, in such an atmosphere, nothing could be done. Sillitoe had been "encouraged" to devote himself to other objectives.

Still, the consequence was that Philby's name was bandied about in public as being the up-to-the-moment unknown "third man" in the Burgess and MacLean affair. Conservative Prime Minister Harold Macmillan had, just this year, publicly expressed his belief that Philby was an upstanding British citizen who had served his country heroically. Others in government openly speculated, even stated as fact, that Philby was the elusive third man, the Communist turncoat who had warned his friends, Burgess and MacLean, that the net was closing on them.

Though Philby had been returned to the Foreign Office, with Sillitoe hoping to keep him close as he built a case, the public exposure of suspicions against Philby had resulted in Philby's indignant resignation. For a number of years, he lived quietly in London, dabbling again in real estate, largely supported by funds from his wealthy family. He had, in his own way, and one Julian did not envy, become a public figure. To no one's surprise, Philby had abruptly moved to Lebanon and worked as a reporter, providing stories to two British newspapers while living with his aging father.

From what Julian was hearing, the entire matter was coming to a head. Colonel Anatolyi Golitsyn had defected from Russia in late 1961. Arrogant, quarrelsome, and temperamental, his had proven a problematic defection, even though he was the highest-ranking Soviet ever to defect. The American CIA had been debriefing him for a year. The matter was of the highest importance, as Golitsyn had been a colonel in the first directorate of the KGB, and his espionage target had been NATO countries.

For months, the debate had quietly raged within the intelligence community as to whether or not Golitsyn was the real thing or, as many argued, a sophisticated Soviet plant, an agent provocateur assigned to spread disinformation and to falsely direct suspicion. Julian understood that Golitsyn had named Kim Philby as a long-time Soviet agent.

Such information from the CIA, who took the defector as genuine, should have been enough, in Julian's view, even given the antipathy between MI6 and the CIA. It wasn't as though Philby's behavior had been above suspicion, or even that Golitsyn was the first defector to name him. But Julian had not been surprised that Roger Hollis, head of MI5 since 1956, had continued to defend his longtime friend. None of this was in the press—not yet. Rather, it simmered in the intelligence community, like a slow-boiling cast iron pot. People in the know, such as members of Parliament and certain senior civil servants, gossiped about Philby on a regular basis.

The winter was proving the worst in Britain since the end of the war, and there was a sharp spike in unemployment. The Conservative government, under

Harold Macmillan, was declining in popularity, and another election seemed imminent, one that the Labour Party would have a very good chance at winning. Labour, especially in its senior ranks, was laced through and through with Communists and hard left-leaning Communist sympathizers. In Julian's opinion, a Labour victory would spell disaster for Britain, especially for its intelligence services.

The good news in all of this was that Labour was led by fifty-seven-year-old Hugh Gaitskell, a man Julian had always found to be quite reasonable and moderate. He had met Gaitskell at a cocktail party some years back, when Gaitskell was a lowly backbencher in the House of Commons. While they were not close friends, they respected one another and, from time to time, had encountered one another at various Masonic lodges. Though Gaitskell's recent change in stance to favor a closer relationship with the new concept of a European Common Market had angered the far left of his party, his position as leader appeared secure.

In such a political and economic environment, a scandal always seemed to rear its head, and one sufficiently tantalizing was about to cause a change in the Conservative government. The consequence was that Gaitskell would become prime minister of a left leaning, dis-United Kingdom.

Julian had grown more and more attached to his young Polish mistress and was disappointed that he couldn't spend New Year's Eve with her. He realized, however, that holidays with Sarah remained appropriate, regardless of how droll or dreadful the people she liked happened to be.

Monika, as always, was disappointed by the news but found a suitable alternative, a party the night before, one for "their kind," Monika said. Though ambivalent, Julian agreed to go, as it was so rare he and Monika went out in public. They pulled up at a large mansion in the best part of Kensington, just a stone's throw from Embassy Row, where most of the foreign embassies were situated, a house that belonged to a fifty-year-old osteopath named Stephen Ward.

It was the first time Julian had actually seen Ward, whose clients, he understood, included Lord Astor, War Minister John Profumo, and members of both Houses of Parliament.

There were rumors that Ward was scarcely more than a procurer of young women for his influential friends, and while Julian led a private life as sexually active and promiscuous as he desired, he did not countenance the increasingly open sexuality of the time, the "Swinging Sixties", as it was known.

He also drew a personal line at providing prostitutes for his associates. He would give Madame Claude's telephone number when the situation called for it, but that was as far as he ever would go in that regard.

They arrived a little before midnight, as part of the night's activities was a mock New Year's celebration, a farce in itself, with man and mistress toasting the New Year a day early, as though the calendar, too, would bend for their convenience. The gathering was not Julian's type at all; he nearly turned away at the doorway. A moment later, he wished he had, for there was War Minister John Profumo with a stunning brunette young enough to be his granddaughter on his arm.

Worse, scattered about the spacious room were at least three young women Julian had seen provided from Madame Claude's stables, and therefore knew to be high-priced call-girls.

There were, perhaps, a dozen others who surely could have been. Other older men walked with young women on their arms who were dressed in London finery and jewels; these, Julian assumed, were the mistresses. He saw his own reflection in them and found it disturbing. Worse was the thought that he'd first had Monika when she was only fifteen.

Just then, Stephen Ward approached with a warm smile. "Monika! So good you could come. This must be Julian, about whom I've heard so much, from so many different sources, though I believe this is the first time we've had the pleasure of meeting. I'm Stephen Ward." He took Julian's hand as he introduced himself.

Ward was a not a handsome man, yet no one could deny his personal charm and warmth. After a few perfunctorily polite words, he took his leave, wandering across the room, kissing the ladies as he went.

Julian located a whiskey and lit a small cigar. The pall of despondency that had settled on him with the bitter winter returned, made all the worse by this gathering of fornicators and his realization that, yes, indeed, he was one of their kind.

Tens of thousands of "commies," as they were openly called, routinely demonstrated, often violently, to ban the bomb, as if unilateral nuclear disarmament would end the threat of nuclear war.

A mop-headed quartet of singers, looking more like girls than young men, was all the rage. Promiscuity was not only rampant, it was expected. The government was adrift and Britain, once powerful, was mired in mediocrity, having fallen without pause from being a world power to a third-class nation. It seemed as if everything Julian had ever known had come unglued.

Rumor had it that Ward orchestrated orgies at Spring Cottage, a place in the country he rented from Lord Astor. That was all very good for university students with no marital ties, but middle-aged men had no business at such gatherings. After all, because of the selection of people at this party, many of them knew one another well enough to chat, and almost everyone knew everyone else by sight or from newspaper photographs. Somewhat dangerous, Julian thought.

Julian wondered for a moment with some concern as to what extent Monika knew Ward. He realized that outside of his company and her putative schooling, Monika had an extraordinary amount of free time. Through pipe smoke, Julian observed Profumo stroke the brunette's rump, then leer down her dress. All much too open. Nothing good could come of this. But then, no one was there for anything good at any event.

Women he didn't know approached in turn to kiss him full on the lips, wishing him Happy New Year, and more than one stroked him sexually. Monika, far from being jealous, seemed to enjoy seeing it and distributed similar ministrations to other men in the room before she returned to his side. If this were about to become an orgy, Julian wasn't sure how he would handle it. Three in a bed was one thing, but fifty?

In the midst of painted faces and wide smiles, Profumo's brunette approached. She was, without question, one of the most beautiful women in the room. There was a raw sexuality about her, a "take it, I'm right here" attitude that made him want to pull her into the nearest corner. She looked as if she'd be good, she acted like she'd be good, and he hadn't the slightest doubt she was good. She absently made circles on Monika's arm with her fingertip as she smiled at Julian.

Her kiss for him was long and sweet, and she did not pull away, finally leaning her head back as she said, "Happy New Year! I'm Christine. Christine Keeler. You really must call me sometime. Monika keeps insisting that we three get together."

"Yes, we must," Julian said breathlessly, feeling on top of the world. Keeler kissed Monika, and he noticed that it was both longer and deeper than her kiss for him. He watched the two women, a little surprised as they caressed one another before separating. A stirring in his nether regions sent a telegram to Julian's brain, telling it that it was no longer on duty and decisions would be made tonight and in the days to follow by other parts of his anatomy.

CHAPTER TWENTY

1963
London

Two weeks after first meeting Christine Keeler at Stephen Ward's party, Julian had been awakened from a sound sleep by the telephone. He answered in a sleep-slurred voice, forcing himself to alertness. The voice in the earpiece was distant, the accent unfamiliar. At first, he couldn't place it. The man was mumbling. Finally, Julian knew who it was. "Tommy? Is that you?"

"That's what I've been saying. Fuck it! Get over here. Make it quick! I haven't much time." He gave Julian his location. "I'm in a telephone booth."

Tommy Harris sounded drunk to Julian. He hadn't spoken with the man in two years. Since he'd returned to Britain a decade earlier, Tommy had done moderately well trading arms and dabbling in intelligence on a contract basis, Julian had heard, as an international intelligence broker of sorts. From time to time, Julian had given him a bit of business to help out, recalling the man's courage in the war. They had not met personally for quite a little while.

"What's this about? It's the middle of the night." Monika rolled away from him and continued to sleep.

"It's raining fucking cats and dogs, and I've been hurt. Hurry, Julian." Tommy rattled off the location of the telephone booth again, adding, "For God's sake, hurry." Tommy hung up.

There was urgency in Tommy's voice that Julian had never heard before. Julian threw on the clothes at hand and then wheeled his Jaguar through the slick streets like a race driver. The phone booth where Tommy was waiting was near the docks, in the East End, a place not fit for man or beast at such an hour or in such vile weather. Then again, Tommy was neither one of those. The bone-chilling, cold rain fell in great sheets that rocked the car. The wipers barely managed to give him a view of the dangerous streets.

Julian pulled to a quick stop beside an isolated phone booth. He hesitated, then reached into the glove box and removed a Colt .380 automatic. He drew back the slide, let it run forward, released the safety, and slipped the pistol into his coat pocket as he exited the car. He'd begun carrying a gun during the war and never quite lost the habit, a development for which, at this moment, he was very grateful.

A gust of wind bearing a great wall of water struck him head on, and he rocked a moment on his heels.

Julian looked about him carefully, then cautiously approached the booth. He eased the door open. Tommy, or perhaps a vandal, had smashed the overhead light, so it was pitch dark inside as Julian pushed on the door and hit something. From the floor of the booth, he heard a groan.

"About fucking time," Tommy whispered.

Julian squatted down, leaning over Tommy and into the booth, out of the wind and rain. He touched Tommy's coat. Julian's fingers turned warm, wet, and sticky. "Jesus. You need a doctor."

"What I need is a Goddamn drink, but a doctor will do. Ambulance on the way; I called them. Lean down. I didn't know who to trust. They'd put me in the hospital, and when I came around it would be too late. Here Listen up. I'm dead tired. Dead—" He coughed lightly, but it quickly turned into a painful spasm.

"Easy, Tommy. Easy."

"Son-of-a-bitch used a sticker. A fuckin' knife!"

"Who?"

"Big guy. Don't know him. Hired help. Lean down. There. That's better. Now, listen up."

Tommy managed the story in a few short minutes. He was dead before the siren of the ambulance could be heard. Julian hesitated, not wanting to abandon the man, but staying made no sense. He drove off in one direction as the ambulance came from the other.

A good mile from where Tommy lay, Julian stopped at another phone booth. Ian Cathcart, he learned, was unavailable, traveling somewhere in India. Julian tried two other intelligence contacts—the ones he usually used when Ian was unavailable—but had no luck.

The phone wasn't answered at one; at the other, a servant informed him the "master" was in Paris.

With no alternative, Julian decided to contact Roger Hollis, who he knew was in town.

He was hesitant to approach the man, as he still harbored suspicions about Hollis and his connection to Philby. But Hollis was the head of the SIS, the top man in British intelligence, and the only man Julian could think of who might make a difference at such a pivotal hour.

Julian drove quickly to the man's residence. He was surprised to see that the head of British intelligence had no guard, plainclothes or otherwise, outside his house. Just after two in the morning, Julian pounded on the door until Hollis himself, dressed in a disheveled robe, answered.

"My God, man!" he said, recognizing Julian. "Come in! Good heavens. Come in! You look like a stray cat from the alley. Can I get you a drink?"

Julian stepped inside, a pool of cold water quickly puddling about him. He decided to restrict the damage to the entryway and stayed rooted. "Yes, a drink would be fine. But there isn't much time."

Hollis gave him a strange look, turned, took his right hand from the folds of his robe, and laid a heavy Webley Revolver on the stand, then made his way to the bar. Julian admired the aesthetic lifestyle Hollis led, with only the bare necessities surrounding him. No one would have guessed, seeing these furnishings, that the resident was one of the most powerful men in the country. Hollis returned in a moment with a whisky.

Before drinking, Julian said, "I have it on good authority that Hugh Gaitskell is about to be assassinated."

Hollis looked stunned. "My God! Gaitskell?" he whispered. "He must be one of the most protected man in the country, after the royal family and the PM."

Gaitskell had a mystical air about him; he was expected to become the future leader of Britain, and hopes were that he would lead a new era of reform and greatness in the country, restoring it to a state of glory. That his life would be threatened was unimaginable.

"Tommy Harris is the source," Julian said. "Those were his final words. I trust him." Giving the name was not something he would normally do, but Tommy was dead, and this was a matter of national security. "He told me he picked it up two days ago, while on a gun-shopping trip to Tirana. One of his sources, who wants to defect, passed it along, hoping this would get him out of Albania. I don't know when it's to take place, but pretty well right away, as Tommy understood it."

"Just where is Tommy now? I'd like to talk to him myself."

"Dead. He'd been stabbed and was holding his guts in with his hands, waiting for me. There wasn't much blood left when I got there. Any doubts you might have should be set aside, given Tommy's murder. It should confirm he was on to something."

Hollis paused for a moment. "I don't see how a second-rate American gun dealer would come across information of such national import, when our entire intelligence operation hasn't heard a peep. Is it possible that Tommy was set up?"

"Tommy had a way of finding things out. Right now, it's not important. We need to move quickly with Gaitskell. If it's a false alarm, all the better."

"Certainly. I'll make the call at once. I'll have extra guards placed at his side at hospital."

"Hospital?"

"Yes. He was admitted earlier today. Some kind of exotic tropical bug, I'm told."

Julian tossed his drink back and then asked, "Tropical, you say? How would he get that in the UK?" The whisky landed in his stomach with a strong glow that spread almost immediately throughout his chilled body.

"No idea. It has the doctors baffled, as well."

Julian thought a moment. It might already have happened. "Could the Soviets be using a disease to kill?"

Hollis curled his lower lip. "I can't see how. Their methods are much more direct."

Julian replied "In this case, they'd want it to seem an accident of some kind, or natural. And, as you said, he's protected very well against the usual, direct methods."

"They've never seemed to much care in the past. You must admit, it does sound a bit farfetched. You've been away from MI5 for many years now. Perhaps you've been reading a bit too many spy novels in the interim."

"You'd have to have seen Tommy to understand. There's more. Tommy says Kim's involved."

"Kim? You mean Philby?"

"Yes. Apparently he's a Soviet mole and has been given this assignment, since he's no longer in government and of little use to them otherwise."

"What rot!! You say Tommy Harris told you this? That's absurd. He was sold a line of nonsense. That's what! It's all a bloody lie meant to slander a loyal British subject! Harris was CIA, wasn't he? They've been trying to pin something on Kim for years, had it in for him since he proved that a string of defectors had been feeding the Yanks bad information. They probably had Harris killed themselves. Besides, Kim's in Lebanon and has been for some time now."

"According to Tommy, Kim was in London last week."

"That's absurd. I know for a fact Kim's in Lebanon."

"What about the police guards?"

"They are at the hospital with Gaitskell, of course, but for you, Julian, for you, I'll see to it.

You should get home before you catch your death."

"I'll be off, then. Thank you."

Julian began the drive home, but he couldn't quite shake the feeling that something had been wrong about Hollis. Why was Hollis so certain about Philby? How could any of them be certain of anyone else? You might have faith in a man, but there was always the possibility. Julian swung a fast U-turn on the empty street, tires squealing as he sped towards the hospital.

He parked the car in the hospital lot and hurried upstairs. Gaitskell was, indeed, well guarded. Hollis didn't disappoint; the entire floor was crawling with uniformed police and detectives from Special Branch. Julian tried to learn if anything had happened to Gaitskell, but the nurses said nothing. He asked to speak to the man in charge. He was no longer a member of a government agency, and his suspicions of foul play, while duly noted by the on-duty detective, were ultimately treated as civilian paranoia, he could see. There was nothing more Julian could do.

Julian arrived home at his London flat after 5:00 A.M., treading quietly so as not to awaken Monika. He hadn't seen enough of her recently, felt he'd neglected his duties. A mistress required more than just a monthly stipend, and their recent jaunt to Ward's had worried him. He didn't want her getting involved with the wrong friends.

He entered the bedroom, expecting to find her sleeping like an angel. Instead, he found her unaccountably absent. He poured himself a brandy to calm his nerves, unable to sleep.

* * *

Hugh Gaitskell died the following day of Lupus Disseminata, a very nasty disease, indeed, one which later would be compared to Ebola. It was tough to diagnose and completely untreatable. No satisfactory explanation was offered as to how Gaitskell could possibly have contracted it in Britain in the dead of winter.

Two days later, Kim Philby abruptly left a dinner party in Beirut, telling his wife he'd be right back, walking through a heavy downpour to the harbor, where he boarded a Polish cargo ship, which left at once for the Soviet port of Odessa.

Julian was stunned when two policemen arrived at his flat three days after Gaitskell's death and requested that he accompany them to the station for questioning. Hollis must have moved fast, he reflected. He was brought to an all-too-familiar room, no windows, a mirror he knew to be two way, a single metal table and three chairs, one of the many identical rooms used for interrogation.

Two men in well-tailored gray suits entered, and, from their manner, Julian recognized them immediately as MI5 even though they showed him Metropolitan Police Special Branch Identification cards.

"Cigarette?" the taller of the two men asked. Julian declined. The other, a squat, mustached, square-headed character, was about Julian's age, the kind of mid-level intelligence operative Julian had come to loath; he took a seat directly opposite him. The taller man continued to stand to his side and slightly behind him. Julian forced himself to check his emotions, particularly his outrage; he knew the interrogation game well, knew MI5's procedures and figured to suffer through a quick round of questioning. He hoped to be free within the hour, with luck.

"So maybe we can start here by asking what you were doing paying a visit to Mr. Hugh Gaitskell at hospital the night before last?" the taller man asked.

"I was trying to protect him. I had heard from a friend that Mr. Gaitskell might be in danger." Julian answered calmly, methodically.

"You show up at the hospital a couple of hours before Gaitskell gives up the ghost and you claim you were just there to protect him, right? Quite a coincidence, isn't it?" the shorter man growled. Julian knew the type. The fellow's hatred of the upper crust, of those born into wealth and title, practically oozed from his pores as he flipped through a manila file.

"As I said, I was concerned for his well being. I received information from a friend."

Julian was growing edgy. The questioning didn't seem to follow one of MI5's routines.

They were setting him up to pressure him; the shorter man was rude and aggressive, far more than they'd allow in a quick interview. From all outward signs, Julian realized grimly that MI5 had—or at least believed it had—incriminating evidence.

"And this information you received was from whom?" the tall one asked.

"Tommy Harris."

"Tommy Harris," the short man said smugly. "CIA. Are you are aware that we found Tommy Harris murdered in a phone booth? We place his time of death less than two hours before you arrived at the hospital. What'd you do for the two hours after you killed him?"

"I—" Julian paused to collect his thoughts. If they were trying to pin him for the murder of Harris, what else were they going to frame him for? Did they have proof or were they just bullying him? "I didn't kill Tommy Harris."

"That remains to be seen," the short man said. "You do admit that you saw him right before he died, correct?"

"I saw Mr. Harris close to midnight," Julian said guardedly. "He told me that Mr. Gaitskell's life was in danger, and I drove immediately to Director Hollis's private residence."

The questioning continued in this vein, with the shorter man trying to catch him in inconsistencies and occasionally throwing out accusations, while the taller man said little.

After an hour, Julian was exasperated by the pair, but they showed no sign of letting up on him.

These intelligence officers questioned people for a living. Finally, the taller one, with a smirk he'd been holding for at least ten minutes, asked. "Perhaps you can inform us a bit about your relationship with one Monika Kurek?"

"Monika?"

"She is in the employment of your company, is she not? Living in London in an apartment that belongs to you? May I ask what requisite skills this old girl has to offer CTC?"

"Monika is none of your business," Julian said.

"Would you think differently if I told you we had proof positive that Monika Kurek is a Soviet operative, a Communist spy?"

A wave of nausea swept through Julian's head as he remembered Mishka's gift of the girl to him, and Monika's almost pathological enthusiasm in bed. Had he been set up? Had he been helping the Communists for nearly a decade, then? "I had no idea," he muttered. "I find it very hard to—" But he knew he was cornered.

The taller man continued. "So, we are to understand that you—a married man with a child, a member of the aristocracy, founder of one of Britain's largest military exporters—brought a seventeen-year-old girl from Poland to England, set her up under the auspices of employment for CTC, a military trading company, as I say, paid for her education, and gave her considerable sums of money, all without knowledge of her espionage activities? Tell me, *Mister* Hardaway, what does this Pole do that our far-less-dangerous British tramps can't do just as well?"

You have no idea, Julian thought, holding the man's stare.

The shorter man stood suddenly, leaned on the table, his face close to Julian's, and said, "Mr. Hardaway, do you have personal relationships with two men, Mr. Burgess and Mr. MacLean, who defected to Moscow in 1951?"

Oh, Jesus, Julian thought. "I knew them briefly."

"And can you describe your relationship with Kim Philby, who defected to Moscow yesterday?"

Yesterday! "Kim's defected?" The men said nothing. "I—I knew Kim from my work in the security service."

"That's right," the short one said. "You were all good chums, were you not? Mr. Hardaway, have you been working for the Soviets as a spy?"

* * *

Monika typically arrived first at the apartment. She'd make herself comfortable and warm the place, as it was usually quite cold except at the height of summer. Sarah Hardaway would arrive late, as usual, and come in with a rush and apologies. Within moments, the two would be naked and in bed. Afterwards, they had the afternoon for cigarettes, gossip, and more sex.

Sarah had met Monika at Spring Cottage on the River Thames. There, Stephen Ward, whom Sarah had met the previous month, had held what Sarah could only describe as an orgy. Over the years, her affairs had grown predictable and sterile. During the war, with a nanny for her son, Christian, and an absentee husband, Sarah had been drawn into an affair with a British major, stationed not far away. "Her major," as she called Reginald Bligh, had adored her, and, for the only time in her marriage, she'd seriously considered divorce. It would have meant giving up everything—title, wealth, station, even her son—but she was certain it would have been worth it. Then, her major had been killed in the Normandy landings.

Sarah had thought she'd never recover. She'd contemplated suicide for several long months. She'd attempted a rekindling of her once-held passion for her husband, Julian, but that had come to nothing. Finally, a mutual friend had introduced her to the charming Stephen Ward, who seemed to understand her from the first. He'd invited her to join him and a few friends at Spring Cottage, the legendary cottage in the woods on the banks of the Thames built by the countess of Orkney.

As much out of curiosity to see the cottage as any other reason, Sarah had gone. Perhaps a dozen couples wandered in that Saturday. By late afternoon, they were disappearing into bedrooms. Nothing more than an arched eyebrow had been necessary to foil the two attempts to pull her into one. Though she did not participate, she was certain that couples were swapping partners. All quite decadent, all very delicious. But she was not quite ready for that yet.

She slept alone that night, then, at brunch on Sunday, was joined by Monika. With her excellent English and that charming Polish accent, she had enthralled Sarah. She'd been startled, a few days later, when Monika had called her at her residence. She was certain she'd not given the young woman her number, but there Monika was, suggesting they meet for tea at a little place she knew.

Sarah had once engaged in a threesome with a member of Parliament and his mistress and had found the experience titillating; but she'd not done it again, considering three to be a crowd for such intimate activities. Stroking Monika's skin that day, Sarah had understood at once what the previous appeal had been. She preferred women.

This had been Monika's first seduction of a woman, and Monika had been surprised at how much it was like seducing and taking a man. The steps had been the same. Except for those orgies in which she'd participated in Warsaw, she'd never touched another woman sexually. She found it neither pleasant nor unpleasant, merely different, though she could tell that Sarah had discovered paradise in her body. Had it been a man, Monika might have been put off by the level of passion she'd aroused. In Sarah, she found no threat.

Mishka had ordered the affair and there it was, as easy as one, two, three. Not even Ward knew his part in the business.

* * *

MI5 released Julian after four hours of interrogation, but continued round-the-clock surveillance.

There was nothing Julian could say to Sarah by way of explanation, and he could only deny the rumors spreading like wildfire through certain quarters of London. Julian hoped that he could manage to quell the chatter before it broke in the press. The last thing he or his family needed was a scandal.

It was nearly a week before Ian arrived from India and returned Julian's call. He had already been briefed. They met at the usual pub, in a back corner booth, late the next afternoon.

"Seems like we've got a bit of a knot to untie," Ian said.

"How was India?" Julian asked, as they eased into the booth.

"Bloody hot. I got sick, of course. Drank gin and tonic all bloody day. I don't understand how the population there can live let alone breed like rabbits. I don't see how anyone can possibly stay alive. Now, tell me about this Monika."

"My Russian bear might have set me up. I'm still trying to figure out how—no, I know how. Why, is what I don't know."

"Could be anything," Ian exhaled, taking a sip of a single malt scotch. "Maybe he just wanted her in the country; maybe he needed her close to your circle of friends. My guess would be that she was another way to check up on you, and through you, she'd gain access to others in the know. You should consider just whom she has met when with you. Or, he might have been doing a favor for a friend. The Reds stab each other in the back all the time, and my sources inform me that our Russian bear has made more than a few enemies in his time."

"He says as much himself. What's your opinion?"

Ian raised his brows at Julian's question. "She's quite a looker. You know she's been running around with a certain Christine Keeler?"

"We met her once, at a party. They seemed to be friends."

"Well, Keeler is far more than she seems. Far more," Ian said, raising his glass again and looking towards the front of the bar. A young couple had just

143

entered; they sat at a nearby booth, their voices taut with young professionalism and youthful lust.

"You realize that Monika's control is very likely this Russian fellow Keeler's been sleeping with," Ian muttered.

"I've been a fool," Julian said, clenching his hands into fists on the table.

"Now, now, the first issue here is to get you out of hot water. It's vital that we keep you and CTC out of this mess. I've done my best to convince MI5 and MI6 that you had nothing to do with Philby. I told them that you yourself have been trying to convince me that Philby was Red for years. You can't imagine the mess that Keeler is stirring up. That's a hornet's nest you don't want to be caught near, especially with that girlfriend of yours, who seems to be mixed up with all the wrong people."

"Did she have anything to do with the Gaitskell murder?"

"It seems not. That was cleverly handled, it appears, by Philby. Why no one is interested in pursuing how a man in the glow of health could suddenly contract a tropical disease in central London quite surprises me."

"How did he?"

Ian screwed an American cigarette into his holder. "It seems clear our dear Kim was behind it. Hugh had simply moved too far right for our Russian friends. The last thing they wanted was a Labour Party leader in favor of Britain's union with Europe. They want us isolated. Easier pickings and all that. And Harold Wilson is the man who would give them what they want"

"And this Harold Wilson?"

"Pink. So pink he's Red, in my view. Hell in a hand basket." Ian was not his usual self.

He looked depressed.

"Can't he be exposed? The man could very well be our next PM."

Ian shook his head. "I'm afraid not. We're looking for a way, but I'm not optimistic." He sipped at his beer and lit yet another cigarette.

"What about 'Operation Matador'? Operation Matador was an ongoing MI6 operation to discredit Wilson and others in the Labour Party considered to be Communists. It was extremely secret.

Ian shrugged. "I wouldn't bet the farm on that working. You read about War Minister Profumo's denial, I take it?"

"Yes. A bloody great lie. I don't see how he can get away with it. I even saw him with Keeler, myself, when I was with Monika at Stephen Ward's home." Realization swept over him. "Oh, my God!"

"Yes. You have no idea how close you are to this entire scandal, Julian. The fact that you didn't know about it is sometimes difficult to believe, even for me," Ian said. "He's been foolish, but then many a man of advancing years has been brought down by a lithesome young woman."

"Keeler has the looks to do it, if anyone does. As does Monika, for that matter."

"Now, strictly entre nous, we are of the opinion Hollis put Ward up to this. And Hollis is your biggest detractor. He's telling MI5 that you had something to do with Gaitskell's murder, and remember, he's head of the SIS."

"I had nothing to do with it. I was trying to save Gaitskell. I have wondered about Hollis myself, for quite a long time. I wonder if he could be the 'fourth man' that they keep talking about?"

"Yes, well, many of us do more than wonder. I believe he placed this Keeler woman with the Russian, Ivanov—that's his name—who worked at their embassy in London. She was supposed to learn about Soviet naval capabilities, while resting between sessions."

"And Profumo?"

Ian looked distressed. "We are led to believe he saw her and wanted her. Never one to say no, she was soon sleeping with the both of them, and, possibly, Ward as well. He's been keeping her these last two years."

"There are no coincidences. She wasn't with Profumo by accident."

"Of course not, and this had nothing to do with spying on the Soviets. There's nothing Profumo could say they don't already know. That was just the first piece of the operation."

"Then what..." Julian stopped and was filled by a great rage. "My God! He couldn't be that diabolical."

"My guess is Kim thought it up. It's got his fingerprints all over it. Hollis knew Ward and what a pervert he was. He had the man fix the woman up with the Russian, then with the war minister. *Voila!* A sex scandal and the end of the Conservative government. But first, their man, Wilson, had to be in place to take over. Kim's parting gift to the country of his birth was not just to orchestrate the scandal but to assure the right man became PM. He went so far as to make a special trip to our hallowed shores to personally see to it, I'm told.

They sat in silence for some moments, then finally Julian asked, "Any chance Ward can be persuaded to talk?"

Ian nodded his head. "The man's a fool, and when pressed, a fool will always talk."

"Then, I wouldn't give two pence for the likelihood he'll survive the summer."

"Nor would I, dear boy, nor would I. But there is a chance that we can trace Hollis another way, through his control. We have reason to suspect that your Russian bear might actually know something about Hollis. Monika, too; she did her little part in this charade. She's been inside the Russian consulate more than once."

"I won't ask doing what," Julian said despondently.

"We're prepared to let her go," Ian said slowly. "But we'll need your help in a few ways.

Let's be frank, Julian. If we wanted to, we could hang you out to dry with this girl as part of the Profumo scandal."

"But you're not going to," Julian said, swirling the liquor in his glass, "because you have a better way to use the situation to your advantage."

Ian gave one of his dry smiles that never seemed to reach his eyes. "First things first.

You are not to let on that you know the girl's a spy. We're going to turn her; but a big part of that is going to be your ignorance. Given the choice of continuing a rarified existence in London or returning to the harsh life of Warsaw, we're fairly sure she'll cooperate." Ian drew on his cigarette, then almost immediately set it aside with a sigh. "We want to pin Hollis's hide to the wall. I should think that your Russian friend knows enough about Hollis for us to nail him."

"You want me to use Mishka?"

"Nothing like that. He's too valuable. Offer him a deal, something he wants. Find a way to get him to talk. Tell him Hollis is on the way out, anyway; he might as well make a profit from it.

From what I hear, this Mishka seems to think he has you in the palm of his hand."

Julian swallowed uncomfortably. "I assure you he does not."

"Well, I'm sure he doesn't. That's where I expect to have you myself, old boy." Ian laughed out loud, and Julian knew that there was more than an ounce of truth in his old friend's words. "You and CTC are simply too important to permit you to be involved in anything that will bring attention to you, or even speculation as to what you do for us. We're going to cover you, but it's not going to be easy. This arrangement with you is one of the most covert operations we have ever carried out, and one of the most significant. Do you realize what could happen to me, even to Tony Eden, if it ever came out what we've done? But there is more, old boy, and good news. We'd like to bring CTC into a closer partnership with the government to the exclusion of others. Part of our renewed trust in you." With that, Ian smiled warmly, and this time it almost reached his eyes.

* * *

Monika Kurek rolled from bed, though she was still very drowsy. It was well after lunchtime, but she'd been out with Julian the previous night and had not returned to her own flat until dawn. Ever since she was a child, she'd found it difficult to awaken. As she crossed the floor to the bathroom, she glanced out the window. It was autumn. The day was predictably dreary and overcast, but warmer than Poland—and for that, she was grateful.

While brushing her hair, she sniffed and wrinkled her nose. I smell of sex, cigarettes, and booze, she thought. She lit a cigarette and all but nodded off. A few minutes later, she put coffee on and took a shower, emerging from the stall feeling born again. She popped bread into the toaster and was just taking her first sip of black Costa Rican coffee when there was knocking at her door.

Irritated for only a second, she realized it was no longer early morning but mid-afternoon—the rest of the world had been up for hours.

Monika rose from the table, belted her blue terrycloth bathrobe tightly about her, and went to see who it was at the door. The moment she unbolted the door, it was thrown open, knocking her back so hard she almost fell to the floor. Two men in raincoats and hats rushed in so fast she had no time to scream. One put his hand across her mouth while gripping her tightly with his other arm.

The second man took her feet. As if this were a well-practiced routine, they carried her quickly towards the window. The man holding her feet swung it open and pulled back so as not to be seen from the street.

The pair stood her upright. And only then did Monika understand what they were doing; it had happened so fast.

The other man removed his hand, and she drew a deep breath to scream for help as she struggled, attempting to free herself from their steel grip. Then she screamed a scream that turned the heads of half a dozen pedestrians. But all of the scream took place as she plunged out the window and fell to the pavement below, her trim body bouncing just once—like a rubber ball that had lost all its air. Her robe fluttered to the floor of her suddenly empty apartment.

CHAPTER TWENTY-ONE

1991
Day Five
London

As Christian drove towards London from Northampton, he considered what Ian Cathcart had told him and tried to make something out of what Ian had not said. Christian mulled over the possibilities in his head, as if he were chewing a bit of tough beefsteak. Finally, just as the rain let up, his thoughts turned to Nicholas Rashidov.

Christian hadn't heard a word from the man during the long months of turmoil within the Soviet Union, though he doubted very seriously Rashidov had failed to land on his feet. Head of the first chief directorate of the KGB, which was responsible for foreign operations and intelligence gathering, Rashidov had been appointed a candidate member of the Politburo two years earlier. Just prior to the Gulf War, the Politburo, an organ of the Communist Party and not of the government, had transferred its power to the Russian government of Boris Yeltsin; it was widely accepted he would return the favor by abolishing the Politburo almost immediately.

Christian had not heard where Rashidov ended up. The fellow had been a fast-rising star in Soviet Russia, and Christian had no doubt that would serve him well in the new Russia.

The KGB itself was due for reorganization, but Rashidov had already tipped his hat to political power, which resided, since the ascendancy of Yeltsin, in the government.

Just one year junior to Christian, the two had hit it off from the first, and Christian believed them friends. They'd first met at a trade conference Christian had attended in Moscow, after Mikhail Gorbachev had declared perestroika the new economic freedom.

When Rashidov and Christian had met, Russia was eager for greater trade, and the company's contacts had been extensive. It was a time of high expectations, most of which were realized for IMSS.

As always, Christian had been taken by the uncommon beauty of so many of the Russian women selected to attend and work at the conference. Many, perhaps all, he knew, were available, working essentially as state prostitutes and spies. He'd been tempted but found the idea of sharing a woman with a long string of men to be distasteful. That, and in the thirteen years Christian had run the company on his own, he'd learned to avoid the honey pots he was routinely offered.

That second evening, Christian attended an exclusive function at the Metropol Hotel, reserved for the vendors most likely to secure contracts. Ian had provided him with a long list of military-related electronics, previously on the restricted list, which IMSS was in the exclusive position to offer to the Soviets. As always, Christian had his eye out for a possible new contact to add to his growing list of operatives. Perestroika seemed to have loosened loyalty to the party, and any number of party apparatchiks had trolled past, offering an inviting smile before taking their place in a seemingly discreet corner.

Just before the serious drinking began about midnight, Nicholas Rashidov approached Christian and introduced himself. Perhaps in his late thirties, he was well dressed in a dark suit and well mannered. Possessed of a good English accent, Rashidov was doubtlessly a graduate of one of the Soviet's charm schools. Clean shaven, he was a handsome man in the manner of the traditional ruling classes of old Russia. He'd readily identified himself as a deputy in the KGB sixth directorate, which was responsible for economic counterintelligence and industrial security.

"Then you've certainly come to the right place," Christian had allowed, downing his first glass of vodka.

"Yes, I have no doubt we Russians will quickly master the essential steps of the previously hated capitalist system." With that, Rashidov had taken out an American cigarette, offering Christian one from the pack. "I'm told we should be great friends," the Russian said as he lit both cigarettes.

"By whom?"

"Why, by my uncle Mishka, of course!"

CHAPTER TWENTY-TWO

1963
London

Sarah set aside her copy of *The Times*. "KENNEDY DEAD," the headlined all but screamed. That was a literal shocker. It had always seemed to her that the American president lived a charmed life, he and his wife. But some Communist Quisling had shot the man down. On second thought, she decided she wasn't so surprised. America was a violent country. Things like the young president's murder were bound to happen.

She rose and stood before a mirror. Could a woman age twenty years in a single, awful summer and fall? It seemed to her that was what the image revealed. She saw the dark shadows under her eyes, the lack of luster in her gaze, how her skin seemed to hang on her. My God, she thought, I'm not yet fifty. When had she last weighed so little? When she'd been in her early twenties? Exhausted, though she was just risen from bed, she sat back in her chair and poured more tea. She had no appetite for anything else, though people were already commenting on her weight loss.

It was remarkable what an old fool Profumo had been, and how widespread had been the repercussions. A war minister, of all people! Engaging in orgies. Running about town with a woman younger than his daughter. He might have survived that, but he lied about it all on the floor of Commons the previous spring. How could he have been so stupid? His affair had been too open; too many people had known to have risked such a great lie. And it was clear, to her, at least, that someone in power was behind making the affair a public scandal. Politics! How she despised it.

Sarah picked up her secret vice, the *Daily Mail*, and scanned it again. It contained a reprise of events that had come to be known as the "Profumo Affair," and brought it all much too close to home. She could only wonder why her name wasn't on display. Stephen Ward, who'd caused all the trouble, had faced trial for living off the earnings of a prostitute. He'd taken an overdose in

August, on that last day of the trial, and was dead. Thank God for his discretion, she thought.

That Keeler person had sold her story to a tabloid for £27,000, but she'd been charged as well and was given a prison sentence. Profumo was out of public life, cleaning toilets or some other such rehabilitative charitable service, the newspapers recounted. The Conservatives were clinging to power; but it was only a question of a few more months before an election had to be held, and Labour would assume power, with Harold Wilson, the backbencher no one really knew, as prime minister.

Though her name had not appeared, there had been references to a young Pole known to be an intimate of Christine Keeler; but Monika's name had never been made public. Sarah sighed and closed her eyes. Oh, how lovely Monika had been. So very lovely! Sarah had never, not in all her life, not once in the stream of lovers she'd taken, considered that she was, at her core, a lesbian. But there it was. The beautiful young Pole had unleashed Sarah's passion in a way she'd never previously experienced.

But, it had been more than sex—much more. It was as if they had formed a union of their souls in a way she'd never known with anyone. It had been nearly spiritual in its nature. Suddenly, her sterile marriage to Julian had seemed a sham she could no longer endure. But what was she to do? Young Christian was away at school. There was her public reputation to consider, if not for her own sake than for his. It hadn't been as if she and Monika could run off and live an open life somewhere. That just wasn't possible. No, all they could ever have was this affair, and, while it lasted, Sarah had not once forced herself to consider what she would do when it ended.

And it had come to an end, an unbelievably violent end, with that poor girl's naked body smashed on stone. Not for an instant did Sarah believe it was suicide. Someone had murdered the poor dear.

It was two weeks after learning of Monika's death that Sarah had finally risen from her bed and attempted to return to some kind of existence.

Her newspapers had been stacked neatly for her and, one by one, she had read each copy of the *Daily Mail* as the fuller story unfolded. The unnamed Polish companion of Keeler was alleged to have been a spy under the direction of Stephen Ward. Ward was suspected of having introduced Keeler to Profumo, at the direction of his un-named handlers, expressly to create the very scandal that had ensued. She'd lifted each new newspaper, experiencing something close to horror that her name might suddenly appear—or a description that could fit no one else.

How close it had all been, Sarah thought. She set aside her tea and made the decision to dress for the day. Had Monika been a spy? Had their affair been something sordid? She replayed her conversations with the young woman and shuddered. Of course she'd been a spy. Much post-coital talk had been about Julian.

Sarah wondered if he knew; the man knew so much. As she selected a dress, she reconsidered the question. She should be wondering, instead, how *much* her husband knew about her and Monika.

* * *

Ever proper, Ian Cathcart didn't quite come out and state his intentions directly, but, instead, made them clear enough, over the course of the following months, by more than keeping his promise of government business. The struggling offices Julian had managed to support in a few countries quietly moved into more illustrious surroundings, grander office towers with expensive furniture, and, more importantly, more staff and budget. The downplayed Concord Trading Company was renamed International Military Support Services and attracted a silent investment from a government body that pumped cash into the company. The company became the discreet darling of the Defense Ministry, with the sweetest of the surplus contracts handed to Julian on a silver platter, making possible the opening of several new overseas offices, a move that Ian vigorously supported. Of course, there was a steep price to pay for this support.

New staff members joined IMSS, using the company as a cover for espionage. Julian's profits grew, and, with that, so grew the danger. Word in Warsaw was that IMSS had become a tool of the British government, Mishka so informed him during their next meeting. Was such a thing true?

Julian had flown to Warsaw in the aftermath of the Profumo scandal. He thought carefully of Ian's words: "Under no circumstances is the Russian to know what you know."

"Business, my friend, is business," Julian said, patting his Russian comrade on the back when they finally found themselves alone. "With our new left-leaning government, let's just say I had to make a few new compromises; part and parcel with them came some formerly forbidden fruit."

By this time, the two had been friends for fifteen years; despite Mishka's ever more evident duplicitous role, Julian still hadn't revealed the Swiss bank account Mishka had entrusted to him to the British authorities. He toasted Mishka at their private booth in Warsaw's only nightclub, pleased to be with his old friend, even with Ian and MI5 riding him, wondering how, even now, Mishka remained two steps ahead.

Julian felt strangely at home in Warsaw, far more so than he'd felt in England during recent months, especially since Monika's death. That was, he was certain, the one topic he should not raise with his Russian friend. The woman had been a spy, a spy sent to him by Mishka.

"Only make sure, in Poland, this forbidden fruit does not cost you your neck. Eh?" Mishka warned. "Now, tell me, is this fruit by chance made with silicon?" The newest development in the West, of interest to the East, was semiconductors made largely of silicon.

"My old friend, your intuition is as sharp as ever. With Wilson in, it's good for business. Far less constricting than Gaitskell would have been."

"Good. Someday, I surely would love to see your country. That would be a sight!"

"If you did ever want to visit England, I'm sure arrangements could be made. And I'm certain you'd have more than a few tidbits with which to make your coming more than welcome," Julian suggested in a half-whisper.

Mishka let out a hearty laugh. "Ah, yes! I would love to see the Abbey in the center of your London. Westminster, no? Where Dickens and Chaucer lie, yes? And where all your kings have been crowned. But, you were saying, you have an interest in certain information?"

"Of course. Of course. If a man needed to come across certain forms of information to encourage his government to give him certain contracts, say, for items made of silicon—"

"Am I understanding you correctly here? You now trade information to your government in exchange for semiconductors? And let me guess. You are looking for information regarding a certain high-ranking member of British intelligence, whose friends seem to have gone to Moscow? The new Holy Grail for you Brits, eh?"

Harold Wilson and Labour had won the election. Britain had become a briar patch for Julian, with Ian, long an ally, now almost demanding free reign over IMSS. Worse, Julian's faith was shaken by his new knowledge about Monika. His son Christian was the one bright spot amidst the shadows that encircled him.

"So I'll put it to you directly. Is Hollis a Soviet agent?"

Mishka nodded. "Tell whoever it is you report to that the answer is 'yes,' most assuredly.

And I personally would be delighted if your control would act on it; and make him pay you for the answer! You know which bank to put it in."

"He'll want more than simple confirmation."

Mishka mulled that over. Then he gave Julian two names, one of which was vaguely familiar. "They are KGB operatives. Squeeze them. They have worked with him and can provide all the information needed to bring him down."

Business now done, the men sat smoking and drinking vodka. "This business with Monika—bad, wasn't it?" Mishka remarked quietly.

"Yes," Julian replied. "It was bad. Did you have her killed, my friend?"

The Russian met Julian's gaze, then said, "No. Not me. I would not do that to you."

"But you sent her to spy on me."

Mishka smiled. "To keep me informed. Nothing bad against you. As you loved her, I thought I'd done a good thing."

"You know who ordered her death," Julian said. It was a statement, not a question.

"Sadly, I do. I just don't know why; and even if I did, there is nothing I can do about it. My God, it is a terrible thing. She was a thing of great beauty."

CHAPTER TWENTY-THREE

1971
London

What pleased Julian most, more than the unprecedented wealth and success IMSS achieved—as a company, while all the time acting in the invisible interests of the JIC—was the way that he and Christian had come to work as a team. His son was, indeed, far brighter than Julian had ever dreamed he would be, and more, he learned the crafts of intelligence and trade with an aplomb unencumbered by Julian's political bent. He would have made a fantastic operative, Julian often thought. Efficient, charismatic at times, at other times entirely inconspicuous.

Julian eventually learned that it was Ian Cathcart who forced Hollis into retirement in 1965. Word on the street was that Hollis was, indeed, Red, and was close to getting caught when he stepped down voluntarily. The confirmation and names Julian had brought from Warsaw had apparently been sufficient to convince Hollis that retirement was better than public disgrace, though why Ian hadn't crucified the man in the press would always be beyond Julian's understanding.

There was, surely, horse-trading at an extremely high level, possibly even as high as the prime minister, to decide how history would remember this circle of men who had nearly collapsed the British government during the Cold War. Julian concluded that the downside of prosecution was to admit that the head of the British Secret Intelligence Service was a Red and had protected the likes of Philby for many years. That would simply have been too much.

Through it all, IMSS continued to prosper. Indeed, Julian realized that he was well on his way to building an empire of sorts. He opened offices in the Middle East, a growing center of intelligence gathering, as well as Hong Kong, where operatives could attract Chinese defectors and infiltrate the Communist mainland, and where IMSS could sell military equipment to China, India, and Southeast Asian interests.

The Americans were the only competition in the region, and consumed as they were by the conflict in Vietnam, they refused, on principle, to deal with most of Julian's customers.

That meant more business for IMSS with Julian, in some cases, buying American equipment through the British government and having it shipped not to England, but to Asia. In a few cases, he purchased goods in Asia, surplus from the Vietnam War, only to sell it in turn back into the region.   A boon for profits, indeed, and, ironically, a boon for intelligence. The enemy trusts no one as much as it trusts the middleman who sells ammunition. If IMSS was to serve as a mask for the SIS, at least it was a good one.

Christian announced his plans for marriage early in 1970, six years after joining the company, and sent Sarah into a gleeful year of wedding planning. Julian hardly approved of the marriage; the girl was, indeed, an aristocrat by breeding but displayed every indication of a low life by inclination. He'd made inquiries and been disgusted at what he'd learned. Christian, however, was intent on her. Indeed, Julian's disapproval sparked a rare argument between father and son.

"She's a hundred-pound whore," Julian had said over a scotch. "Not a proper wife, not any kind of wife, in point of fact."

"And you should be one to talk," Christian answered, his mouth slanted. "I'd rather marry a British whore than have to import a foreign one."

Christian had walked away as Julian closed his fists. It was the closest he'd ever come to leveling his son. But as he calmed himself, he was glad he hadn't. The apple doesn't fall far, he'd thought. I'll give the boy five years, and then we'll see who was right.

During the wedding preparations, Julian traveled an exceptional amount, even for him. Christian, who had in recent years handled much of the travel for his father, felt a need to be close to the wedding, to help Evvy, his future wife, with decisions on flowers and seating arrangements. Julian marveled at how the world was changing. In his day, he would have gracefully ignored any wedding preparations as a matter of principle.

Mishka told Julian that he had entertained the idea of attending the wedding, but said there was no way for him to leave the Eastern Bloc legally. Julian was pleased to see the relationship that had developed between his son and his old friend, and increasingly left Warsaw to Christian's management. The Russian had taken the son under his wing, as easily as he'd taken the father, referring to him as "Young Christian." Although Julian had never asked, he assumed Mishka had no children of his own, as Julian had never heard of a wife or children, even in the Russian bear's most drunken moments.

It seemed to Julian that Christian enjoyed his time behind the Iron Curtain. Julian saw in his son the same excitement he'd felt at first, augmented by the new power that IMSS wielded. No longer was this a struggling trader, one of many setting up shop in Warsaw, competing for business. IMSS had emerged as the dominant player in the world security market, and Christian was adept at wielding this power, knowing when to exploit it, when to feign indifference. He had a confidence and grace that Julian admired, and Julian planned to turn over control of IMSS to Christian, once the bloom was off the marriage and the boy had his head about him. Julian planned to remain on as chairman.

Christian was married with all the splendor of an earl's grandson. Julian couldn't deny his aging father the triumphant grandeur of presiding over the nuptials. The ceremony was held at Westminster Abbey, and was attended by some fifty lords and ladies of various ranks, along with many members of Parliament. Also in attendance were the best and brightest of British society. The press turned out in droves, and the event was widely covered in newspapers and magazines.

A few months later, Julian greeted the news that he would soon be a grandfather with enthusiasm. Christian told him at the office while preparing for yet another trip to Warsaw.   "Congratulations!" Julian exclaimed joyously. He sent his secretary to buy a few boxes of cigars and paraded through the halls of IMSS. "I'm going to be a grandfather!" he told everyone he encountered— man or woman—as he stuck a cigar in the person's mouth.

Later that day, Julian arranged to take Christian to the airport himself, then telephoned Sarah to have Evvy stay with them at the country estate while Christian was away. En route, Julian decided the time had come to share certain secrets with his son. He told Christian about the Swiss bank account into which he had placed money and certain documents for Mishka over the years.

"Not just his cut from the deals we make with him," Christian said, "but he gives you pounds and dollars himself to take out of the country?"

"Yes."

"I've never heard of such a thing. He's playing a deadly game."

"As are we, if they figure out we are his bankers. If they arrest him, that will take them about one second to decide. But that's the game I've played almost since meeting him. Over the years, he's given me very important information. Usually, it was against his enemies or potential enemies, but some of it served no purpose I could see, other than to weaken the Soviet state."

"But why? It makes no sense."

"It does, if he intends to defect."

"Does he?"

Julian nodded. "In time, I'm convinced. Be prepared should he ever hint at it."

"I will."

"There's more." Julian related his drunken night with Mishka those years before, the time Mishka had told him that he was heir to the throne of the czar.

"That's absurd! The czar's entire family was murdered. He's dreaming!"

"Yes, I know. But over the years, Mishka has given me documentation in support of his claim to put into the Swiss bank safety deposit box. It's certainly convincing on its face and would, at the very least, if it ever came to light, make a serious case in his favor. He's touched on the subject, from time to time."

"To what end?"

"I think he believes an earl would be in a position to approach the British government about recognizing his claim—and rendering him discreet assistance."

"But you won't be an earl for long."

"He doesn't know that yet. But I think that's why Mishka will defect when he's ready. He intends to do his very best to reclaim the throne."

"I don't see that happening. The days of the ruling monarch in Russia are long over."

The windshield wipers snapped back and forth several times before Julian spoke. "We were born into a world of Russian communism. But, in fact, it is a very new and not especially stable phenomenon. For centuries, Russia was ruled by a czar and the church. When communism falters, as it surely will in time, there will be change; a well-placed heir to the throne might find himself just the man. I wouldn't rule it out by any means. And it's our secret, my boy."

Julian dropped his son at the curb. "Don't stray too far in Warsaw," he joked. Christian looked at his father, nonplused, but Julian returned a knowing gaze that elicited a smile from Christian.

"Far is okay, but not too far," Julian admonished. Chairman he might be, but Julian still had his sources. He knew that, in the span of a single married year, Christian had already begun to keep a mistress in Warsaw. He recalled Christian's hypocritical admonishments, espoused when Christian had only been engaged, not married. The recollection made Julian laugh to himself. He, too, had been an arrogant youth, assured that he'd not fall victim to his father's failings. It was only much later that Julian learned what he'd once considered faults were, in some ways, his father's best qualities.

"And say hello to Mishka. Tell him he should be watching you more carefully." Julian grinned and drove off quickly.

* * *

Julian was waiting at the gate the following week as Christian stepped from the airplane. As they shook hands, he led his son aside. "What is it?" Christian asked. "Is Evvy all right?"

"She's fine, my boy. It's the earl. He died last night."

"Ahh. That's it. He was—what? Eighty-five years old?"

"Eighty-six. A good and long life."

"How did it happen?"

"A stroke in his townhouse." Julian glanced about. "You might as well hear it from me. It's in the tabloids. He was with a young lady."

Christian smiled. "You're serious?"

"Quite. Apparently, he'd kept the young lady for the last several years. She's only forty-five years old now."

Christian grinned. "Why, the randy old dog! And all the while he behaved as if he'd given it up."

"Yes. An excellent cover. We should all be so lucky."

They drove through the night to Julian's estate. Christian's mother greeted him at the entrance and expressed her regret. "He was a dear man. I'll miss him terribly."

Christian was certain that was true. Ever since his mother had lived on the family estate during the war, there had been a bond between his grandfather and his mother. It had been a natural part of his life, and he had instinctively believed such a bond would form between Evelyn and his father; but it was clear that was not to be.

Evvy was lying down when Christian entered their rooms. She rose and expressed her sympathy, then said, "So. Your father will be earl now."

That struck Christian as an odd thing to say at such a moment. "Not for long," he answered.

Evvy gave him a strange, piercing look. "What are you talking about?"

Christian removed his coat and went to wash up. "Not now. This isn't the time for it."

His wife followed him. "Tell me! What do you mean?"

"Father intends to disclaim the title under the Peerage Act."

If Christian had struck the young woman his strongest possible blow, the physical effect could not have been greater. She gasped. "What are you saying?"

"He's disclaiming the title."

"Why would he do that?"

"He doesn't want it. He views it as a hindrance, a throwback to days best left in the past. I agree with him."

Evvy stood speechless for a long minute, staring at her husband in disbelief. Finally, she said, "You knew?"

"I've always known. He told me when I was still in school. My God, Evvy, those days are over. What does he want with that damn title?"

"And you *knew*?" she repeated.

"Don't be so shocked. Surely, I mentioned it to you."

"No, never. Not once!" She looked wildly about the room before her gaze fell on him again. "I blame it on your days in that left-wing dump of a university. The London School of Economics is a hotbed of lefty intellectuals."

"Well, perhaps not. Father asked me to be discreet since neither of us wanted to hurt the old man's feelings. It makes no difference, Evvy. It's just words."

Evelyn retreated to her dresser and sat down heavily. She placed her hand on her stomach, though she did not yet show the baby that was growing inside. "And what of our son?"

Christian laughed. "We don't know that it will be a son, my dear. It might very easily be a lovely little girl. But if it is a son, so what? My father doesn't want the title. I certainly don't. It's a new world. What really matters will be his, not some honorific granted the family centuries ago. The thing's more a curse than a blessing. We're well rid of it. And what do you care? Your father's still a duke; if it's really so important to you, have everyone call you Lady Evelyn. You're entitled."

"You deceived me," she said.

"I certainly did not."

"You most certainly did," she insisted, standing regally. "And I shall never forgive you for this. Not ever." Evvy turned away.

* * *

There was much to do at the family estate, and it was now Julian's primary residence. With Christian increasingly running the company, Julian found himself spending more time there than he cared to, but it was necessary. He'd given up instructing the staff not to refer to him as "My Lord." What was he to do? It was engrained in them. The earl is dead; long live the earl.

As the day for the birth of his first grandchild neared, Julian received word that his declamation had been registered. As just the third peer to ever renounce his title, the newspapers ran several articles about his decision. No one, from what he could see, understood in the least why he had taken this step.

He spent his nights with paperwork, wondering why, with all his late father's abilities, the man could not have been better with accounts.

It was on one of these late nights, Julian sitting by the fireplace, reading his own family's history from centuries before, that Mishka telephoned. It was an extraordinary event, as it had never happened previously.

"My condolences on the loss of your father. I regret I could not extend them sooner," Mishka said. Julian recognized his friend's voice immediately.

"What an unexpected surprise! Thank you."

"I haven't had a chance to speak with you in ages, old friend," Mishka said. "I was pained to hear about your father. So you now face the world as an earl, eh?"

"I've decided against that," Julian said. "I think the title is dead, buried with my father."

There was a pause, then Mishka said, "You should reconsider. Such titles are important to common people. It gives you the ability to do things you could not otherwise, and provides you with access. I urge you to rethink this."

"I appreciate your thoughts, but my mind is quite made up in this regard. The days for such things are long gone. The sooner this family is rid of it, the better."

"I see." Mishka left a powerful moment of silence. "I have a favor of you. A very important favor."

"Anything for my oldest comrade."

"You will have to come to Warsaw."

"Christian's been handling the region and is about to leave on a trip there, in any case. Can't he take care of it? I'm still preoccupied with the business of the estate. My father, I regret to say, was not much of a businessman."

"Young Christian is a wonderful man, and I enjoy my time with him. You must feel honored to have someone like him as your son. But there are still some things he cannot do. I am afraid this is one, eh? There is a powerful person who, how should I say it, wishes to visit the West? For an extended stay."

Another silence hung between them.

"Are you certain this is a secure line?"

The Russian laughed. "I believe so. But if I'm wrong, I'll soon know, won't I?"

"I think that's out of my league, these days. Perhaps I could contact some-one in the government. I do have friends in that business—"

"Let us be frank," Mishka answered. "*You* are in that business. It is common knowledge among those in a position to take an interest in such matters. I have had, many times, to explain why you were still in Warsaw, many others to explain why you were still breathing. But I cannot pass this mission to just anyone. You understand? The most sensitive mission of my life, eh?"

"I—"

"Old friend, would I ask if it were not important? I ask this favor. I have not asked such a favor of you, ever. I am sorry to ask at such a time, but it must be. Events dictate it, not I."

Did the bear want to defect himself? Julian thought. Or was it someone else? Julian knew he couldn't ask. "I have a great deal to do here. The red tape around an earl's death is enough to make even your bureaucrats squirm. Some laws have been in place for hundreds of years."

"It will be a quick trip, I promise."

"Give me a few days," Julian told him. "I'll get there as soon as I can."

"Thank you," Mishka said.

* * *

When Christian heard that his father was planning to go to Warsaw, he would have none of it. "I'll go," Christian insisted. "Whatever it is, I'm sure I can handle it."

"No. No. You've got a baby coming soon. Could be anytime, couldn't it?"

"Evvy's date isn't for a couple of weeks."

"Take it from someone who almost missed the birth of his only child: be there in the waiting room. If you aren't, you'll regret it your entire life."

"I should go. You have so much work here with the estate."

"That will wait. Be there for your wife. I could use a week away. England is the worst place in the world for me to mourn the passing of your grandfather. He was an earl here, a public personage, but he was also my father."

"If you insist."

"I do. And so does Mishka."

CHAPTER TWENTY-FOUR

1991
Day Six
London

Hannah set the morning edition of *The Times* on the breakfast table. "More bad news, dear," she said. She sat and picked up her teacup as she watched Christian flip the front page to the stark article below the fold.

IMSS REMAINS CENTRE OF INVESTIGATION BY CUSTOMS
By Tim Barclay

IMSS and its chairman, Christian Hardaway, son of the late earl of Carlisle, one of Britain's most respected counter-espionage operatives of the Second World War, remains under investigation by HM Customs and Excise, following the recent discovery that electronic timers sold by them had been used at the Lockerbie Bombing of Pan Am Flight 103 just over two years ago.

After investigators interviewed more than 15,000 people, examined 180,000 pieces of evidence, and researched in more than 40 countries, there is some understanding as to what blew up Pan Am Flight 103. The bomb was made out of the powerful plastic explosive Semtex and was activated by a timer. The bomb was hidden in a Toshiba radio-cassette player, which, in turn, was inside a brown Samsonite suitcase. But the real problem for investigators has been who put the bomb in the suitcase, and how did the bomb get on the plane?

The investigators believe they received a "big break" when a man and his dog were walking in a forest about 80 miles from Lockerbie. The man found a t-shirt that turned out to have pieces of the timer in it. Tracing the t-shirt as well as the maker of the timer, investigators felt confident they knew who bombed Flight 103—Abdelbaset Ali Mohmed al-Megrahi and Al-Amin Khalifa Fhimam, both Libyan intelligence operatives.

Tracking of the timers revealed that IMSS had purchased them in 1987 from the manufacturers, Smiths Industries, and supplied them as part of a contract to the Yugoslav government agency, TransJug. It is known that the Yugoslav authorities had regularly done business with Libya, among other terrorist-sponsoring regimes.

A spokesman for IMSS denied that the company had knowingly supplied these timers to Yugoslavia for export to Libya. But documentation received by The Times shows telexes and internal memos discussing the translation of the manuals into Arabic and provides airway bill numbers of shipments, including these timers.

A representative of the Board of Trade confirmed that, in such circumstances, it would be usual to suspend export licenses granted and withhold the granting of any further licenses. Mr. Hardaway's passport has been requested by HM Customs and Excise, and it is understood that he will not be allowed to leave the country until the investigation is completed.

Elton Frazer, MP, has already listed a question on this matter for the weekly Questions to the Prime Minister in the House of Commons.

"Well?" Hannah asked.

"Now I know why my solicitor keeps calling. They want my passport." Christian exhaled so strongly that the pages of newspaper fluttered.

* * *

Raymond Philips had been at his desk since shortly after his return from Bangkok, feeling refreshed and ready for whatever was to occur, as he always did after a debauch. He'd read the initial Times article more than once on the British Airways direct flight to London, quite pleased with how events were shaping up. His role, as he now saw it, was to make certain that while the boy Christian was destroyed and, hopefully, imprisoned, IMSS remained with him at the helm. The possibilities, in that event, were limitless. Wealth, influence, even a title would all be within his reach. What was essential was that he remain close to the boy, as if tied to him, so that he was the key, indispensable executive when the axe fell.

Preparing the report on the timers Christian wanted was the kind of intelligence disinformation operation at which Philips had always excelled. It had, after all, been he who had obtained the models and serial numbers of the timers in the first place, and seen that the information found its way to *The Times* reporter. Now the task was to deny Christian the information for as long as possible while the storm increased in intensity. Philips began by telling Christian that the files could not be located.

"I don't care if you have to tear this place apart. Those files are here somewhere."

For two days, Philips supervised the search for the records, knowing all the time where they had been secreted, since that was where he personally had put them. His hope was the search would never find the reports or that the government might execute a search warrant and seize them. But, just in case, Philips took copies and began preparing his eventual report to Christian. It had become a question of putting the information together in such a fashion that it was of little, if any, use to Christian, at least until it was too late. For that challenge, Philips worked late into the night.

Weeks earlier, Philips's most satisfying bit of creativity had been to locate the serial numbers of the timers used on the ill-fated Lockerbie flight and substitute them for others in the company files. These documents he copied then set aside. They would confirm the first article to Christian. He had done the same with certain Israeli attacks, locating the timer serial numbers from Israeli files, and then substituting them for others in the IMSS files. These he also copied and set aside. That should give the boy indigestion, he'd thought.

Philips pressed on to the real work.

He took out a notepad and, in pencil, recorded the dates of the trips Christian had taken abroad in the last two years. The list included every capital of Europe and the Middle East, as well as a smattering of Asian and South American cities. Most importantly, there were several trips to Yugoslavia, which was a recognized transit point for countries to the East.

Next, he took the serial numbers of those specialist timers he had previously prepared.

These could only be sold to specified nations, typically those in NATO. He searched for overlaps and found several. On six occasions, IMSS had sold these controlled timers to authorized nations when Christian had been present in a country for which the timers were prohibited. Philips prepared receipts for each of those trips, listing the timers as having been the subject of those trips.

With his doctoring in place, the records would show that a specific lot of timers, for example, had not gone to an authorized nation like Sweden—when, in fact, it had—but had gone to Belgrade, instead, from whence, it was reported, they'd found their way into the hands of the Palestinians.

He did the same for a trip to Riyadh, careful to use the same serial numbers he'd given the newspaper. Philips then prepared a large listing of other restricted timers and saw to it the files said Christian had provided them to the government of Lebanon. The implications of that would be self-evident. Philips then drafted a cover letter for Christian, expressing his surprise at what the files revealed, while assuring his continued support, though in measured terms.

Any sufficiently detailed investigation able to secure the complete cooperation of the nations involved—an all-but-impossible contingency—would reveal that the subject timers had never been sold to the countries in question. But even in the very best of circumstances, such an enquiry would take years. Christian would be destroyed long before that, assuming there was even the energy to carry out the investigation to that degree. Most of all, the actual end users' names had been eliminated from the IMSS files, though he supposed that duplicate information existed somewhere. In this modern age and in such a large company, they *had* to exist. He had no idea where to look for the correct records.

The irony—and joy in it all—was that Christian would not know that he was being set up because he knew he had not sold these timers, as the report and his own company records said he had. He would deny all guilt and, the more insistently he denied his guilt, the guiltier he would appear.

Philips drafted the report in his own precise handwriting. Later that evening, after his secretary had left, he laboriously typed it on her typewriter with his own hands. Satisfied with his handiwork, Philips slipped the report into his jacket pocket, put his handwritten draft through the high-security shredder, and relaxed in the chair.

As to the timing, Philips had given this considerable thought. It was essential for Christian to remain off balance, unable to come to terms with what was happening to him. While meeting with Khaldun, an idea had surfaced. Philips didn't dwell long on it; once these things were decided, it was best to just get on with it. When reaching for the brass ring at his age, one pulled no punches. It was a shame, really, but what else was there to be done?

Philips lit a cigarette, realizing, in that moment, that he needed a patsy on the off chance that the boy survived long enough to make a fight of it. Any number of possible candidates came immediately to mind. He would see to it *The Times* had this report before Christian, when the time came; then he'd decide who'd take the fall.

CHAPTER TWENTY-FIVE

1933

Moscow

For a man of Mishka's achievements, a desire to work in the NKVD was unusual. It was peopled with various thugs, survivors of its precursors. Most of the top students chose posts in central government ministries or the party itself, positions that had the potential to lead to the highest ranks, possibly the Politburo, even—for some—the Standing Committee. The NKVD—Stalin's newly reorganized and renamed secret police—was chartered as a force for the detection of practices counter to the interests of the state. Mishka sensed in the act of reorganization a deeper purpose than simply protecting the revolution. Stalin's paranoia was more complex and all consuming.

When interviewed, Mishka claimed—presciently, as it developed—that the future of the Soviet Union lay in the success of the NKVD. His argument was that a young state would face challenges when the zeal of revolution faded to the reality of class change. While life was considerably better, there would invariably be detractors. He told his selection committee interviewers that the reborn NKVD was a unique body politic, reporting directly to Stalin, and should eventually extend its reach to monitor both national and international attempts to undermine the revolution. He asked only that he be permitted to serve in this great cause.

Mishka's true motive was to be at the forefront of any anti-nationalist movement, to understand the strengths and weaknesses of such movements, and to discover whether czarist supporters would be there to shore up a counter-revolution. And, if so, when. In appearing to serve the revolution, he would instead be serving his own personal cause. Mishka was accepted, and following training was placed as an assistant under the tutelage of Lazar Kaganovich and moved to a single room not far from Red Square in Moscow.

Mishka took to Kaganovich immediately. In fact, he wondered if Kaganovich had not been, in another life, a nobleman like Mishka, and watched his parents murdered and his wealth stolen while he helplessly looked on. Kaganovich certainly had the heart of a killer and the profound hatred to go with it. Mishka found himself admiring the man, though he admitted that Kaganovich's paranoia bordered, at times, on a form of insanity. Still, Mishka served faithfully, keeping documents in order and applications to the state for additional resources free of mistakes, patiently ingratiating himself to the aloof Kaganovich while awaiting promotion.

In Mishka's first years with the NKVD, the organization emerged as one of Stalin's darlings, and budgetary requests were a matter of formality. Kaganovich had convinced Stalin, who in fact required little convincing, that anti-revolutionary seeds were sprouting across the Soviet Union and a strong, always brutal hand, would be required to secure the growth of their cause and protect Stalin in office.

Kaganovich was prone to tirades, especially when under stress, and Mishka often encouraged them, ingratiating himself in so doing while gaining more and more responsibility. The paranoia could not but help influence Mishka. In Stalin's police state, no one was secure. For years, Mishka expected arrest or execution around every corner, even at the hands of his colleagues, because that was the way it worked. In every face, he saw recognition; from every mouth, he heard the words, "Georgi Alexandrovich, you are the heir to the imperialist czar and you are under arrest!"

Mishka earned one of the most prestigious jobs in Kaganovich's organization and excelled in the work. With nearly free rein, Mishka expanded his own network of intelligence agents, dispatching recruits to Kiev, Leningrad, and the European border. He sent agents to infiltrate every part of society, hundreds of them, and he managed them loosely, allowing them to send back any information they could, leaving them to work in their environments for weeks on end without communication.

But his death squad he monitored daily. Mishka had not felt the exhilaration he experienced when he ordered a murder since he'd scored on the football field in Kiev and been carried on the shoulders of his team.

Kaganovich rose in Stalin's estimation and became the leader's most trusted confidante.

His tactics were well known—violence, Siberian exile, murder, sometimes one, sometimes all.

Kaganovich sat behind a desk with his pistol on top of it, beside his pen; he did not hesitate to use either to kill. For Mishka, this meant only more and more authority. When Kaganovich became a full-standing member of the Politburo, Mishka, for all intents and purposes, assumed the role of running the counter-revolutionary forces within the NKVD.

The secret work of murder allowed Mishka incredible freedom. Kaganovich and his direct commander, Stalin, required no explanations. Mishka kept his death tolls on ledgers, a strict accounting in number and name only, with no justification for the deaths he ordered ever written on paper. The assassins themselves were uninformed about reasons for their work. The neat split between intelligence operatives and executioners in Mishka's force gave him complete reign. The intelligence agent was assigned to another mission. The execution was carried out. The death left no record, save for the family's grief and the small, handwritten name in Mishka's thick ledger.

As the political purges of the expanded, with Kaganovich's paranoia fueling Stalin's orders and the death count soaring, Mishka found himself in the enviable position of jury, judge, and executioner. Mishka filled his first ledger and started a second, thicker book, the kind government accountants used, with gold-embossed letters on the front of the black leather cover: LEDGER.

Although he loved the people of Russia, he knew that they would only rise against Stalin and the Bolshevik revolution when they realized these so-called Communists were butchers, lacking in the virtues of the czars of old. In time, when enough blood had been shed, Russia would long for the days of the czars, Mishka believed. The sacrifice of lives was a necessary evil to take unto himself the power of the czars, and for the good of greater Russia. The czars were noble, brave, and just. The Communists were peasants, imitating royalty with only a thin veneer of ideology to justify their brutality.

Mishka killed in an effort to free the people of Russia; the innocents he murdered did not die in vain.

Then, one morning, a disturbing question came from Kaganovich. Had Mishka heard of a pro-czarist movement under a nephew of the former czar? Was it real? Yes, Mishka replied. In fact, Mishka had heard rumors, but his operatives had found nothing to substantiate the claim—much to Mishka's disappointment. Yet the movement remained a possibility. It was commonly known to the White Russians in exile that a nephew had escaped during transfer to Moscow after the revolution, and there was documentation to support the claim. "Kill him," came Kaganovich's order.

It was, Mishka thought with amusement, a most peculiar situation. He was being ordered to eliminate himself.

The event filled Mishka with despair. With every round of purges, Stalin, the Man of Steel, became more entrenched in power. With the passing of each decade, the steamroller that was the Soviet state systematically destroyed every remnant of czarist Russia. Mishka came to doubt that a counter-revolution would ever be launched, let alone succeed. He was doomed to the life of a butcher.

Slowly, however, he came to realize that such was not, necessarily, a depressing thought. It had taken a number of years before Mishka realized his own joy in killing, in the power of life and death. He killed brutally, often personally, patriotic words on his lips extracting a cruel vengeance for what he deemed his own damned fate. An eye for an eye was not enough.

Love, for Mishka, became an act of equal cruelty. He satiated his sexual desires with prostitutes. He also used the wives of officials who feared his wrath. The women themselves came compliantly to his bed, in most cases, but others came with genuine passion, inflamed to be taken by a man with the power of life and death, with so much blood on his hands.

In his work, Mishka discovered false pretenders to the czarist throne, groups with plots to take over sections of the Soviet Union and force Stalin to recognize them as independent states, dissidents devoted to building a new party. He slaughtered them all, often interrogating them beforehand, a skill he had honed but also one for which he'd inherited a natural proclivity. He knew how to instill such fear in the heart of a human being that answering his questions seemed but a small price to pay to escape the fear and pain, if only for a few moments. After a few hours with Mishka, most longed for death.

He usually interrogated with only one guard present, a soldier Mishka had promoted due to his support of Mishka without question, a man Mishka doubted would be betray him Boris Zhirinovsky.

Kaganovich continued to assume greater power in the government, working closely with Stalin and giving Mishka protection from the increasingly precarious nature of Moscow politics. When Kaganovich and Stalin purged the Soviet government of their enemies in the late 1930s, Mishka was never suspected, never made a target when almost every official in a position of authority was murdered. In fact, Mishka remained outside Moscow, carrying out his own puppet trials in Kiev and slaughtering hundreds of people he'd disliked as a boy, some of them his old classmates, patriots he knew had never uttered a word against the Communist state. By then, murdering had become pure joy for Mishka.

* * *

Working along the Polish border after the German invasion of France, Mishka had been among the first to see the threat of a Nazi assault against Russia but did nothing to alert the capital. Instead, he sent his most trusted deputy, Boris Zhirinovsky, into Poland as a spy. Zhirinovsky had been a childhood friend in Kiev. Mishka had recruited Zhirinovsky into the NKVD from a meaningless political post. Zhirinovsky owed him everything.

Zhirinovsky, who had already made repeated contacts with the Nazi regime, returned to Moscow in secrecy. The pair met at Mishka's home, a large penthouse near the center of the city with a balcony view of Lobnoye Mesto, the "Place of Skulls," a circular platform where public executions had been carried out in the days when his ancestors ruled the country. Behind it, the domes of St. Basil's Cathedral rose like a bunch of radishes into the dark sky.

The apartment's only splendor was the view. Mishka had intentionally decorated it with sparse furniture, made it a proper Communist apartment despite the excesses he'd witnessed among some of his fellows. Mishka refused to allow himself hedonistic pleasures, poor substitutes for what he would eventually enjoy as the rightful ruler of the mightiest nation in the world. He preferred to live as a peasant, to remind himself of his purpose, of the boot that had cracked his mother's cheekbone and the bullet that had taken his father's life, of the millions in the countryside starved during Stalin's inept attempts at restructuring the agrarian life of Russia's peasants. Thousands of years of history could not be changed by a single hand or a single idea any more than a smart man, with no royal blood, could lead a country to greatness.

Close to midnight, Zhirinovsky knocked at Mishka's heavy wooden door. He carried only a large black briefcase for luggage. Mishka answered the door himself and embraced his old friend in a hug, almost lifting him from the ground.

"It's been a year, hasn't it?"

Zhirinovsky's back was covered in sweat from the humid, August night. "Almost, I think. In Poland, you stop counting after a few days. Life is hard there under the German occupation."

"Show me the documents," Mishka ordered impatiently.

Zhirinovsky opened the briefcase and removed a docket of papers, passing them to Mishka, who studied them for several minutes before breaking the silence. Mishka laughed heartily as he produced two glasses. He took a bottle of the best Russian vodka from his icebox. He poured two long drinks and toasted Zhirinovsky.

"To our long lives. So what else? Do they have plans for us if they manage to conquer us?"

"We'll be subdivided into Nazi colonies, like everywhere else. A German military governor will be installed, but they know they'll need support from our military, and they will certainly want to install a Russian leader—a symbolic figure, someone who can keep the people at bay and help them clear out the Jews."

"Kaganovich would relish the idea. Though he's a Jew, himself, he has a hatred for the people that rivals Hitler's. He would love to send these people to their deaths. Tell me more."

Zhirinovsky pointed to the sheets of paper he'd brought, which contained a careful listing of the forces the German army would unleash against Russia. He gave Mishka a brief summation.

"Excellent!" Mishka proclaimed when the briefing was concluded. "You've done an extraordinary job. I'll report this to Stalin personally. I am certain you will be commended. It is a difficult time in Moscow, now. We believe we have destroyed the counter-revolutionary plots, but still, in Moscow, trust is an endangered animal. Do you have answers to the letters I sent?"

" Here," Zhirinovsky said, removing a single large envelope from his brief-case. Mishka checked the German seals on the backs of the envelopes; they had not been opened.

"You've done a great thing for the revolution, Boris. I am proud of you. Have you read these?" Mishka waved the envelopes.

"Of course not! The seals are unbroken, aren't they?"

"Yes, but did you read my letters and perhaps read these before they were sealed?" Mishka smiled. "Boris, if you did, it's no matter to me. The messages in those letters were on Comrade Stalin's direct orders."

"I would never betray your trust, Mishka." Boris lowered his head, almost as a subject to a king would, and Mishka was filled with a pang of fear that Boris had, indeed, read the letters. Sending those communications was an extremely dangerous move. He should have made the journey himself, present-ed himself in person to the Reich as the rightful czar of Russia rather than in secret letters, letters that could easily pass into the wrong hands.

"This is meant for Stalin's eyes only," Mishka said. "I will give it to him tomorrow, myself, along with a commendation for your work."

"Thank you," Boris said, raising his eyes to meet Mishka's.

"What was the name of your contact?"

"Excuse me?"

"In Germany. Within the Reich. I want to know more about his background. Who he is, in fact. You know we have extensive intelligence on the Nazis."

"Reinhardt Gehlen. He is the head of all intelligence with regard to the So-viet Union. He has the Führer's ear."

The two men shook hands, each holding the forearm of the other.

"We may have changed the course of history, my friend," Mishka told him. "One can only hope, for the good of the revolution."

Mishka tore open the letter as soon as Boris had left. It was signed by Field Marshal Walter von Brauchitsch, the commander-in-chief of the German army. It was an expression of interest in the claims of Georgi Alexandrovich Romanov to the throne of Russia. The field marshal requested further information, proof of the claim, and—possibly—a meeting "to confirm that the interests of the Reich and the interests of the czar are, indeed, aligned."

The six months of correspondence had finally yielded results. The Germans would do business with the rightful heir to the throne of the czars. It was not Mishka's first effort to contact the Germans for support, but it was the first that had earned the attention of the Nazi upper echelon.

Mishka summoned a squad of secret police, and they arrived only moments after Zhirinovsky had reached his apartment. Mishka took personal charge and ordered the men to enter the apartment. They had Zhirinovsky's hands cuffed behind his back before the man could understand what was happening.

As with so many others, recognition that Mishka had come for him struck Zhirinovsky with a rush of terror. "I—I have done nothing, Mishka. Why have you—It is you that have something to hide!" Zhirinovsky's outrage quickly turned to frightened blubbering.

"Nonsense, traitor," Mishka said, silencing Zhirinovsky by slamming the butt of his pistol into the man's jaw. The man fell to the ground. Zhirinovsky regained speech just as two of Mishka's henchman bent Zhirinovsky over, head to the floor, in a kneeling position. Mishka put his boot on the man's cheek and looked down. It was Mishka's favorite position for murder, the same pose in which, long before, a captain had shattered his mother's face. He loved the look of pure fear that swept across a victim's face, turning the skin a paler shade.

Zhirinovsky began to yell again, to cry, screams of "no!" amidst his pleas for mercy. Mishka lowered his gun and pointed it at Zhirinovsky's temple. He fired a single shot. A pool of blood oozed from the man's head, mixing with brain matter and bits of bone. Mishka lifted his heel from the man's lifeless face and walked away without once looking back at his former friend's body.

CHAPTER TWENTY-SIX

1971
London

Christian lit yet another cigarette and resumed his pacing of the waiting room. Everything had seemed normal until a few minutes ago. Now, he wondered. Evelyn's pregnancy had seemed to proceed normally. His wife had grown larger and larger, and become more and more difficult to live with. Though she'd promised to behave herself, he knew that she'd continued smoking on the side and drank at least half a bottle of sherry a day. Her behavior troubled him deeply, but there'd been nothing more he could do about it. He'd tried and, as always, she'd gone right ahead and done exactly as she wished.

Evelyn had gone into labor several weeks early, shortly after his father had left for Warsaw. Christian had taken her to hospital, as arranged, and been by her side during most of the protracted labor. At one point, the doctor had suggested a Caesarian procedure, but Evelyn had shaken her head violently, side to side. "No scars! No scars!"

Christian spoke to the doctor, who seemed to him a bit of a wimp, and asked the man's recommendation. "The C-section is recommended in lengthy labor but it's not required. If she wants to bear the pain, there's no harm in it."

At the moment, however, it seemed there might very well have been harm in it. Nurses were rushing about, and the strange looks he received sent chills down Christian's spine. His wife, the baby, or both, were in serious trouble. But when he asked, he was given the reassurance that all was well.

It was then that his office assistant, Brian Reynolds, arrived in a rush. Not long out of university, he was serving an apprenticeship with IMSS. Julian had placed him with Christian. "Careful what you say now," he'd cautioned. "The boy's father is a member of Parliament."

But Reynolds had proven to be no problem. He was eager to learn, discreet; Christian was sorry that the time was fast approaching when Brian would leave the company. He looked up as the young man rushed into the room, brandishing a sheet of paper in his hand.

"I'm a bit busy at the moment, Brian," Christian confided.

"I know, sir, and I'm sorry to bring such terrible news to you at this time. Better you read it. I haven't the heart."

Christian took the paper and saw it was a telex from their Warsaw office. It read:

I regret to advise that Julian Hardaway's body was discovered early this morning in Warsaw. He appears to have been the victim of foul play. Authorities are not cooperating, though they say there will be no difficulty returning his body to London. I have attempted to learn details and will try through informal channels today, but a curtain of secrecy has descended over the incident.

We at this office wish to extend to Christian Hardaway our deepest regrets and condolences. Your father was a fine man and will be greatly missed.

Please advise as to transportation details. A coded message will be sent daily each afternoon, advising of what, if anything, we are able to learn of the circumstances.

—P. W. Preston, Manager

Dead? That it wasn't possible was Christian's first reaction. Holding the paper, he found he was unable to move. Then he heard a voice coming from a very distant place.

"Sir! Sir! Can you hear me?" It was Brian.

Christian nodded, then handed back the telex.

"Have you any instructions, sir?" the voice asked.

Christian slumped onto the couch, shaking his head slightly, unable to speak.

"I'll see to the details, sir. You needn't worry. Everything will be taken care of."

At some point, the young man vanished; Christian couldn't recall later the exact sequence of events. He remembered that he was alone when the doctor entered the waiting room, accompanied by a grim-faced nurse. "Mr. Hardaway?" the doctor said.

Christian looked up. His wife. His child. "Yes?" He managed to stand up, his legs nearly buckling under him.

"I regret to inform you that I have bad news." The doctor paused.

"Yes?"

"The baby was stillborn. We did everything we could. I'm very sorry."

Christian was numb. Dead. His father and now the baby. "What was it?"

"Sir?"

"A boy or a girl?"

The nurse scowled at the question. "A boy, sir. I'm very, very sorry."

"My wife?"

"She's fine. Tired. Distraught, as you'd expect. We're taking her to recovery. You can visit with her for a moment, if you'd like."

"Of course. When she's ready."

Dead? His father was dead. Christian found it unbelievable. The man had always seemed so permanent, so knowing. A death in bed with a young woman, the death the old earl had experienced—now that was something he could grasp, but this. The telex only said "discovered." Nothing more. Preston was a good man. He wouldn't send via an open message anything that he knew beyond what the officials reported. Christian would have to wait to learn more. But that word—"discovered"—seemed to Christian to hold possibilities at once limitless and unsavory.

And there was this. Christian had been scheduled for this trip, and his father had taken it in his place.

"She's ready now, sir," the nurse said, a little bit too pleasantly, bearing in mind the circumstances. "This way."

Christian followed the woman, his mind racing with speculation as it fought off despair. He found Evelyn in a private recovery room, looking haggard and old. For a moment, Christian believed he'd seen her in old age. He took her hand. "I'm very sorry, dear. Wasn't your fault. You mustn't think that."

Funny that those were his first words, Christian thought later. Perhaps it was because he believed the exact opposite — that it was her fault, in every way.

She was crying. "So hard, Christian. So hard! Don't ask it of me again. Please?"

"Yes. I understand."

"They said it was a boy. This will be very hard on your father."

Had he time to think, to prepare a response, Christian knew he would have said nothing; but this, on top of the news, had severed his usual restraint. "Father's dead, Evvy. I just received the telex from Warsaw. I don't know the details, but he'll be spared learning of this."

"Dead? That can't be. Oh, that's simply terrible!" she whispered.

"Sleep, if you can. We've much to grieve about later. But, for now, just rest."

She whispered something, as if to herself.

"What?"

"I said, 'You're the earl now.'"

"What?" he repeated.

"Your father disclaimed the title, but it's evolved to you."

"Evvy—Not now. This isn't the time."

She gripped his hand fiercely. "Promise me you'll keep it. Promise me!"

Christian looked at his wife in disbelief. How could she be speaking of such trivia at a time such as this? Could she be so shallow? It was his sudden realization that, in fact, she was that elicited a harsh reply from him. "My father wouldn't have the thing, and neither shall I!" With that, he turned on his heel and went home.

Over the following days, Preston, true to his word and nature, sent Christian private, encoded messages. There was, however, little to report. Christian's father had checked into the hotel and gone out that evening, but no one knew to where or to meet whom. Early in the morning, his body was found lying in an abandoned apartment building. He'd been suffocated.

Later, when Preston returned to London, he met with Christian. "The official version, sir, not made public, but widely known in key circles, is that your father visited a specialized bordello where he engaged in rough sex involving asphyxiation, to heighten the sensation, and was accidentally killed."

"That's absurd!"

"Yes, sir, it is. But it's meant to discredit him. I've leaned on all my sources, and it's clear they aren't telling the truth about what really happened. I don't know where he went or what he was up to, but that was normal. I often didn't know when either of you would be in the city."

That was certainly true. What an awful business this is, Christian thought. "Anything else?"

"The truth is, he was killed by someone who subsequently went to a great deal of trouble to cover up the facts. I'm sorry. Perhaps, in time, someone will defect, and we'll learn the story."

There was no reason to ask who'd want to kill the man. The list of enemies was limitless.

But Christian's father had gone to see Mishka, and he'd had dangerous dealings with the Russian for years. Christian decided to risk the question. "What about— Kirov?" Preston was well placed enough in IMSS to know about Mishka. If not the details of their business arrangements, Preston knew enough to realize the Russian had played a role in their business dealings, though Preston could have had no idea of the man's true place.

"I can't say that he was even in the city. And— well, sir, I've come to believe they were genuinely friends. I can't imagine he'd have anything to do with such nasty business."

At home, Evelyn's bed was closed to Christian. He'd expected no less. Over the coming years, on three occasions, when they were both intoxicated and returning from a party, they had sex. Each time, they did not speak of it the next day. And each time, it did not mean the resumption of wedded relations. She'd made it clear to him. If he wanted her body, he'd take the title. He decided to pass. Other bodies were readily available to him.

As for the title, without a male heir, it would die with him—and good riddance.

Of far greater significance was the murder of his father. Who had killed Julian Hardaway, and why? Christian was never entirely satisfied that the murder had not initially been meant for him and that his father had been killed by default. It was the one great mystery of his life, and, before his time had passed,

Christian was determined to learn the truth and exact his revenge, whatever the cost.

CHAPTER TWENTY-SEVEN

1940
Russia

The German-Soviet pact secured a portion of Poland under Soviet rule. Stalin, already seeing the possibilities for expansion, annexed Finland almost as soon as Hitler had swept through the rest of Poland. Stalin's vision of a Europe split between Hitler and himself only demonstrated his naiveté, in Mishka's opinion. Mishka understood instinctively that Hitler would not stop before he'd conquered all of Europe and Russia.

After receiving Zhirinovsky's report, and in order to act on his plans for collaboration with the Germans, Mishka maneuvered to be assigned to the Belorussian front as commissar. With his help, Germany would have no trouble defeating the Bolshevik army. The move had proved ridiculously easy to manage. All he'd had to do was suggest to Kaganovich that there remained traitors within the Red Army. And the closer the Germans came, the greater a threat they represented.

Kaganovich supported him. As the primary intelligence gatherer, Mishka had strongly skewed his reports on Poland to indicate that Stalin couldn't trust the current military command to resist German attempts to turn them into traitors. "They are weak with materialistic longings," he reported.

Mishka relocated to Bialystock, Poland, expecting to establish a center of operations close to the German line. But he found himself unable to resume communications with the German High Command. He thought, perhaps, he had rid himself of Zhirinovsky too quickly. He had the occasional opportunity and, as part of the pact between the nations, met from time to time with Russian-speaking German officers, but always in the context as the commissar of Belorussia.

Mishka could trust no one and was isolated all that long spring and into summer, traveling constantly along the Belorussian front, submitting frequent reports to Moscow and Stalin that the Germans were remarkably quiet, even when they weren't. He knew an invasion was coming, though he never said so, hoping, instead, that an invasion would quickly succeed, while Stalin slept in his capital, worried about the Politburo.

And Stalin did sleep. Any insinuation that the Nazis might be on the verge of invasion was quickly dismissed by the leader. Stalin was still basking in the limelight. Not only did he hold Russia in a tighter grip than any czar in memory, he had been named Man of the Year for 1939 by the American magazine *Time*.

The thought of simply defecting appealed to Mishka, often with an all-but-irresistible pull. He believed he could persuade the Germans that he was the czar's heir and would find himself at the head of an anti-Communist Russian army. But to take such a risk, he would be leaving a position of power and walking into an abyss. While in this state of mind, he finally reestablished communication with Zhirinovsky's German contact.

Mishka's first meeting with General Reinhardt Gehlen came after several subtle but clear requests, and had nothing to do with Mishka's great lineage or his desire to claim Russia. Revealing that information was too dangerous at this stage of the game, Mishka decided. Instead, Mishka approached Gehlen in the simple guise of a traitor. He planned to demonstrate his belief that Germany possessed the superior military machine, that he had information that might help them, and that he expected someday to live in a position of prominence in a Nazi world.

The meeting proved uneventful. Gehlen gave absolutely nothing away, yet asked dozens of questions about Soviet-controlled Belorussia. How was Stalin defending it? Did he honestly believe he could hold it? Why was Mishka, the commissar—a high-ranking official in the Soviet scheme of things—risking his life to give Germans information?

Mishka answered well, if not honestly. He said he believed Stalin's rule was rotting from within. Millions had died in the famine. And in the government purges of the late thirties, Stalin had murdered not only his enemies, but also many of his friends. More enemies rose in the ranks, and the old dictator had few friends left. The military and middle classes had been liquidated, and the current colonels had been lieutenants not long ago, while the current majors had been sergeants, at most, and almost none had any military school background.

Gehlen asked bluntly for the third time. What did Mishka want?

"I, General, want only what is best for *me*. I am happy to continue sending intelligence reports to Moscow that show no signs of German invasion, but we both know those are lies."

Gehlen raised an eyebrow at him, the closest he would come to admitting the plan for a Nazi attack.

"I believe I could be of tremendous help to your organization. Russia is quite a jewel for a crown, but not one to be taken for granted."

"And all this just to be a prisoner of war?" Gehlen laughed.

"I expect that there will be a place for a Russian Nazi in the next regime?"

The two men shook hands with something that, if less than friendship, was certainly beyond treaty. Mishka returned to Belorussia by night, disappointed at the meeting. He would have to await events.

* * *

A year before the German offensive against Russia, Mishka met a young woman named Kristina Shaposhnikova. Her father had recently been named a marshal of the Soviet Union and was newly appointed as chief of the Soviet general staff. He had held the position of deputy chief since 1937 and was one of a handful of senior army officers who'd survived the purges. It was Shaposhnikov whom Stalin had charged with rebuilding the army, and Shaposhnikov was going about the task furiously. For several years, Shaposhnikov had commanded the Leningrad Military District, and it was in Leningrad where Kristina lived with her mother.

Mishka had gone to Leningrad on the direct orders of Kaganovich, who wanted a private report on political conditions there. There were rumors of collaborators with the Germans; Mishka's job was to stamp them out, a task he fulfilled with relish.

That summer of 1940, Kristina was twenty-one years old. They met at one of the many party functions Mishka sponsored. Lovely, with large, luminous eyes, she would not initially meet his eyes when she spoke, so shy she was. When he learned the name of her father, Mishka made his decision. Once the food and vodka were gone, the party had quickly wound down. He caught Kristina by the sleeve of her coat as she prepared to leave.

"Stay," he commanded. To his surprise, the young woman set aside her coat and sank into a chair. Once everyone had left, he told her to come to the couch where he sat. "Why are you in Leningrad?" he asked. "Why haven't you joined your father in Moscow?"

"I'm here to serve the people," she responded in a voice so quiet that he could hardly hear her.

"You live with your mother?"

"I did. She died last month."

"You are married or have a boyfriend?"

"No."

Mishka weighed his choices. Although she was shy, she was also very docile and seemingly ready to follow any strong man. Her father was powerful, too powerful to offend; he was also very busy in Moscow, and, if he truly loved his daughter, she would not have been left to live alone in Leningrad. Shaposhnikov was well known as a man who put his career and loyalty to Stalin above everything.

"You are mine now. Into the bedroom. Prepare for me. I'll be with you shortly."

In fact, Mishka was not at all certain how the girl would react to such an approach. It was with some surprise that he watched her rise meekly from her chair and cross the room to the bedroom. It was strange. He never thought it would be so easy.

Mishka made a short telephone call to add the girl to the manifest of the train he'd be leaving on first thing in the morning. Then he went into the bedroom and quickly undressed. He'd not had a woman in some time, and found himself highly aroused. When he crawled into the bed, Kristina spoke. "Please, sir. Be gentle. It is my first time."

That had been much more than he'd expected. As for her shyness, he was bold enough for the both of them and would lead the way in bed.

Kristina left Leningrad as docilely as she submitted. He took her to his apartment in Borovichi and arranged for them to be married that week. Afterwards, he wrote her father to inform him, presenting theirs as a genuine romance, the marriage rushed because of the uncertain times with Germany, and begging the marshal's approval. A week later, Mishka received a letter of congratulations and a case of caviar. That was it.

Ten months after that first night in Leningrad, on the very day the Germans launched their invasion, Kristina gave birth to a healthy young boy. Mishka could not have been more pleased. A son. An heir.

He named the boy Nicholas, for his uncle, the last czar to rule Russia, but had the birth registered with Kristina's maiden name to take advantage of the connection to her father and to conceal his role as father. Such caution was, by now, instinctive in him. He doubted it was needed, but there was no harm in it. But the family connection proved worthless. General Shaposhnikov's health deteriorated, and he was moved from his post and given command of the KGB military academy, a position he held until he died in 1945, just six weeks before the victory. Mishka never did meet the man.

Kristina proved a disappointment, as well, albeit a convenient one. She became ill with tuberculosis and died shortly thereafter, leaving Mishka to care for their hardy son. At this point, Mishka believed his best chance to become czar must wait on Stalin's death. In the meanwhile, it was wise to keep the fact that he had a son a secret. It might be that, some day, he would sit on the throne of All the Russias and would be in a position to train his son to replace him. But he'd come to understand that day might never arrive. In that case, it would be up to the boy to fulfill the dream of restoring the Romanovs to power.

In Moscow, Mishka selected a childless couple to raise his son. The boy's putative father would be Mikhail Rashidov, and young Nicholas would take that name for the time being. Rashidov was senior in the Communist Moscow City Committee, which ran the capital, and was not a man of great ambition. He'd set his sights early on to simply survive. He already owed much to Mishka and, when Mishka explained that Mikhail would have his patronage and protection in exchange for raising his son, Mikhail was delighted to accept. Not that Mikhail had a choice. But the couple had long wanted a child and Mikhail's wife, Ludmilla, took the boy, Nicholas, to her bosom as if he were her own flesh.

Mishka instructed that the boy was not to be told who his real father was, and Mishka was to be identified as a long-time family friend and "uncle" to him. Mishka would be the boy's favorite visitor and would see to it that every path was cleared for him. In time, when it was right, Mishka would reveal to Nicholas the boy's true identity.

But, all that was to come. For the time being, there was much to do.

* * *

Well over three million Germans marched on Russia in the summer of 1941, a mere three weeks after Mishka turned his son over to the couple. He had assured Gehlen that only minimal preparations had been made against any attack, and had urged the Nazis to strike before Stalin could consider better defensive tactics.

In six months, the Germans had Russia overwhelmed and nearly took Moscow before a bitter winter and a surprisingly resilient Russian people managed a counterattack. Mishka warned Gehlen repeatedly that the Nazi war machine must continue to strike until Stalin was dead. That meant taking Moscow in the first wave of victory. If they allowed the Red Army to regroup, victory would no longer be certain. Mishka risked everything on a quick German victory and had come to fear he'd risked it all for nothing. Germany's failure to secure victory that first summer placed Mishka in an awkward position. In Russia, intelligence and the NKVD had taken a backseat to the machines of real war.

Kaganovich had little time for him. Mishka stayed with the Russian army for the most part—what was left of it. His contacts with Gehlen were as frequent as circumstances and the volatile front permitted, although, from his perspective, not especially productive. He hoped to make a friend of the man but found Gehlens abstinence from alcohol and women difficult barriers to overcome. The German was pious—at least in his professional life—and was rising quickly in the intelligence apparatus of the German army on the Eastern Front. As the campaign against Russia turned from stunning success to catastrophic failure, Hitler's insistence that Russia be won strengthened, and Gehlen, with his ties and deep understanding of the Soviet Union, became increasingly important to the Führer.

Gehlen surely knew Germany was failing by the time of the defeat of the German forces at Stalingrad. By January 1945, Mishka's meeting with the recently promoted Major General Gehlen had taken a strange turn. Mishka had, at first, come to Gehlen as a supplicant; but their roles had reversed as the war moved on. Mishka found himself receiving a nervous Gehlen when the German crossed the border and arrived at a remote Kiev dacha for an audience. Gehlen confessed that he wanted out.

He was willing to offer information about the Third Reich, the kind of information Mishka had once given him—battle plans, intelligence on weapons stockpiles, and organizational hierarchy. But both men knew there was nothing Gehlen had that Russia needed.

Hearing that Gehlen was no longer married to the Reich, Mishka initially thought to kill him.

It would be a much-needed coup for him. He could manufacture a story about luring the German's chief intelligence officer on the Eastern Front to a secret meeting. Gehlens usefulness was exhausted, and the man knew far too much about Mishka. It was an obvious decision.

Then Gehlen, perhaps talking to Mishka because there was no one else left to whom he could talk, told Mishka of his liaison with the OSS in London. Mishka's interest was piqued.

"The Americans?" Mishka asked in disbelief. "What do they want with you?"

"The Americans need an enemy. That's what keeps their economy alive. Germany is almost gone, Japan about to collapse. So who do you think is next? The Communists! By vilifying the Communists, they'll be able to keep their wartime economy afloat for the next fifty years. Russia is to be their coming great crusade. And I have the key to that. No one else has an organization built to spy on the Soviet Union. I have the entire operation in place and years of intelligence to give them."

It was true. Gehlen was a superb administrator, and the Russian knew his agents were everywhere in the East. "My friend," Mishka said with a warm smile. "I see a way for both of us to not only live through this war, emerge as heroes, but also to get rich from these politicians and their paranoia." As Mishka continued to explain, the smile on Gehlens usually expressionless face grew, as he allowed Mishka's political intelligence and his infinite capacity for deception to develop a plan for the both of them.

It was genius, sheer genius.

CHAPTER TWENTY-EIGHT

1969
London

Nicholas Rashidov drew the curtains in the windows of his apartment near the Soviet embassy and opened the windows over the garden below. It was spring, and, despite the constant complaints of Londoners about their city, he found the air this morning remarkably clear and invigorating.

The woman whom he'd brought home the previous night was already gone, thank God.

He hated the task of seeing them out the door in the morning. They always wanted to talk, about anything, but most of all, about their presumed relationship. There was none, of course, but that was not what they wanted to hear.

Rashidov had been the assistant commercial attaché in London for just over one year and would remain in that post for another two. The time, thus far, had been well spent, in his opinion.

His already fluent English was now almost perfect, and the slight Russian lilt made it very attractive.

But Rashidov was not satisfied with simply doing well. He needed some brilliant intelligence feat in Britain that would attract the notice of powerful figures in the KGB. He knew he was being watched and that much was expected of him. Perhaps today, he mused, as he stepped into his morning shower. He had a meeting with the young American that morning. Perhaps today is the day. As he lathered his hard body, he whistled a traditional Russian folk tune.

The death of his parents in a car accident while he was at university had struck Rashidov hard.

Until the moment he had learned of it, he had had no idea how much he had depended on them, their love and their support. Everything Rashidov knew about politics, about advancing his career, he'd learned from his crafty father, who'd survived Stalin, Khrushchev, and all the changes since.

His father had been a survivor and shown his only son the way.

Rashidov had found himself alone. Well, not alone entirely. He had his uncle Mishka Kirov, who had rushed to his side upon learning of the tragic accident. The man had offered himself as surrogate father and expressed the desire that the two of them share a closer relationship.

Rashidov wasn't certain he really wanted that. His uncle had been a protégé of Lazar Kaganovich, who had survived the post-Stalin purges, but only just. He was now living in disgrace somewhere in Moscow. Rashidovs father had expressed the opinion that Mishka had been lucky, indeed, to escape elimination in the purges.

"Why is that, father? He seems a jolly enough man to me," he'd asked. Before his father answered, he'd noticed the look his mother projected toward him, a look of conveying caution and fear. He was certain of that.

"They were closely allied, he and Kaganovich."

"But Kaganovich survived; why not Uncle Mishka?"

"Yes, you are right. Why not? Enough about this."

But Rashidov had never shaken the odd conversation or the tangible fear that had manifested itself in that small apartment that night. Once he was well established in the KGB, working in the Lubyanka Building, he'd been in a position to learn more about his uncle, especially since no one knew of their relationship and everyone was willing to share what they'd heard and the swirl of rumors about the man.

The picture had not been pleasant; but then, none of the stories about Stalin's henchmen were ever pleasant. He'd employed scores of murderers and, every few years, unleashed the murderers against themselves to thin the ranks and weed out anyone potentially disloyal. Only the very lucky and the very wily had survived; and, in Stalin's regime, it was difficult to believe that any form of luck existed.

His uncle was a murderer, albeit an officially sanctioned one. Rashidov knew that much.

Such a man was not unusual, given the history of the new Russia. But Uncle Mishka was a man whom Nicholas Rashidov had heard relished death, often inflicting it himself, even when executioners were available. If they'd had no relationship, this was a man Rashidov would normally have stayed well clear of. Given the man's history and past associations, Rashidov could not see how Mishka could help him; instead, the risk was that he would hurt or maybe even end his career.

But there was something strangely needy in so brutal a man. From earliest childhood, Rashidov had sensed that Mishka saw in him a son he'd never had. Rashidovs parents had encouraged closeness to the man, but something about Mishka had kept Rashidov a bit distant, though he feigned that closeness. The older he'd become, the more he'd pretended at the intimacy Mishka so strongly desired. Had it been up to him, he'd have had nothing to do with his uncle. But it was not up to him. Still, since his association with Mishka was not acknowledged within the KGB, Rashidov could see no harm that had come to him because of Mishka.

Dressing in his best suit, Rashidov stepped out of his flat, walking briskly to his meeting. Today, he thought. Let it be today...

* * *

Nicholas Rashidov had met Mitchell Seaver the very week he'd arrived in London from Russia.

It was only natural that Rashidov should meet the man. Anyone holding his position at the Soviet embassy would be known as a KGB operative, a junior one, to be sure, but an agent well respected and marked for better things. America might be the greater enemy, but Britain was more closely situated, with a significant left-leaning population, not to mention the many Soviet sleeper plants throughout British society.

Seaver, himself, was officially working covertly for a corporation well known to be a CIA front. It was not anticipated that the bright young American would ever function other than in the open, so no effort at this point, in what should be a promising career, was made to conceal the connection to the Company, except on the most superficial level. In fact, it was useful for Seaver to be known by the right sort of people as a CIA agent, as one of his many jobs in London was the recruitment of operatives for the Company. Because of that, one of Seaver's responsibilities was to go to the many social functions that would also be attended by Soviet and Eastern Bloc operatives.

This was not a good time in Mitchell Seaver's life. Married the year he joined the CIA, and right out of Yale, he had quickly fathered two children. It was important, for the kind of career he envisioned, that he be seen as a stable family man. And Seaver had played the role to the hilt—upon reflection, perhaps too much so. His wife had complained about his many long absences. But most of all, she told him that she deeply resented being a showcase wife at CIA functions. "The children and I are not trophies for you to put on display whenever it suits you."

He'd reasoned these were complaints that would pass, so had been shocked the previous year when he'd been served with divorce papers one evening as he left his Langley, Virginia, office. It was humiliating. And it became common knowledge throughout his department within minutes. Worse, it developed that his wife had been having a fairly open affair with some bird colonel in the Pentagon. As bad as that proved to be, much worse was the eventual divorce settlement. He lost the house, for which he was ordered to continue to make the mortgage payment, custody of the children, and was ordered to pay both child support and alimony.

The bitch had destroyed him financially and professionally in a single coup. If he lived as a pauper, scrimped on every cost, he might just manage to exist. But what was the point? His ex-wife was allowed to return to the court every year to request an increase, which was certain to match any increase in pay he received. Seaver was, in short, well screwed.

His sympathetic section leader had arranged this posting to London, where it was possible for him to actually live with the added station income he received plus a generous amount of non-accountable expense money. But once he returned to the States, it was back to the poor house.

Seaver's anger, he soon realized, was not just with his now former wife, but also with his country. How could it have such draconian laws? He'd done nothing wrong; it had been his wife with the round heels, not him—or, at least as far as she could have known. When had it stopped being a man's world? So the night Seaver met Rashidov at a Soviet embassy function, there had been something discernable in Seaver's manner. The perceptive Russian had noticed it at once. In the weeks since, they'd met several times, each of them dancing the dance they'd been taught in craft school about how to recruit an agent.

Only, by now, it was becoming clear who was leading and who was following.

They met that day at a pub named 1802, near the museum at Canary Wharf. It was not a part of London that either man usually frequented, and no one would know them there. Seaver arrived first, considered what to do, then went for a slow walk around the block. When he next reached the front door, he spotted the Russian at a corner table in the rear, with a view of all the entrances to the pub.

Rashidov had actually arrived much earlier and spotted Seaver when he'd first approached. He'd been amused when the man had elected not to be seen as the first to arrive. Once Seaver was out of sight, Rashidov had gone inside and ordered a coffee with a brandy, since he couldn't stomach British ale. Seaver arrived five minutes later and ordered a pint of light ale.

Today was the day for straight talk, to Rashidovs thinking, so he cut straight to the chase.

Yes, Seaver confirmed, he was willing to accept money in exchange for information. "There are some conditions," he said.

"What are they?" the Russian asked.

"You will always be my control."

"Done. It is in my interest to keep you to myself."

"I want your word you will not reveal my real identity, not even to your superiors. I know you can give me your word and then promptly break it. But I believe you to be a man of honor and that you will keep it. I also believe I will learn if you break your word, and that will be the end of my cooperation."

Again, this was no problem for Rashidov. The last thing he wanted was for anyone to know the name of one of his potentially most important informants. "Done. You have my word. I will not reveal your name and will keep what information about you I must give as vague as possible."

"Finally, each month you will deposit ten thousand dollars into a Swiss account I've established. Should you ever fail to make a payment, I will consider our relationship terminated."

And so, the bartering began. In the end, Seaver settled on three thousand dollars. "But before we make any payment, you must prove to me your sincerity. I cannot justify such a sizeable payment without results," Rashidov told Seaver with a good degree of honesty.

Seaver knew that. In Rashidovs shoes, he'd have made the same demand. From his inside jacket pocket, he extracted a list. "I expect a bonus for this. It's the names of ten of our agents in the Eastern Bloc. Remember our agreement."

Rashidov took the list, recognizing two names as men under suspicion, unable to avoid registering shock at one of the others. "You are certain?"

"Absolutely. You can take my word or you can do some checking yourself. You'll see I'm right."

The two never spoke about this subject again when they met at public functions. Before leaving the pub, they established their method and frequency of contact. They saw each other at various functions over the next two years, but neither spoke to the other. One month after that meeting, all ten agents were dead, and Seaver was pleased to find a bonus payment of ten thousand dollars in his Swiss account. From that point on, he found his greatest difficulty was in spending his added income in such a way so as not to attract attention.

For Rashidov, the acquisition of a senior CIA operative was to launch his career on a trajectory about which he could have only dreamed previously. He kept the man's real identity a closely held secret and, since the man's information was consistently reliable and useful, he was never pressed for a name.

No matter how far he rose, Rashidov remained Seaver's control and conduit for information, not all of which he passed along. Bits here and there often proved more useful to him personally than they might have been to the state.

CHAPTER TWENTY-NINE

1950
Warsaw

Mishka was considered a hero by the Russians who occupied Poland, but he found the work of his NKVD—now a far larger organization under the leadership of a new Moscow bureaucrat—far more interesting. War changes all nations, and, inside the Soviet Union, a new guard had risen.

Mishka found himself on an interesting fringe of the Soviet hierarchy as head of the NKVD in strategically vital Poland. In his new role, he was in constant contact with the border, with agents and double agents, who, with the beginning of the war of attrition between America and the Soviet Union, found themselves the center of their nation's attention.

He moved to Warsaw, near the city center, occupying the apartments of a former nobleman, these being restored at a frenzied pace, replete with servants befitting his position. The NKVD had become Russia's most powerful organization, and his portion of it, in Poland, was not without benefits. From his new position, Mishka dispatched countless agents to the West via Berlin.

Nonetheless, Mishka slipped into despair. His initial plan with Gehlen had failed. Mishka feared that his prime had passed him. Perhaps he, the last czar, was destined to die in anonymity, a hero of nothing.

Gehlens modus operandi at war's end was simplicity itself. Gehlen produced his records and offered them to the Americans. These represented years or intelligence gathering on Russia, German sympathizers, and other intelligence organizations—once this information had been negotiated for and accepted, he would surrender to the Americans and offer himself and a cadre of his men to them in exchange for their freedom. The Americans had taken the bait. What else could they do?

In September 1945, Gehlen, though technically a prisoner of war, had been flown to the United States with the records to which he'd led the Americans, these concealed in waterproof drums, buried in the Austrian Alps. There,

Gehlen had exposed certain OSS operatives he knew to be Communist sympathizers, ushering in the new reformed Central Intelligence Agency.

In July 1946, Gehlen had been released to the West Germans. He'd gone immediately to Munich, where he'd launched the South German Industrial Development Organization, employing, initially, 350 handpicked intelligence agents. His organization was known simply as the Gehlen Group. It was, in fact, the only spy operation against Russia the Americans' had. They funded and supplied it with all its needs. Once in place, Mishka had reestablished contact with the German. Everything was set.

An intelligence veteran himself, Mishka was stunned by the audacious operations the Americans launched through the Gehlen Group. He was equally impressed, in time, with the massive transformation of the NKVD into a new organization, the KGB. Flocks of agents trained to speak effortless English and dressed in perfect Western attire passed through Warsaw on their way to infiltrate the West. All enjoyed Mishka's bacchanalian hospitalities. Mishka, known as one of the minds behind the early NKVD, and revered in most intelligence circles, took the departing agents through Warsaw's underground nightlife. And while the Poles had no idea of real pleasures, the agents were pleased to have a final night of old-fashioned, Communist-style fun before passing through the Iron Curtain to the cold depravity of the West, where there were no subtleties of relationship and drunkenness was out of the question in case a single word caused their downfall.

Mishka's English, learned from his Uncle Oleg, was rusty. At every opportunity, he practiced with the agents. The ones going to England spoke almost flawless British, while those destined for America let the language lilt and drag in their mouths; yet none of them had ever left the country before. Mishka learned that there were entire towns built in the Gulag to resemble cities overseas, like Hollywood sets, of London, New York, and Washington. The agents in training lived for a year as they would in the West and spoke only English. Teachers were not plentiful, but enough foreigners had come to join the Communist cause that the schools were possible. The teachers were rewarded with homes in Moscow, when not working, and the latest in Soviet automobiles.

The Brits were being fools, Mishka believed. They had once thought that Hitler would stop with Czechoslovakia, and again they deluded themselves, believing that the Soviet Union would respect peace in Europe. They even began to send businessmen, nobles dressed in the clothes of successful capitalists and no doubt reporting back to Her Majesty, but untrained and unbelievably gullible.

The first one he met, the one whose dossier had been thick as a Tolstoy novel by the time he arrived, was the perfect example.

Julian Hardaway was one day destined to become an earl and had served on the German desk in British intelligence during the war. He had been given a proper education and was even a soccer fan like Mishka himself. So Mishka was to have a British friend. Perhaps Julian Hardaway would be a friend like Gehlen, a friend not afraid to cross borders. And if he wasn't, there would be more English arriving any day. The Brits were indiscriminate, children of an island nation that had collapsed because of its lust for empire, its desire to connect again with a continent. Here was a man he could have worked with to rule Europe, if circumstances had been different, if history hadn't fallen apart.

Mishka liked the man. And, after all, it was better that the first trade ventures with the West following the partition of Europe between communism and democracy pass through Mishka's own hands than through the hands of others.

Mishka's relationships with the Soviet agents in transit paid off. Reports of the good work being done in Warsaw were sent to Moscow; and when Moscow realized that direct communication with the Motherland was often difficult and dangerous, Mishka's stock again rose. Poland was far more porous. Mishka became the primary control for the agents who passed through Warsaw, particularly those placed throughout Europe. Though he was little more than a glorified relay, Mishka saw all the communiqués that passed from the West to Moscow. He was as well informed as anyone on the progress of Soviet intelligence in the West. He was, in fact, at the very heart of the Cold War.

At about the same time that Mishka met Julian Hardaway, Gehlen resurfaced, as they'd arranged, now in a very interesting capacity. Once his Gehlen Group was fully functioning, the German himself traveled to Poland in secrecy to meet with Mishka. As always and as agreed, he was ready to deal. Even better, Mishka discovered, Gehlen had passed along the information Mishka had created for him, the story of a surviving Romanov heir still alive somewhere in Russia. The Americans had been led to believe there was an underground movement in the Soviet Union aimed at restoring the czar. One of their potential strategies for regime change was to help this hidden organization return the czar to power. If, of course, they could find him.

"The Americans are a nightmare," Gehlen observed, "but at least I'm not being tried at Nuremberg."

"Are we in a position to resume our 'trading' business?" Mishka asked.

"Yes. And, as we discussed, this time we make a profit." Gehlen frowned and lit a cigarette.

"I can pay you handsomely for information on Russian missiles. It doesn't even have to be correct—the Americans won't know any better and, in fact, don't care. It's all about reporting to the Pentagon for them. There is even some kind of bonus for having the most information; nobody checks for accuracy because they can't. The Americans are flush, as they say."

Mishka and Gehlen smiled, almost in unison.

* * *

At the time Burgess and Maclean, two of the highest-placed Soviet agents in England, defected, Mishka's plans were unfolding remarkably well, especially given Stalin's mental decline and increasing paranoia. With his network of agents and connections to both the CIA and England's MI5, Gehlen had alerted both governments—at very high levels—of the existence of a rightful czar, but without revealing his actual identity.

Mishka was surprised at the level of support the so-called "Free World" seemed prepared to offer an aspiring monarch. Apparently, they were desperate for anything but communism, and the perceived stability of a pro-West czar was alluring. In his times of despair, it was the support Mishka believed would come from the West that gave him hope.

Through Gehlen, Mishka fed a steady stream of information to the Americans, some of it true, most of it false. But Burgess and MacLean caused Mishka to pull back. The pair possessed far too much intimate information from British intelligence to report to Moscow, and Mishka could not be certain exactly what they knew. Their debriefing would most certainly include rumors of a czarist pretender who was highly placed, perhaps even within the Soviet intelligence apparatus. When he received such a query from his superiors, Mishka was forced to concoct an entire charade and murder three of his own men to pacify Moscow. Still, he sensed that there might be suspicion concerning him.

Bowing to pressure from the director of the KGB and Kaganovich himself, Mishka reluctantly returned to Moscow, distancing himself from the potential time bomb of Polish intelligence. Thankfully, two years passed without incident. So close to the wellspring of power, unable to exercise much himself, Mishka grew frustrated and dangerous. Old Stalin would die soon, he knew, but there seemed no way to orchestrate a coup to his advantage.

Over the long decades of his ascent within the party, Mishka had always considered every possibility. Once his German option collapsed through Hitler's folly, he looked to the time when Stalin died. He had done his very best to see that the reign of the Man of Steel was relentlessly bloody. Surely, no man in history was more hated and more feared.

But what to do?

Mishka had never been able to rise to the Politburo, which would select Stalin's successor. Kaganovich had never once even suggested it. In fact, when the Politburo was replaced by a presidium of thirty-six members, Mishka had learned of the change along with the masses. He knew that Moscow saw him as a bloody, yet skilled, intelligence operator, but nothing beyond that. Such an appraisal had insulated him from reprisals, but it also kept him an important step away from the kind of power he required to orchestrate a coup.

Though he believed the British, with their history of a monarchy, would be most receptive to his position—especially as he was linked by blood to the House of Windsor—they were in no position to make it happen, only to lend support. After the war, his best hope lay with the Americans who had the money to make it possible, not to mention the military—if they were willing to use it. But he knew the Americans would never support him in a coup in Moscow without proof that he had Russian support. That support could come from the people themselves or from the political leaders, and he lacked both. Holed away as a high-level bureaucrat in the KGB, he had no way to garner that support.

He watched in bitter frustration as Stalin grew ill, stricken by a stroke. He continued to watch, unable to do otherwise, as Nikita Khrushchev positioned himself to take power while, at the same time, Mishka's old mentor, Kaganovich, fell from favor.

There was potential for chaos, as had nearly happened when Lenin died. Without a rightful heir, without a throne, a nation simply couldn't exist. But in the end, chaos failed to emerge; and with the peaceful transfer of power to Khrushchev, that moment in history deserted Mishka as well. By then, he longed for nothing so much as to return to Warsaw. At least there, he could rule his own kingdom, be free to make money, free to plot, and possibly to find his way to the throne—if not him, then his son.

Khruschevs plans for him, Mishka decided, must have been engineered by one of the telepaths with which they were experimenting outside of Moscow. They answered his prayers and turned his worst nightmares into reality all at once.

Mishka was returned to Poland to open the Soviet Union's first foreign trading company, Polymot, serving as director general. Under the cover of special regulations, the Brits and other European countries had been conducting business with the Poles since the end of the war, and now, in this Brave New post-Stalin World, Russia was going to exploit it more aggressively. Mishka was seen as just the man for the job.

In Warsaw, the reborn Mishka found himself becoming closer, in many ways, to his British friend, Julian. Mishka worked to renew contact with Gehlen - The Americans held Gehlen in high esteem, though, in the end, Mishka decided it was more likely word would leak back to Moscow, and he'd end up with a bullet in his head. Still, he was coming to believe that his personal triumph could only come from the outside.

But the crafty Gehlen had shifted sides again and was now working for the West Germans.

The two finally met outside of Potsdam and shared a coffee. The German told him that he would be glad to pass information along, from time to time, and would appreciate the same from Mishka, and the Russian left it at that. He asked the man for a high-level contact at the CIA, but Gehlen warned him away from the agency.

"The CIA has a very highly placed double agent. Your friends have been most effective in that. Go through the FBI. Get to Hoover, if you can. Tell him I sent you; give him my code name, 'Red Rover.' Cleanest people in America, the bureau. It seems to be the only American agency your people have never penetrated."

Perhaps sensing where Mishka was headed, or believing it to be the desire of all senior men in the KGB, Gehlen promised to help if Mishka ever wanted to defect in exchange for sworn secrecy regarding their former relationship.

CHAPTER THIRTY

1991
Day Seven
Langley, VA

The years as a traitor had been, in large part, good ones for Mitch Seaver. In time, his former wife remarried, and he was freed of both the alimony and mortgage payment. His children were finally of age, and child support had come to an end. His career did well, also, and he rose steadily in the ranks of the CIA. As he entered his middle years, he no longer drew on his Swiss bank account, and the money there simply grew and grew. Sometimes, he wondered where and how he would spend it, but that did not stop him from adding more to the growing pile. It was nice, every so often, to visit his bank's branch office in the nice, warm Cayman Islands and count his money before burning the bank statements and records on the beach.

Nicholas Rashidov had, from all Seaver could tell, been true to his word, and no one but Rashidov himself knew that he was the Soviet's most deeply placed mole within the Company, and its most valued asset. In time, Seaver took to feeding Rashidov just two or three bits of information at a time. On occasion, he was able to blow an operation to eliminate a competitor for a promotion he sought; Seaver took special pleasure when that was the case. But for the most part, Seaver fed interesting, and—perhaps—valuable information about CIA activities and plans in various parts of the world. The Company squandered its resources so widely and had its fingers in so many pies that he had a wealth of information from which to draw. An amusing point had come when Seaver had been sent word that he'd been made a KGB colonel and, should he ever need to defect, he'd be given his very own dacha and pension. The following year, he was told he'd been made hero of the Soviet Union.

As the CIA grew in size and budget, it seemed to all but self-destruct. James Angleton, the head of counter-intelligence, had become obsessed with the idea that the Company had been penetrated by a Soviet mole named Sasha. Even before he was a traitor, Seaver had watched the man's behavior with amusement. In his mind, everywhere Angleton looked, he saw Soviet agents. The careers of many fine men were destroyed by his paranoia. In point of fact, Angleton's suspicions rendered the Company's Soviet division virtually inoperable. Angleton was convinced, as well, that every Russian recruited by the Soviet division was a Soviet plant; no defector was trusted. The situation did not improve with Angleton's resignation in 1976. In time, Seaver no longer feared being caught. The only way he could be betrayed was by the Russians; as long as his identity was secret, that would not happen.

Seaver followed Rashidovs career with interest, realizing that the higher the Russian rose, the more secure was his own position, though that was not how he saw himself at all. He was a clever man, cleverer than the rest; when it came right down to it, his own country, wrapped in all its self-righteousness, was no different from the Soviet Union.

The culmination of his career came shortly before the start of the Gulf War, when he'd been promoted to deputy director of the Directorate of Support, which provided the mission-critical elements of people, security, information, property, and financial operations. He was in a position to divulge everything the Soviets could possibly want and more. He had imagined that was how it would play out until he vanished into an obscure—but very wealthy—early retirement on some remote, warm island.

Then the Soviet Union began to crack at the seams. Seaver no longer believed any CIA projection that had held Soviet Russia to be a juggernaut, even as it was clearly collapsing, trusting only his own analysis. In his view, Gorbachev couldn't last another year. It looked as if the drunk, Boris Yeltsin, was about to take control of a non-Communist Russia, a state greatly reduced in power, size, and wealth from the soon to be late, great Union of Soviet Socialist Republics.

This left Seaver with two serious concerns. Would his secret remain a secret? He'd lost track of Rashidovs career since the previous winter. Was the man backing the wrong horse and staying with the party? Or had he jumped to Yeltsin? Or was Rashidov waiting on events? Seaver didn't know.

His other concern was money. Though he was secretly a very wealthy man, his was hidden wealth. For the moment, however, there was so much more opportunity open to him for earning a great deal of money in his new CIA tasking. In the aftermath of America having driven Saddam out of Kuwait, it was time for some of the largesse the emir had been giving to IMSS and the Brits to come to America. America's own corporations could provide whatever the Kuwaitis needed, and Seaver would receive his lucrative cut from the deals because of his place on the board of directors of International Trading Partners.

With Christian Hardaway on the run and IMSS under suspicion, the path for ITP into the emir's deep pockets should have been easy. Seaver had made a special trip to Kuwait City to make certain of it. Instead, Raymond Philips—Seaver considered the man a shit—was sucking up to the emir's boy, the Palestinian Khaldun. From what Seaver was hearing, IMSS, even in its current precarious state, was about to receive a substantial contract. That just wouldn't do.

In his hotel room, Seaver opened his briefcase and took out a file on Khaldun. There was enough dirt on Khaldun to undo any man, though with Arabs one could never be certain. Behavior that would scandalize a Westerner was often seen as nothing more than an amusement. "Well, let's see how amused the emir will be," Seaver almost verbalized.

London

Though Christian decided to remain away from the offices of IMSS, he stayed at his townhouse - the idea of joining Evelyn at their country home was too much. Hannah urged him to remain with her, but the last thing Christian wanted was to implicate his lover in unfolding events. The second *Times* article, along with the government demand for his passport, meant this was just the beginning. It would, in short, become much worse before it got better.

Unless...

Thursday was an atypically lovely day for London in March, and Christian retired to his small garden with his morning coffee and a summary file. One of the advantages of serving as CEO of Britain's most comprehensive private intelligence network was that he was privy to so many secrets. As a result, from the very start, he'd been shocked at the turn of events. How could those in power have allowed such a circumstance? Surely, they understood that he was in a position to destroy a great many of them.

Over the years, he'd been made aware of and documented one misdeed after another, not only of politicians, but of the Civil Service and SIS operatives. And he knew the location of offshore accounts brimming over with cash never reported to inland revenue or explained to constituents.

And it only began there. Christian knew of any number of missteps by the security services, misdeeds never disclosed, lies purported as reality. The evidence of failure and mistakes were scattered about the globe and through the decades. He knew them all.

This master list would have to be his trump card, he knew, only to be played if all else failed. On a notepad, he listed some of the most egregious misdeeds or salacious activities. Once he was finished, he perused it at leisure. Until this moment, he'd never really dwelt on the shabby nature of so much of what he knew. He'd always put his country first, as his father had taught him. Others, it seemed, were not so patriotic. The items on his list would be a bombshell, if released.

Christian briefly considered how he'd manage that, feeding the stories to the press and certain investigative agencies at just the right pace to keep the scandals of others in the press, while his own problems slowly vanished from public view. Those not yet named in stories would be only too eager to be of assistance when he next called.

Only for a moment, Christian thought about contacting Philips and putting him to work in the files Christian had always maintained for just this sort of contingency. But he stopped. It occurred to him that whoever was in back of this might desire precisely that response from him. The true purpose behind his nightmare might be far more wide reaching than the mere destruction of a wrongly implicated man and IMSS. The launching of the attack could well have been intended to precipitate his counter attack, with all the devastation it would create. If that were the case, then the source of his trouble was certainly foreign.

The list of adversaries, in that event, was a bountiful one, but the CIA and KGB came immediately to mind.

His sources told him that Mikhail Gorbachev was on thin ice in the tottering Soviet Union.

One even claimed that Russian communism was in its last days, though that struck Christian as wildly optimistic. Still, there were signs that the end was coming in that part of the world.

Though he was now called president, a name that suggested greater power, Gorbachev's actual influence was slipping with each passing day. He'd unleashed glasnost and perestroika, with all the unintended consequences that inevitably went with them. Glasnost simply allowed public criticism, which undermined his rule while gaining him nothing in return. Given human nature, people very quickly assumed they had a natural right to speak their minds. Perestroika allowed open capitalist dealings, which had proven profitable to IMSS, but only served to feed the appetites of the corrupt party apparatchiks.

Frankly, it seemed to Christian that the Soviet leader had no idea what he was doing.

Gorbachev certainly had no idea how to use power. Glancing down at the list of misdeeds he'd jotted down, Christian wondered if the same could be said about him.

Old Joe Stalin had it right in one key regard. If one wanted absolute power, it was incumbent upon the leader to keep the populace terrorized relentlessly. Gorbachev simply didn't have the stomach for that.

None of that meant that the KGB hadn't launched this operation against Christian. It could be seen as a last hurrah before they were phased out, if that was what was happening. More likely, it would be seen as a means of asserting their power, a demonstration that they still exercised influence over foreign affairs.

Christian had learned long ago, however, not to try to understand the rationale behind any KGB actions. Sometimes, they were for the good of the country, more often for the good of the party or even that of the KGB itself. On occasion, however, they were simply the power play of a key individual. Only long after events had transpired was it possible to decide which was, in fact, the case.

Even then, one could never be perfectly certain. So his troubles could have originated almost anywhere in the interwoven layers of the Soviet Union.

But the attack upon him and ISS might just as easily be from the West. Mitch Seaver's presence in Kuwait continued to strike Christian as a false note. The timing and location were all wrong, given Seaver's recent promotion. The more Christian considered it, the more certain he was that something was amiss. There was no doubt in his mind that the Company would like nothing more than to destroy IMSS and see all that business, not to mention the private intelligence-gathering opportunities, go to their own nominees and not to the British.

Christian did not undervalue the enormous success of his company—IMSS—as an intelligence gathering operation. The British security services had their faults, but in nearly every case over recent decades, they'd more accurately gauged what was really taking place than had their American counterparts.

That was, in no small measure, a consequence of the information he had sent them.

From the first, IMSS, by its very nature, had great advantages over the CIA's operational arms. Once Ian Cathcart and others in JIC had reached the conclusion that his father's company would be an excellent vehicle for information, bearing in mind MI5's penetration by the Soviets, they had thrown their resources behind the effort. IMSS had always had a single hand at the tiller, and Julian had shown himself an excellent administrator. There had been a well-connected board and experienced staff for the tasking. As required, they brought in specialists from the various branches of the British military or security services to perform specific intelligence operation or to run long-term missions.

The system had been efficient and very, very discreet.

The Americans had gone about establishing and operating International Trading Partners in a very different way, one that reflected greater priorities than simply gathering intelligence in the guise of selling military and security hardware. The company was managed by a large board of directors, comprised of politically connected retired generals and admirals. It was also replete with former politicians and Washington power players. In the corridors of power, such seats had come to be viewed as patronage. The most recent addition was a former senator, quietly garnering all the support he could for a run at the White House.

In addition, ITP employed prime contractors such as Raytheon and General Electric to perform standard operational tasks, throwing in the occasional spy when needed. There was no single hand on the tiller. Lobbyists ran rampant through the offices of ITP, securing direct business to the benefit of those who retained them.

Christian knew that Mitch Seaver was close to the former senator and several others on the board. How, or if, that was influencing events, Christian had no way of knowing.

But the source might not be foreign at all, Christian was forced to consider. A highly placed mole in British intelligence could be behind what was transpiring. Or elements within the British government itself might have decided to close down his operation. There was certainly no love lost with Lawrence Skinner, head of the SIS, and Skinner was in a position to do something about IMSS, though Christian would have anticipated a more obvious course of action. The nation's security services had never liked the fact that IMSS existed and had worked relentlessly, over the years, to discredit it and him. Perhaps they'd finally been given the green light.

But he refrained from calling Philips for another reason; Christian no longer trusted the man. None of this should have come as a surprise to him. One of the man's jobs had been to head off publicity or, at the least, alert Christian when something was amiss. Philips had failed in both functions, this time; such could not have been coincidental. Christian realized he'd given the man too much freedom in recent years, and really could not say, with confidence, what the man did with his time.

Christian finished his coffee then called his personal secretary, Pauline, on her direct line.

"Hullo, sir," she said, answering. "How are you holding up?"

"I've had the drunk, now I'm ready to make heads or tails out of this."

"I wondered when you'd call."

"I want you to put your thinking cap on. List the likely suspects, if you would. Also, include anyone recently with an axe to grind with me. And keep this to yourself. Not even Raymond is to know. What's he up to, by the way?"

"He's had the boys scurrying about, searching for files. They're all complaining about it."

"I've asked him for a report on those timers. I know we didn't sell them. The documents should say that. Keep your eyes and ears open, and prepare that list for me, if you please."

"Yes, sir."

"And use a public telephone to contact me."

In the kitchen, Christian rinsed his cup as he considered what to do next. He'd promised to drop his passport off at his solicitor's office that day, so he'd have to go out. What else to do while he was gone? Just then, the doorbell rang. He considered ignoring it, but decided he had to come out of hiding sometime.

Standing on his doorstep were two men in Cecil Gee business suits. The older one, a man perhaps fifty years old, spoke first. "Are you Mr. Hardaway, sir?"

"Yes."

"I'm Deputy Inspector Farragut, Special Branch. This is Detective Sergeant Connors. Might we have a word with you, sir?"

Farragut was a large man, gone slightly to seed. His eyes were a piercing blue, and Christian suspected they'd been an advantage in his career. The number two, Connors, was a spare man, some years younger, with a clipped moustache and a bland face.

"In regard to what? I'm really quite busy, as I'm sure you know."

"I assure you that you will want to speak with us."

Something in the man's manner convinced Christian, and he let the men in, then led them to his parlor. He considered against offering tea. "Please, be seated. How may I help you?"

"I'm afraid we have bad news, sir." Farragut eyed him evenly as he continued. "We regret to inform you that your wife, Lady Evelyn, is dead."

For an instant, Christian was stunned. Of all the bad news he'd anticipated, this had never entered his mind. "Dead? Are you certain?"

"I'm afraid so, sir. She was found early this morning, not far from here."

"Near here you say? Found? What do mean by 'found'?"

"I'm afraid I must ask. Where were you last night?"

"I was with someone early in the evening. I can give you the name, if necessary. I then came here sometime after midnight. I'm not certain of the hour. What happened to my wife?" he asked,

"She was murdered, sir. Stabbed, I'm afraid."

Oh, Evelyn, Christian thought. You poor dear. Look what you brought upon yourself.

"Could you say why she might be coming here?" Farragut asked.

"Here? I don't think she would be coming here. I didn't speak with her at all yesterday. The last time she was in this city house was—let me think. Five or six years ago, to the best of my knowledge."

"Why is that, sir?"

"Ours was not an unusual arrangement, in our circles. She lived her life; I lived mine. We were friends if no longer in love, as we once were. Divorce was out of the question."

"This name you mentioned providing. This would be your lady friend?"

"Yes. I don't think she'd object to that description."

Farragut cleared his throat. "And your wife? She had a—" He seemed at a loss for a moment.

"Lover? Yes. She'd been seeing an attaché of some sort at the Soviet embassy."

"How would you characterize their relationship?"

"Superficial."

The younger policeman spoke for the first time. "It must have been awkward for you, your wife seeing a Soviet employee, given your line of work."

"Potentially, I suppose, but these are changing times. Am I under suspicion? If so, perhaps I should call my solicitor?"

Farragut spoke. "I shouldn't think that would be necessary, sir. It has the appearance of a street crime, though, as you know, this is not that sort of neighborhood. Still, we would like to speak with your friend."

"What time was she—When did Evvy die?"

"We put it at about ten last evening."

"Let me give you her name and contact information. I was with her at that time."

Connors spoke again. "Of course you were, sir. We anticipate that's what she'll say."

CHAPTER THIRTY-ONE

1968
Moscow

For all the disappointment that his life had become, and continued to be in his quest for the throne of Russia, Mishka took great delight in his son, known to all as Nicholas Rashidov.

Mikhail and his wife, Ludmilla, had proven excellent choices as surrogate parents. Mikhail was sturdy and cautious, the ideal Soviet city bureaucrat. Mishka had helped Mikhail's career along to assure that he attained sufficient senior party status so that young Nicholas would qualify for the best party schools. Mikhail's ambitions were limited to the city of Moscow, and that made the task easier.

In all, Mishka was only required to actually liquidate two officials who stood in Mikhail's way. Mikhail's wife had been a doting mother. Mishka had no complaints about either of them.

Young Nicholas grew to be a handsome, fit, inquisitive young boy. Had he known his true lineage, doubtless he would have taken great delight in knowing how much he resembled his namesake, the last czar of All the Russias. As it was, he resembled neither of his putative parents, though no one commented on it. The war had been a turbulent time, and many acts that would, otherwise, have been unthinkable had occurred. No one asked questions, certainly not of a connected senior city party official.

Nicholas entered school shortly after the end of the war. It was an all but officially private school, reserved for the party elite. Nicholas proved an adept student and was the pride of the school, with his handsome features and excellent manners. Whenever possible, "Uncle" Mishka attended school functions to praise the boy on his progress. Mishka also called on Nicholas at home, whenever Mishka was in Moscow, and made certain, through gifts and pleasant excursions, that the boy was closely bonded to him, at least as close as he seemed to be to his "parents."

In 1956, the year Nikita Khrushchev secretly denounced Stalin and his cult of personality, young Nicholas entered the prestigious Frunze Military Academy for a two-year course. With an excellent library and the fresh scent of freedom Khrushchev was bringing after the crushing oppression of Stalin, the students were encouraged to expand their thinking. Nicholas studied foreign languages, operational-tactical disciplines, Marxism-Leninism, and—though a bit tongue in cheek—the history of the party and political work, with an emphasis on the history of war and military art. Again, the young man excelled in every task and had, by then, caught the eye of KGB recruiters.

After two years at the academy, Nicholas was accepted into the Lomonosov Moscow State University, the oldest and most respected university in the Soviet Union. He was there for seven years, graduating ultimately with a PhD in economics. At the university, he studied history, largely free of party doctrine. His facility in languages was noted as he became proficient in English, French, and German. Six months at a KGB "charm" school in the Urals that was built to resemble a British Market town had all-but perfected his command of English.

In all this, Mishka took enormous pride. At each necessary step, he had quietly interceded to be certain the young man was selected for the next rung in the ladder of success. So as not to diminish the young man's self-confidence, Mishka made no mention of his secret assistance to the boy's education and career.

To assure secrecy, Mishka arranged to have Mikhail and Ludmilla killed in a motorcar accident, once Nicholas had moved into a dorm at university. Mishka had gone there immediately to comfort the grieving young man.

Mishka was able to use his power to assure that Nicholas was recruited into the KGB at the age of twenty-four, where his first assignment was at the Lubyanka as assistant to a division head. There, he was at the center of the KGB's world-wide operation. A bachelor himself, Mishka was pleased to observe the young man's endless stream of attractive female lovers.

Mishka had cautioned Nicholas since he was a boy to avoid entanglement with women. "They are here for our pleasure. You have no need of one until such time as you want a son. And, for that, you must wait until your career is approaching its zenith." The boy, that later became the man, had listened well.

Indeed, Nicholas paid careful attention to everything his "uncle" told him and had always found the advice to be sage. After three years in the Lubyanka Building, Nicholas was informed that he would be posted to the Soviet embassy in London as an assistant commercial attaché. He was filled with excitement upon telling his "Uncle" Mishka.

"You've done very well. Excellently, in fact. This is an important stepping-stone for you.

Just keep in mind that the British are not stupid. They will know what you really are and why you are in their country. They do the same here. They will attempt to ensnare you. Beware."

"I'll be careful, Uncle. You know me," the handsome young man grinned.

* * *

It was not possible for Mishka to leave the Soviet Union, so he settled for monitoring his son at long distance. Mishka's contacts and resources were, at once, considerable and excellent; therefore, doing so was no problem. He even had brought to him still photos and film of Nicholas going about his affairs on the streets of London. It seemed to Mishka's discerning eye that the handsome man fit perfectly in British society.

If Khrushchev had accomplished anything, Mishka believed, it was to diminish any chance Mishka had of ever ascending to the Romanov throne as czar. The crude man had sufficiently lessened the heavy hand of the state, rolled back the worst abuses of Stalin, such that the people were largely content with their lot. Revolution was the last thing on their collective mind, not when they could put their name on a list and, in a few years, receive a car.

Only in the oppressed nations of the East did revolt seem possible. Yugoslavia had managed to slip the Soviet noose even when Stalin still ruled. Hungary had rebelled in 1956 and was crushed. Czechoslovakia had attempted reform just that previous spring. In his own domain of Poland, Mishka could feel the pulse for freedom beneath the apparatus of party power. He recalled the time the Queen of the Netherlands visited Warsaw and had asked one of her official Polish escorts if he were a Catholic. The man's response had been, "Believing, Your Majesty, but not practicing."

"Oh," said the queen, "I suppose that's because you are a Communist."

To which the Pole replied, "Practicing, Your Majesty, but not believing."

But the kind of counter-revolution Mishka needed would not begin there, at least he did not think it would. He required discontent within Russia. He had murdered countless thousands to make it happen. Then that country clown Khrushchev had come along and changed it all.

Most of all, Mishka feared what would become of his dream. He had pledged to his mother that he would not rest until he was czar. With each passing year, with his own power fading, that seemed less and less likely. Only in the West did he believe lay the possibilities of supporters. He'd planted the seeds. For decades, he'd floated the story of a czarist faction within Russia, bandied about the idea that an heir was on hand, if the time ever came or could be made to come. But the West was fickle, the British security services infiltrated with traitors—many of Mishka's own making—the CIA riddled with turncoats. Whom could he trust?

Mishka felt in the depths of his very soul that the time would come. The Soviet Union was corrupt through and through, the economic system untenable. Too many of the people under the Communist thumb wanted out. It was only a question of time. He just didn't know if he had enough of it left. It might well come down to his son, he realized. Mishka's lot might be to prepare the way for the boy.

Mishka pondered still again when he should tell Nicholas the truth, reveal himself as the young man's father, that Nicholas, through him, would be the heir to the Russian throne. It would have to be soon, before his son's career took its natural course, and Nicholas began to set limits on his ambition. Soon, Mishka thought, soon.

CHAPTER THIRTY-TWO

1991
Day Eight
Paris

"May I join you?" Moussa Khaldun asked of the seated Raymond Philips.

"By all means. I've taken the liberty of ordering your usual scotch." It was late afternoon, and the Hemingway Bar at the Paris Ritz was almost empty. Khaldun settled into the rich leather armchair and took a sip of his drink. "How are matters in London?" he inquired.

Philips stretched his neck a moment, as if his tie were too tight, then responded. "All right, I suppose. I'd hoped they'd have arrested him by this time. They've not even served a search warrant."

"You're concerned?"

"No. I just wish it would go a bit faster. I think I've prepared the document that will do him in; and the beauty of it is he requested it himself. I'm just not certain what to do with it."

They discussed the possible transition of control of IMSS to Philips in the near future and how it would come about. "It can be seen, initially, as something temporary. Don't get too eager, Raymond," Khaldun cautioned.

"I understand how these things are done. The army wasn't exactly a tea party, you know," Philips reminded. "So, why are we meeting? I should be in London and am, in fact, returning the moment we are finished here."

"I've presented to His Excellency, the emir, my proposal that, despite his recent infatuation with the Americans, he place an order with IMSS for three hundred million pounds."

Philips tried on his best poker face. "My word!"

"Yes. I believe I can keep it quiet until you are in control, at which point you can announce it as an example of what the company will accomplish under your leadership."

"Yes, I see that. Thank you, thank you very much."

The Arab leaned forward. "My position with the emir remains sound, but I've heard rumors of change. And, of course, the man's health is not the best, as you know."

"So what is your cut?" Philips queried, getting to the point.

"Ten percent."

Philips was astounded. "You can't possibly be serious!"

"I've never been more serious. I must make it while I can; if I cannot with you in charge, then why should I assist you?"

"But, that's outrageous! Five, perhaps. But ten is out of the question! The sheik will want his share of this pie—but at least he adds his on at the contract signing."

"You talk as if it's your money."

"In a sense, it is. If I bleed off that much, then we make nothing."

"No one will know, not until you are firmly in control and it's too late." Khaldun sipped his drink. "You are free to adjust your bid, however."

"How much?"

"I could manage another fifteen percent with the emir. He's preoccupied these days. The women of Kuwait spent some time out of the country during the invasion and have returned with silly ideas—like the right to vote."

"All right, then. I see your point."

"It's a small enough price to pay for what you are getting personally. I'll prepare the emir for a higher bid from you next week. When do you expect to take control?"

"That depends. I'm doing my best to nudge things along."

"Good. This moment won't last long." He finished his drink. "If you have time, I understand a fresh consignment of Romanian youngsters has arrived. Care to join me?"

"I only wish I could. I must get back to London. Next time."

"Of course. There is always next time."

CHAPTER THIRTY-THREE

1963
Moscow

When Mishka had dispatched Monika Kurek to England as a spy, he did not have in mind the downfall of the British government. In fact, that consequence was the very last outcome he could imagine. He simply wanted a plant, a useful tool, someone in place to keep an eye on Julian and Julian's involvement with the British government.

Mishka's thought was to find a way, through her, to test the waters about his possible defection to England. He had always believed that once Julian had become an earl, given Julian's family's history with the nobility of Britain, that he would be best placed to put Mishka's desires before the right sort of people. After all, the British royal family and the Romanovs were related and shared a common heritage. Surely, Mishka would be welcomed.

Mishka was more than ready. Too often, he found himself drinking beyond recognition, with the first vodka downed before noon and the last long after midnight. He had been seeing the older Kurek sister, Victoria, the one he'd first given to Julian, finding that he enjoyed her more after her affair with the Brit. She had roused his spirits of lust and, with her father, Kurek, struggling to save his family from destruction, the sister had been easy prey.

This Julian, a bountiful man, ambitious and righteous, had a weakness for beauty. Could English women be that ugly, that boring? Mishka believed he had found the Briton's weakness, his lust for feminine beauty and talent, both wonderfully abundant in the Eastern Bloc.

Mishka planned to send Monika with Julian to England from the first. Though she would be Mishka's private agent, she was officially on the books as a UB, a Polish intelligence operative, and he'd had to disclose her existence. Others would give her orders, in theory, but Mishka made certain she would remain a sleeper agent in all senses of the word.

The night he'd introduced her to Julian, Mishka had let slip his true identity, that he was the czar, the rightful heir to the throne. He had hoped to draw some response, but that had not happened. Worse, the Brit didn't seem to believe him. Mishka needed to find a way to safely inform Julian as to his heritage and his ambitions. Monika would become close to the man and report back to Mishka through a secure channel. Mishka had briefed her on a high-level intelligence plot to secretly acquire British war plans by acting as a czarist pretender and claiming that the plan was backed by Moscow.

The girl knew no better.

He needed for Julian and the Brits to believe him if his plan were to work. Mishka's thought was to assure the support to his claim by Britain, taking material and financial support from the CIA, and then to defect at the right moment. He would lay claim to the Romanov fortune with Britain's blessing, relying on his own financial reserves in the meanwhile. He was certain Julian would help him, once convinced, indebted to Mishka for years of cooperation, for his wealth—and for Monika.

Julian had already become an accomplice through the millions of pounds Mishka had asked the man to deposit in the Swiss account. What Mishka feared was that the Brits would never believe he was a legitimate defector without, at least, support from one of their own. More likely, the Brits would treat him as a double agent, assuming this was one of those complicated operations at which the KGB was so adept. In recent years, there had been a witch-hunt mentality at the American CIA. Mishka would find himself permanently suspect unless he played Julian right, and he helped him.

Mishka had hoped he wasn't overestimating the power of nobility.

After the Profumo affair became public, Monika's communications to Mishka altered. The information she'd sent in the time she'd been in London had never been especially useful, but her messages had become different; Mishka wondered if he could still trust her. He'd seen the advantages of her association with the upper crust, coaxing information and planting seeds for him in the minds and through the rampant cocks of Britain's ruling elite. But he'd never wanted her caught in the middle of a spy scandal.

Fortunately, from what the woman reported, Julian had never once mentioned the fact that Mishka was a Romanov. Between what he had told the man and the cover story he'd given Monika to plant in Julian's ear during pillow talk, Mishka had thought to cause Julian to raise the issue, or at least to pose the possibility to someone in the royal family. But nothing had happened.

Mishka realized that he had held the information too closely. He'd played too tight a game with Julian. But to have done more was to have risked too much. Before Mishka could exploit Monika's relationship to his advantage, perhaps have the girl provide him with a more accurate story and solicit his assistance, it all unraveled. Somehow, Monika had been activated by others, without his knowledge, and had become involved in the scandal that brought down the Conservative government and placed their man, Harold Wilson, in power.

Or perhaps it had simply taken place primarily on its own, though he could not believe that. Too much had happened on KGB orders for her small role to have been happenstance.

Making Wilson PM had been a great coup, and the careers of others were made because of it. But to cover their tracks, those who directed the coup had ordered Monika murdered in a way that would look like suicide.

* * *

Julian's visits to Poland became less frequent after the Profumo affair, and Mishka could only guess at the reasons and if they were related to the scandal. One thing was for certain: IMSS was expanding rapidly. The company had received an infusion of capital from somewhere, most likely the same source that seemed to give IMSS all but limitless access to military supplies—Her Majesty's government.

Electronics, once impossible to acquire, magically appeared at Mishka's doorstep, goods no one else could obtain. He heard from sources around Europe that similar transactions were happening in every country open to British trade. More significantly, IMSS was expanding its foreign staff, bringing on board men from British intelligence or the military.

IMSS might as well have put a British flag at every door.

Young Christian Hardaway seemed poised to take the helm, an excellent heir to his father's business, in Mishka's opinion. The young man was tall, confident, masculine, and intelligent, a skilled negotiator who spoke his mind without ever revealing his strategy or appearing arrogant, a man who commanded respect. Though he was nearly thirty years the boy's senior, and the two couldn't have hailed from more different worlds, Mishka felt a camaraderie with the young man who addressed him with affection, if laughingly, as "Uncle."

"Uncle Mishka," Christian had said on his first solo visit to Warsaw. "My father says that your word is law for us here. You are our eyes and ears."

"You have many eyes and ears here," he'd told the boy, laughing. "I, however, may be the only one with your best interests at heart."

"That is exactly what my father said," Christian responded.

"Enough of business, young Christian. What has your father said of the real Poland, eh? It seems he has you to bed by midnight every time you are in Warsaw with him and doesn't tell you that we only just wake up when the clock, how is it said, strikes twelve?"

Mishka had spared no expense. And whatever it was the boy had enjoyed in Britain had obviously not prepared him for pleasure behind the Iron Curtain. They dined and drank like kings and then retired to a special event Mishka had planned to introduce this young aristocrat to the finer things in life. He'd filled a ballroom with the best in champagnes, vodkas, caviar, and women, a dozen of them. To this, he brought only Christian and the IMSS general manager for Poland, P. W. Preston.

Also attending were the head of the KGB in Poland and the current director of procurement.

"We'll call this our company Christmas party," Mishka laughed, opening the ballroom's double doors to reveal the contents. "Ladies," he snapped his fingers above his head and the women rose—blondes, brunettes, along with a tall redhead.

Mishka yelled, "Music!" A string quartet began to play a waltz. The Russian invited his guests to choose their favorite women. He knew that the girls would take care of the men.

"Christian, these are special for you—our guest of honor."

"There are things an uncle can do that a father can't, or shouldn't," Christian said, laughing as he tried to take in the women all at once. He danced with them one after the other, while they undressed him and themselves. The musicians switched to light jazz. Almost on cue, the room gradually emptied as the men and their chosen women went to their rooms.

CHAPTER THIRTY-FOUR

1991
Day Eight
London

Since the first article had come out defaming IMSS, Christian hadn't managed more than two hours of consecutive sleep. His infrequent calls to the office elicited the same sad story: contracts were being cancelled or put on hold left and right. There had been a rash of staff resignations as well.

There was a time he'd have given the collapse of the family company his full attention; for the present, such was secondary to his own survival. If the cards played out as they lay, he believed he'd spend most of his remaining years in one of Her Majesty's prisons; either that, or, more likely, his life would be cut short to save someone embarrassment.

Christian had continued calling his network of contacts, both those in country and those abroad, searching for any information that might allow him to understand why, suddenly, he'd been damned by the British government and caught completely off guard in the process. Blindsided. But his queries were to no avail. Contacts either avoided him or had nothing to offer but speculation. He could conjure enough of that on his own. What he needed were facts.

Within the United Kingdom and, in particular, within the British government, Christian was decidedly persona non grata. It was almost as though there'd been a circular notifying the entire intelligence and political community that he was blacklisted.

The daily newspaper articles on the matter had become ludicrous, in his view. *The Times* had run a piece of journalism malfeasance in which their designated hatchet reporter, Tim Barclay, opined that Christian and IMSS had, for decades, sold to the Russians expressly against government orders. Nothing was further from the truth; IMSS had sold to the Russians *because* of government orders.

The only conclusion Christian could make with any certainty was that IMSS had outlived its usefulness as a spy organization, and Her Majesty's government was suffocating the company, quickly and methodically.

The brutal murder of Evelyn had stunned him. He'd gone to the coroner's to identify her and been distressed to see the look of horror locked on her face. The detectives, Farragut and Connors, had both been there, watching his behavior and reaction very closely. He decided that was the extent of modern investigations—see if the suspect acted suspiciously. When they'd attempted to question him again, he'd waved the men off, saying he had a funeral to arrange.

The headlines in the tabloids that morning had been horrible. *The Daily Express* banner read, "Lord Slays His Lady with Family Sword." *The Daily Mirror* wrote, "Hardaway Suspected of Killing Errant Wife." Only the *Guardian* had suggested he might be innocent by reporting her affair with the Russian and hinting that something sinister was afoot. Reporters had yet to find him, but it was only a question of when.

The telephone rang. For a moment, Christian considered leaving it, but this number was known to only a few. So he answered. "Hullo?"

"Sir, this is Pauline. I'm calling from my home."

"Yes, very wise." In his misery, he'd forgotten her assignment. "What have you got for me?"

"Well, Philips has prepared a report for you on the suspect timers."

"Yes, I told him to trace those we've been accused of selling improperly. I've not seen the report, as yet."

"That's because, although he's written it, he's not provided it to you, and I know why. I heard from the cleaners that he was using his secretary's typewriter after business hours a couple of nights ago. I had maintenance move that typewriter to my office before his secretary came in the next morning. I then unfurled the ribbon and read what he had typed. I made a transcript for you."

"You can do that?"

"There are in-house security rules about disposing of typewriter ribbons and carbons so information does not get out of the building. I had to get to the office before his secretary and had to remove the typewriter—maintenance told her it had been sent out for repair. I can send the transcript to you, if you like, but it's pretty damning and won't make pleasant reading. It confirms we sold the Lockerbie timers and others. He says that our records have the sales taking place at, or shortly after, you made visits to various embargoed countries."

"'Our records,' you say?"

"Yes."

"That's absurd! I haven't personally arranged a sale of anything, let alone timers, in more than five years! And if the timers for the Lockerbie flight were connected to us, we'd have heard about it some time ago. That was easily the most investigated bit of sabotage in British history."

"Yes, I understand, but the appearance is just dreadful, and I don't know if you'll even get a chance to tell your side of it. I was not surprised to learn they cannot trace the Lockerbie numbers on any of our records. But I've some good news. I checked the backup records kept in storage and found one sale to Yugoslavia mentioned in Phillip's report that occurred during a month a lot were sold to Sweden. I pulled the Swedish transaction and went through it, line by line. We sold them timers, the very ones Philips's report says went to Yugoslavia."

"He's forging documents, then?"

"Yes, but obviously, he can't get rid of everything. He can't remove all the records we have of our sales. There are just too many of them. They are in accounting, in sales; even our auditors may have copies. I went to records to pull the hard copies of the Swedish sale."

"They're missing, I'll wager."

"Yes, they were. I pulled the file for Yugoslavia, and there appear the same numbers as in the report."

"So, he's hidden the evidence that exonerates us and doctored the files of those that condemn. But surely, he knows, given time, we can prove his report wrong. That's why he hasn't given it to me yet."

"Officially, we're still searching for the missing files. I'd say the report is meant for public consumption. You'll get your copy on the same tray you get the morning newspaper reporting it. The government will act at once, and you'll have no time to respond. I don't think he expected anyone to learn of the report so early, giving us time to produce contrary information."

"He hadn't planned on you, Pauline."

"What do you want me to do now, sir?"

"Make several copies. Find all the records you can. Keep me informed. Good job. Watch your back now."

"Yes, sir. And my condolences on your loss. Sorry. I should have said that straight away."

"Thank you. Just you be careful. Someone's playing very rough, and I don't want you to get hurt."

So it's Philips, Christian thought as he rang off. He had to admit it caught him by surprise, though, in retrospect, Philips was the obvious choice. Christian had never considered the man to be a risk taker; yet that was what Philips had done, taken on the risk of his life. Christian wondered, for a moment, if Philips had murdered his wife. Could Philips be that ruthless? He realized he'd never really known the man, taking in all that stiff upper lip bravado at face value.

But Philips wasn't the enemy, merely one of the tools being employed by someone else. Christian didn't intend to waste a single moment fighting the man. He would either put a stop to this nonsense immediately, or take his medicine and go to goal, or fight back publicly by releasing an endless stream of scandal, or run like hell.

The problem with the final option was that it had become a very small world, indeed.

CHAPTER THIRTY-FIVE

1971
Warsaw

Mishka's correspondence with J. Edgar Hoover's office lasted for two decades, an amazing amount of time. For the first five years, a patient Mishka only alluded to the possibilities, the wealth of information available to him and his connections with the anti-Communist underground in Eastern Europe. He was convinced, at the time, that this was his final chance. He used Gehlens code name "Red Rover" and, once contact was established, Mishka admitted that he was a high-level KGB operative working in Eastern Europe.

At the same time, Mishka extended his tentacles into Eastern Europe's anti-Communist underground, not as the eyes and ears of Moscow, but as a czarist supporter seeking other like-minded souls. There were few remaining, but Mishka inflated the numbers in his reports. A counter-revolution was brewing, he told the FBI.

Gehlen had been right. None of the information he released to Hoover's FBI ever reached him in reports by America-based spies. The FBI was clean. It was then Mishka arranged for direct correspondence between the Romanov heir and Hoover. But over the years, this had been a delicate dance. The timing was never right, not with the ebb and flow of history and relations between the Americans and Russia. The two—the Romanov heir and Hoover—would go a year or longer with no contact at times, followed by a flurry of letters; but nothing came of it. Mishka was infuriated with American intransigence. They had the power to fulfill his lifelong dream and destroy their greatest adversary in the process. Why did they dawdle?

Mishka believed that he had become quite close to his son, Nicholas, in the time since the tragic death of his putative parents. Mishka had certainly worked hard enough at it. But creating a close emotional bond with anyone had proven difficult for him.

He'd lived his life maintaining his distance with only the pretense of friendship, for he never knew who events would demand he kill. It seemed to him, at times, that the young man was playing the same game. When Mishka considered his life, it seemed to him the only real friend he had was Julian Hardaway.

It had been a mistake, Mishka came to believe, not to have raised the boy himself or, at least, not to have told him from the start that he was his father, that they were joined in blood. The bond Mishka sought could not be created artificially. A son loved and adored his father; that was the way of the world. Mishka had thrown that away in his paranoia. But given Stalin's reign, what else could he have done?

Now his son had been returned to Moscow to serve as the newly appointed chief of the British department in the KGB. The time had come to tell Nicholas his true family history and the future that lay ahead for him. Mishka could scarcely contain his excitement as he prepared for the meeting.

* * *

Nicholas Rashidov examined his office with approval. The view was not all he'd hoped for, but proximity to his chief was excellent. When he'd received word in London that he was being recalled to Moscow and that he'd been named to head the British department of the KGB, he'd been thrilled.

Rashidov was under no illusions as to his situation. It had been the wealth of information provided by his American CIA agent and the unexpected death of his principle competition for the slot that had made this promotion possible at such a young age. Moscow, with a position from which he could garner true power, was just where he wanted to be. Regardless of the reasons, he was grateful.

From a practical point of view, his appointment seemed inevitable, at least to Rashidov. No one had better experience with the British than he, and he also brought to his new position an educational background that set him apart from the others. What remained was to do a superior job and make the personal contacts that would matter over the years to come. There was nothing like a well-placed mentor to assure a rapid rise. He intended to make appropriate contact with several potential supporters. A fortuitous marriage would help, but he had not come across the right person yet. These were uncertain times, and he first needed to determine which way the wind was blowing before taking such a step. The worst thing he could do was to make a marriage into a family that subsequently fell into disgrace.

With all these matters in mind, he glanced at his watch and sighed. There was no getting out of it. His Uncle Mishka had scheduled a private dinner for the two of them, telling him he had important information to impart. The old man had gotten on Rashidovs nerves recently. Khrushchev had been too lenient with these old killers and should have made a clean sweep of them. That would certainly have solved the problem.

He had considered turning down the request, then avoiding his uncle thereafter. No one he could think of was aware of his relationship with the man, though he was certain it existed in the security file kept on him, housed in this very building. The man could hurt his career, Rashidov was certain. If only there was some way to be rid of him. For the moment, he'd have this meal, but best to end their association this night.

* * *

Mishka had arranged for dinner at one of Moscow's most exclusive restaurants. Within its walls, the conversation would be innocuous. Afterwards, with each of them smoking a fine Cuban cigar, they would walk in nearby Gorky Park. Only in such an open area could Mishka be certain no one was listening. The amusement portion of the park would be closed at such a late hour, but it remained well lit and secure for his purposes.

Since even before the revolution, Muscovites had taken to picnics in parks or outside of the city as the opportunity to speak frankly. It was an old joke among men such as himself that, when a subject arose that required discretion, one would ask, "Do we need to go to the park?"

The boy looked good to Mishka, Nicholas was tall, elegant, assured. Nicholas was the new Russian the party was always talking about. In this case, however, his son was, in fact, an old Russian, the kind of leader the Communists had murdered en masse and sought to crush permanently.

It was at such a moment that Mishka was all but overwhelmed with the sense of his mission. Tonight was pivotal. Events might yet place him on the throne. But in the eventuality that such did not occur, his son must be prepared and possessed of the same fire in his belly that had burned within Mishka these many decades.

Seeing Mishka, Rashidov smiled, then walked briskly to his uncle before embracing in the traditional Russian manner. For an instant, Mishka felt a tinge of doubt. Had the smile been less than sincere? Did he detect some hesitation in the boy?

"Over here," he said, his arm still about the well-dressed young man. "We have a booth. You must tell me all about London. I have never been there; I want to know everything. Start with the women, no? Are they as willing as I hear?"

By now, the men were seated. Rashidov had expertly scanned the room and been dismayed to spot a senior KGB officer seated in a corner. That was the problem with public meetings like this. Someone was bound to see you.

Mishka insisted on placing the order for both of them. "They cook the old way here," he told his dining companion. "I know the best dishes."

Rashidov examined his uncle critically. Mishka had aged a bit in the three years since Rashidov had last seen him. He'd put on a kilo or two; nothing serious, but it was apparent. Otherwise, the man was tall, fit, and handsome, with a certain elegant bearing about him. Looking into the mirror as he'd dressed earlier, Rashidov had been startled to see how much he resembled him.

Perhaps he should find out if there were some family relationship between them before breaking off permanently with the man. No, he decided. There was no reason to know. It would change nothing. The man was a hindrance to his career.

"Tell me," Mishka said, after the first course was served, "did you have occasion to meet Julian Hardaway, as I suggested?"

"Yes. Twice. Briefly, both times at embassy functions. He was as charming as you said, and is well regarded by our staff. He's been very useful over the years."

The older man's eyes twinkled. "Yes, more than you can know. But he works with the other side, you understand?"

"So I have found."

"And his son? He's about your age, I believe. Did you ever meet him? His name is Christian, and he's on target to take over the family company."

"No. It never came up."

"Too bad. That should prove a worthwhile friendship. Make the effort, when you get the chance. He travels to Warsaw a great deal these days. Perhaps you could come over for a meeting."

"I think not. I have my new position to solidify."

"Of course. I should have considered that. Maybe I can persuade the boy to come to Moscow. He comes occasionally, in any event."

The men turned to their dinner as Mishka quizzed his son about London and Britain in general. Rashidov was only too happy to share some of his adventures. In many ways, the years had been a lark. "Did you meet any of the royalty while there?" Mishka inquired.

"Of course. I met the queen, once or twice, at her annual garden party and at a Buckingham Palace reception. I did also meet a number of lords and such. Pompous, silly people, if you ask me."

"That's the party line, and perhaps those you met are, in fact, as you say; but my experience has always been that breeding shows. A ruling class tends to do things in a superior way, since they are educated and trained to it."

Rashidov laughed. "That sounds unorthodox." At that moment, he noticed his KGB section chief staring at him, obviously wondering who he was with.

"Perhaps. But true, in my experience. The party has been overzealous in that regard."

The meal was as good as either man could expect. Rashidov had forgotten how much he missed Russian fare and over ate. When coffee was served, he passed on dessert. "Too much already, uncle. Too much."

Mishka laughed. "We'll go for a walk then. The park is across the street. It will do us both good."

Perfect, Rashidov thought, wondering what the old man was up to. "Yes, sounds good."

It was a brilliantly clear night, the air was brisk, and both men pulled their evening coats closely about them. Winter was gone, but spring had yet to arrive. Off the pathways, the ground was soft.

They were all but alone as they strolled from light to light, walking leisurely and speaking of the meal—until Mishka fell silent. At that moment, he handed the young Russian a cigar and the two lit up before resuming their walk.

"Did your parents ever tell you how I came to know them? How I came to be your uncle?" Mishka asked. They had reached the Moskva River and turned to follow its course beside the park.

"No. I don't recall ever asking. You were just always there."

"Was there anything about my relationship with them that struck you as odd?"

Now that's a question that could lead to trouble, Rashidov thought. There had been several occasions that came readily to mind. He was certain that both of his parents had feared his uncle, but had always dismissed that as the result of his uncle's fierce reputation. "No," he said without hesitation. "Nothing I can think of."

Mishka chuckled. "Good answer. They taught you well at trade school. Let me tell you how we met. It was early in the Great Patriotic War. I took an infant to them and asked them to raise him as their son."

For a moment, Rashidov failed to grasp what he was being told. Then, it came to him. "You gave *me* to my parents?" As was the case with any child, Rashidov had occasionally considered whether he was adopted or not. In Russia, for his generation, it was not such an unusual thought. There had been many orphans caused by the terrible war, far more than the state could ever handle efficiently. Informal adoptions had been commonplace, though with a family member, whenever possible, which prompted his next question. "Are we related?"

"Yes, Nikki, you and I are related. But I was not related to those you thought were your parents." Mishka paused to let the thought sink in.

"What do you mean, Uncle?"

"Let me tell you the story. Just listen for now." Mishka related meeting his wife, presenting theirs as a wartime romance, how the two of them had been swept away with love for each other. "Such things were commonplace in those days, not like now. There was no time. No one knew if he would be alive the next day. We filled what time we had with all the passion we could."

"Your wife was the daughter of Boris Shaposhnikov, marshal of the Red Army?"

"Yes, she was. We had a son. Kristina, tragically, never recovered from the delivery. I was in no position to raise this child, you understand. I was a commissar, always at the front, always on the move, and I had no family to whom I could give my son to raise." Again Mishka paused to let Rashidov take it in.

After a moment, the young man said, "You gave your son to my parents to raise. That's what you're telling me?"

"Yes, Nikki. I'm telling you I am your real father."

Rashidov stopped in his tracks. A flood of memories rushed over him. It made so much sense. Suddenly, every unanswered question of his childhood was gone. His doting mother, his loving father, the man they seemed frightened of, vanished in a moment, replaced by this man, one of Stalin's executioners.

"I see. Why did you not tell me sooner?"

"I considered it before you left for London. I had not told you previously out of respect for your parents," he lied. "As long as they lived, I did not want to burden you with what might have been conflicting emotions."

A thought crossed Rashidovs mind. Could such a thing be possible? He recalled how his uncle had suddenly appeared when his parents were killed in the car accident, how often he'd seen the man after that. He made a mental note to pull the file on the accident. If it was a whitewash or unavailable, then he would have his answer.

"Yes, of course. It would have been very hard on them." Better they were dead. Yes, for you, old man, that would be better.

"I know this is a lot to take in like this. If there is anything you want to ask me, now would be a good time."

"How did you pick my parents?"

"Good people I knew. Childless. Living in Moscow. They were a natural and easy choice. I was able to help your father's career a time or two, as well, to see that you gained entry to the best schools."

That caught Rashidov by surprise. And what about his career? The unexpected death of the primary competition for his current position popped into his head. Could it be possible? Other fortuitous events came to mind as well. "And me?" he asked. "Have you helped me along?"

Mishka smiled. "You are my only son. Of course, I've helped. What else can a father do?"

Rashidov found himself suddenly angry. Could his success be that simple? Had all his hard work been for nothing? Had he moved so rapidly up the ladder because of this butcher? "I never asked for your help. Not once."

"Of course not. Nor would you. It is to your credit." Mishka stared at the river a moment as he drew on the cigar. Finally, the moment of a lifetime was here. He turned to face his son. "Prepare yourself. Let me begin by telling you your true name. You are Nicholas Georgi Romanov. Nicholas is for your great uncle. Georgi is my true first name. And Romanov is our true last name."

"Why—? You have me confused."

"Then, allow me to unconfuse you. Listen. This is the story of your family. It will take a while to tell, so be patient. All your questions will be answered."

And so, Georgi Alexandrovich Romanov, heir to the throne of Russia, told his son their story. With each passing event, the mask of control fell away from Rashidov, until, by the end, he concealed nothing. In all his life he'd never before heard such a tale, never had his jaw stay open for so long.

When he was finished, Mishka tossed his cigar into the river. Rashidovs was still pressed between his fingers, cold and unsmoked.

The story had sounded incredible to him, as well. He wondered how Nikki would take it. "There are documents," Mishka added. "I've had them placed in a bank lockbox."

"You're telling me that you are the czar of All the Russias?"

Mishka smiled. "That I should be. That, with your help, I hope to be."

"You joined the KGB to advance this—this cause of yours?"

"Yes. And did all I could to make Stalin's reign one of terror. I hoped that he would be overthrown; or, failing that, when he died, an opportunity would present itself. But it did not."

"I see no such opportunity now."

"No. So we must create one, or at least stand prepared when one presents itself. This system we have is unnatural. It cannot endure."

A wave of fear swept over Rashidov. "Who knows about this?"

"No one."

"If this story is true—"

"It is."

"If this story is true, then you and I are in great danger. They will not allow the legitimate heir to live, not one so closely connected—"

"Yes. Another reason why I waited for you to reach manhood before sharing our history with you."

Rashidovs mind raced with implications. "Documents, you say? How did you get them out of the country?"

"Ahh. My friend Julian Hardaway. He took them for me. He also opened the account."

"Then, he knows."

How much to tell? Mishka considered his response. This was, after all, his own flesh and blood. "I've told him, yes. My thought for years was to quietly generate British support in the right circles."

Rashidov drew a sharp breath. "Then *you* are the source of those stories we keep hearing, about an heir to the throne who is seeking backers for a coup."

"I suppose. These efforts are never as secure as you'd like. Word is bound to leak. Julian is a lord in his country. If he can get the aristocracy there to support us, anything is possible."

"You're mad!" Rashidov said. "That's insane! You'll get us both killed with your craziness."

Mishka drew himself up. "Without risk, there is no prize, and this is the greatest prize of all—to restore our family to its rightful rule!"

"What about my career? Don't you see? I'd be throwing it all away."

"Quite the contrary. Do well; advance. You will soon find yourself in a position to influence events to our favor. And if this cannot be done in my lifetime, then do it in yours. What matters is that we succeed!"

Rashidovs mind raced, and he was silent for a long time. "You really believe this man, Hardaway, can help?"

"I've always believed he could."

The young man paused, then said, "Then I must meet with him. I want to assess how realistic this all is. Get my own sense of the man. You understand?"

"I suppose. His son, Christian, is due in Warsaw in a few days."

"Not the son. This Julian, who has helped you. I need to see him."

"All right. I can arrange it. Perhaps this will set your mind at ease. Think on this, my son. Consider what I offer you—the throne of Russia, the power to set our troubled country right, to find our true place in the world, then to pass it all to your son. What greater power and glory can a man aspire to?" Mishka impulsively reached forward and hugged his son. "My Nikki! I've wanted to do that for so long!"

CHAPTER THIRTY-SIX

1991
Day Eight
London

After speaking with Pauline and leaving his townhouse, Christian realized that London had already turned warm for the year. The city had been damp and dank, but today, London was transformed and had become bright and cheery. The sun was positively dazzling. Couples—arm-in-arm or hand-in-hand—were everywhere, basking in its warmth. Christian parked in his usual spot in the underground car park, then walked briskly to Hannah's townhouse.

He rang the bell and the door sprang open. There was Hannah in all her breathtaking beauty. "Give me a kiss, handsome," she said, "then I've got to hurry back to the kitchen. Dinner's almost ready." They embraced and kissed, far too briefly in Christian's opinion, then she was off in a dash, calling back, "Make yourself at home. I've just opened a bottle of wine."

Hannah was dressed in something fitted, made of silk, and Christian was immediately aroused. But instead of doing the obvious—there was time enough for that later—he crossed to the bar and poured two glasses of wine, gulping his down at once and pouring another before taking a glass to Hannah. He patted her well-rounded, firm behind as he set the drink down.

"Hands off the chef. I wield a nasty wooden spoon, you!" she warned with a smile. "Seriously, almost done. You can set the table, if you like; then we'll chat as we eat."

A few minutes later, they were digging into the main course as Hannah made small talk. But in Christian's view, there was no avoiding the unpleasantness. For more than a week, such had been his life. He was surprised he even had an appetite.

"How are things at the office?" he asked.

Hannah finished chewing before speaking. "You have a friend in Douglas."

She meant Douglas Hurd, foreign secretary. "He adored your father and considers you both old school, salt of the earth, that sort of thing—and doesn't believe a word of nastiness about you. He's instructed every agency to give you and IMSS the benefit of the doubt, and he's ordered his own inquiry into the source of the information to *The Times*. He's of the opinion someone is plotting against you."

"That's good to hear. I don't know as it will be enough, but reassuring, regardless. That 'someone' is Raymond, I'm afraid. Perhaps not him alone, but him for certain." He told Hannah what he'd just learned from Pauline.

"No good deed goes unpunished, I suppose," Hannah observed when he was finished. "Didn't you consider firing him for some bit of business over young boys?"

"I don't think it ever reached that point, but there was talk."

"And this is how he rewards you! He disgusts me." She stood up and went into the kitchen, emerging with a bottle of port.

"My solicitor tells me I need to make a formal statement concerning Evelyn. I suppose I should get it over with. If I delay, it makes me look complicit."

She looked at him with those beautiful eyes. "I talked to the police already. I don't think either of them believed a word I said. Can you tell me how she died? I only know what I read in the papers."

"Stabbed, I understand, with a dagger or military-style knife, the kind they sell at camping stores everywhere. I'm told I'm not really a suspect; the killing fits a mugging gone bad. But this, along with the other business, has raised eyebrows."

"Why was she there? Was she coming to see you?"

"She wasn't all that close. It happened on the other side of the park. I believe her Russian lover lived nearby."

"Have they talked to *him*? I'll bet not. They want to put it on you, if they can."

"I wouldn't know; but either way, he has diplomatic immunity and won't say anything, assuming he even meets with them. I've been thinking about her murder, who would have done it and why."

"You don't think it was random, then?"

"No. It was meant to put the heat on me. I wouldn't be surprised if some 'eyewitness' doesn't step forward in the next few days and pick me out of a lineup."

"My God! That's positively evil."

"Yes. That's the word for it." Christian tossed back the rest of his wine, then got up and went to the bar in search of a more serious drink. "You seem worked up tonight."

"You can say that. I quit my job today."

"You what?"

"Resigned. I'll have to be your kept woman now. I've nowhere else to go." That was not strictly true. Hannah's future was financially well secure.

"What happened?"

"I've been snooping about on your behalf—openly, I add in my defense. I wasn't out to be a sneak. Skinner took exception and complained to Douglas. My boss was brought into the show and told me to stop, calling into question my loyalty. We had words, and I submitted my resignation. Now, I'm a free woman, available at your every whim and fancy."

"I wish you hadn't done that. I can't believe that I've put you in such a situation. I don't want you hurt on my account."

"I think Skinner can't wait to see you undone. He's talked against IMSS for months now."

"Do you think he's part of this?"

"I don't know, though I've wondered. He could have managed to ease you and your company out over time; but this has happened so quickly and so publicly, he's making it clear to everyone he's had nothing to do with it. And I am inclined to believe him. He's not stupid."

They quietly cleared the table and retired to the sitting room.

"You'd be better off without me, you know," Christian said. "I'm poison for everyone right now."

"I'm a grown woman, Christian. I choose those with whom I spend my time and those with whom I do not, thank you very much. And if this catastrophe is what it takes to bring you to me once and for all, then for me, it's a blessing in disguise."

When she said those words, Christian loved her more than he'd ever loved any woman. It was a strange sensation for a fifty-year-old man to discover such depths of emotion within himself.

"The foreign minister is furious about the whole ordeal. Douglas is just beside himself, but there's nothing more he can do at this time."

"I just wish I understood *why* this was happening." Christian sipped his drink and tried to relax. The muscles in the back of his neck felt stiff as wood, and he had the desire to simply keep his eyes closed and sleep right there on the couch. An image of himself looking much older, the pepper washed out of his salt and pepper hair, leaving it pure gray, his thin body dressed in a prison uniform, snapped him to attention. "I wonder if they'd give me a white collar institution or if they'd put me with the other traitors in maximum security."

Hannah's temper snapped. "Don't talk like that! And don't waste your energy thinking about the 'why' of it. Figure out the 'who' and make an end of it. That might still be within your power."

"Yes. You're right, of course. I need to stop this immediately. The longer it plays out, the harder it will be for me. I've drawn up my Doomsday list of scandals, but I don't know about using any of it."

"Why not? No one I can see is actually helping you, except for Douglas. You know all the dirt they've covered up over the years, the absolute shits they've protected. How can they leave you out to dry like this?"

"I've been through all that. But it might be that whoever is behind this *wants* me to counterattack. The true intent in all this could very well be to force me to use what I know. The scandals would rock the nation, bring down the government, put both major parties under public suspicion."

"I see your point." Hannah lit a cigarette to calm herself. She'd quit smoking two years before, and he was disappointed to see she'd started up again. "Christian, I don't think they'll send you to prison," she said, covering his hand with her own. "And I'm not saying that because I love you. You *do* know too much. They can't risk it."

"You're saying they'd kill me instead?"

"Oh, I doubt that. No, they'd say you had a breakdown; they'd have a quiet hearing, bundle you off to some rural clinic, and pump you full of drugs for the rest of your life. I've heard stories."

"Yes. And I can put faces to those stories."

They sat silently for some minutes. Then Hannah spoke. "We should run, Christian. Once out of the country, where they can't touch you, all they can do is take the company apart. I doubt they'll pursue you. You told me a lot of your money is in banks overseas. I'm free now. Why should we stay?"

"Perhaps you're right—and it just might come to that."

"You can't wait too long. The more time passes, the more deeply committed they'll become to a course of action. Better to just vanish now. We could find a villa in Tuscany, maybe Capri. We could have a family, Christian. You could— you could do something else. I know you enjoy the life of a powerful executive, but maybe we'd be happier with a simpler existence."

It was an enormous temptation, an option he'd considered seriously since he realized he was under suspicion for Evvy's death. But it just wouldn't work. "It would tell everyone that I'm guilty. On top of that, my father died for this company. I'm not going to let anyone just wipe us off the map."

What he didn't say, what he'd never told her, or anyone else, was that he would never rest until he had avenged his father's death

"We may have no choice, Christian. Please? Just think about it. You can go ahead. I'll follow." She put out her cigarette and lit another. "Have you considered the possibility that the CIA is behind this?"

"My first thought. I told you I saw Mitch Seaver in Kuwait. That was very odd."

"If it is ITP, I don't know if there's anything you can do about them. They've got the Americans on their side. Our government won't stand up to them, if it comes to that. You'd have a losing battle on your hands. Why make the sacrifice?"

"Why?" Christian's temper flared, not from anger but from exhaustion, and because that question was the same one he'd been asking himself all week. IMSS was a sinking ship. He couldn't guarantee that it would survive another three months.

But he couldn't just walk away. His father had passed the office down to him, along with a thriving business, a business built on trading with the enemy. At the time, Ian Cathcart had assured his father that Julian was doing his country a service, that his father had contributed an incredible amount to British intelligence and was considered by many, behind closed doors, to be a national hero. It had all remained the same with Christian.

Christian had been determined to continue his father's work. Under Christian's guidance, IMSS had grown ever larger as the world had become much smaller. Now the world seemed like a chessboard with one player—the U.S.—mere moves away from mate, while the Soviets grumbled and bared their teeth on their way to defeat. Christian had moved IMSS into the Middle East as early as he could. There was money to be made, oil money. And whether it was the Egyptians, the Kuwaitis, or the Saudis, they continued to buy British. The Americans had left IMSS's customer base alone because of the Arab-Israeli conflict, and the only success ITP had in the region was in picking up the deals IMSS wouldn't do, the Iran-Iraq war, for one, where the Americans supplied both sides on a grand scale.

He'd seen the thinking in British intelligence, the unhappiness with the role his company played. He'd wanted to hedge his bets in the event the name of the game was changed, though he'd expected to be given a gentleman's amount of time to transition his company. He'd already started, just in case.

With the troubles in the Soviet Union, Christian had begun a campaign to bring IMSS into the next century. He'd thought that it would evolve into a security company, of sorts, instead of primarily a government contractor. The old British intelligence operatives that populated the company's executive staff were perfect for consulting on everything from overall national security to transportation issues, such as airlines, airports, and even oil tankers. And there was personal security for high-ranking dignitaries in constant motion.

Before the Gulf War, and then the article in *The Times*, he'd been on the verge of inking anti-terrorism consulting deals with Malaysia and Japan. A new field was opening up in corporate security as well: safety, defense against corporate espionage, even anti-terrorism training. A world with only one superpower was no safer than one with two; to the contrary, it was more dangerous. In the old days, the threat was a nuclear war that never came. Now, there were terrorists, renegade armies, and assassins. It was harder to defend against a single determined attacker than the bombs of an entire nation. Danger was everywhere.

Ironic, Christian thought, that what he'd envisioned as his crowning achievement, bringing the company into the twenty-first century, would be ruined just when it was finally within reach. And that he'd been accused of selling to terrorists! He, of all people!

Despite his grim evaluation of events, Christian still believed, in his heart of hearts, that he would, miraculously, rebound, find a way to make IMSS into a company that would foster a measure of global security. He still believed he'd turn out the hero, not the victim of someone else's game.

"I can't just walk away, Hannah. Not yet. Not just like that." He moved closer and kissed her, moving the hair from her eyes. She teased him, bringing her lips to his chin. She leaned away, then returned, kissing him full on the mouth.

"I love you," he told her, whispering the words. Her eyes watered, and he felt a tear trickle down his cheek. He realized he'd never said those words to her before. In fact, he hadn't said them to anyone in more years then he could remember. The last woman he'd said that to had been Evvy, a different Evvy, an Evvy he barely remembered. And he himself had been a different man.

CHAPTER THIRTY-SEVEN

1971
Warsaw

Julian Hardaway pulled his overcoat tightly across his shoulders, turning up its lapels. It was cold and windy, colder than he'd anticipated. He stood in the stoop of a quiet apartment building, careful to remain still in the shadows as he waited. Mishka had told him this meeting was important, urgent even. Julian wondered, once again, what it could be about.

Julian had anticipated, for some years, that the Russian bear was ready to defect. Why not?

The Soviet Union was rotten to the core. Mishka's mentor, Kaganovich, was in disgrace, and the man had just about managed to get through this last decade with his life. Mishka's best years were behind him. He had no future in Russia, and no family about which Julian was aware.

Julian thought for a moment of all the darkened streets in which he'd waited to meet some very dangerous people over the decades, in every corner of the world. He could have been an earl and lived a life of comfort, serving in the House of Lords—had that been what he'd wanted. Certainly, every man he knew, except his own son, would have followed that easy course. But there had always been an unrest in him, a need for service, the need for adventure. And, if the truth were truly told, it was the adventure that had driven him over the decades. Had this all been about adolescence, an unwillingness to fully embrace the responsibilities of adulthood? It was a troubling thought that struck him to the quick.

Julian spotted movement down the street, but nothing he could put a name to. A gaggle of leaves fluttered and bounced their way along the street towards him, driven by a sudden gust of wind. He resisted looking at his watch. He'd been waiting less than five minutes, and Mishka was normally very punctual. Looking at a watch only made the time move more slowly.

Ever since Monika's death eight years earlier, he'd reconsidered their relationship. Clearly, Monika had been an operative. He'd been a fool to take the young woman at face value. Mishka had been more wily than he'd thought, placing her closely to him like that. To what end? He'd replayed every conversation with the young woman and come to a startling conclusion. The theme of a Russian czarist faction within Russia had come up again and again. Clearly, Mishka had been serious when he'd claimed to be the heir. If it were true, the man was playing a dangerous game. Julian had passed along the information to Ian Cathcart, but nothing had come of it.

Julian had never for a moment accepted the coroner's verdict that she'd committed suicide.

He was certain, in his heart, that while Mishka had planted the young woman on him, she'd been killed on the orders of others. There'd been a number of mysterious deaths surrounding the Profumo affair. What was one more?

But how could he be certain Mishka hadn't given the order? The Russian had killed thousands in his lifetime, what was one more? Still, her death had ended one source of embarrassment for him. In many ways, this was a sordid life he'd picked for himself.

A figure stepped under a streetlight and stood so he could spot him. Nicholas Rashidov! Now that was a surprise. He'd last seen the man in London at an embassy party. What did Nicholas have to do with Mishka? Clearly, this was whom he was here to meet. Julian stepped onto the sidewalk and walked towards the man under the circle of dim light.

"Mr. Hardaway," Rashidov said as the men met. "I am sorry to have brought you to such an unappealing location. My uncle could not make it and asked me to meet you and bring you to him."

Julian recalled the man more completely now. They'd spoken briefly, a time or two, in London. The young man had been assigned to the Soviet embassy at a much lower level than Julian would typically have contact with. "Good to see you again," Julian said, extending his hand. "Who is your uncle?"

"Your friend, Mishka."

"Ah! I do believe you are the first relative of his I've ever met."

Rashidov nodded. "My uncle could not get away and sent me down for you. The party is here, on the third floor."

Julian looked around the barren streets. There were no commercial businesses of any kind.

On closer examination, though, he realized the building they were standing beside had once been a hotel. It appeared abandoned to him, but so much of Warsaw did these days. "Party?"

Rashidov grinned. "You know these old Russians. No matter how pressing the matter, you must have some fun first. It won't be long. Here" He opened the door at hand. "Up the stairs. The elevator is not working."

Julian stepped inside, out of the cold. Above him, he could now hear the muffled sounds of contemporary music. He groaned inwardly. He had no stomach for a drinking bout or an orgy. The men mounted the stairs, the music growing in volume with each flight. On the third floor, a pair of doors were all but pulsating with the beat of the music. Rashidov shrugged, as if they must both bear their fate. Julian opened the door and stepped in.

The room was smaller than he'd anticipated. Gaudy in its décor, it reeked of hashish. He felt the rush of arms grabbing him from each side and was unable to offer any real resistance before he was thrown to the wooden floor. His arms were pinned, and, before he fully realized what was happening, a plastic bag had been slipped over his head, drawn tightly round his throat. He struggled at first but realized it was useless. They had him.

Finally, he stopped struggling and was surprised how calm his mind became. So this is how it ends, he thought, as the air ran out, if only Christian—if only—.

And then it was dark.

* * *

Mishka cursed the aging Syrena he'd commandeered. Polish women might out-fuck Russian women, but this Polish car was clearly inferior to any Russian-made vehicle. Rain splashed against the windshield, and he squinted in order to see more clearly as he raced through the night. Of course, the car had no wiper blades. That would have been too much to expect. Still, he'd reach the coast within the hour.

He wondered once again if he were being wise.

At the time, the reaction of his son, Nicholas, to the news that they were heirs to the throne of Russia had seemed normal. The young man was a trained KGB agent and knew how to contain his emotions. So when Mishka had seen the shock in his face at the end of the tale, he interpreted that the boy had accepted what Mishka had told him. Nicholas's immediate analysis that this information placed them in danger had been an accurate assessment of the situation and was certain to more closely bond the two of them. Even his request to meet with Julian had been perfectly logical. It was only natural that he assure himself of the steadfastness of Mishka's longtime friend, the only other man in all the world who knew their secret.

So Mishka had called his British friend, told him where to be hours earlier, but not telling him whom he would be meeting or why—only that it was important. And now, Julian, his friend, was dead, murdered.

And what a miserable death it had been. He'd been suffocated, his body taken to a seedy hotel room, set up to serve the vices of perverted men. They'd slipped women's stockings on his friend, smeared lipstick on his lips, and turned his murder into a deviate orgy. It was disgusting. And Mishka had absolutely no doubt who had done the killing—none whatsoever.

Mishka glanced at the speedometer, coaxing a few more kilometers per hour out of the ragged engine.

Had the time truly arrived? Mishka had always believed he'd know when he'd need to defect.

His escape plans had been in place for years, and there was plenty of money on hand and in his Geneva account. Now that the moment had seemingly come, he was not so certain. Logic and experience told him that by the time he'd decided the moment was perfect, others in the state security apparatus would have reached the same conclusion. It would, in fact, be too late.

What could Nicholas have been thinking? Mishka asked himself for the thousandth time.

Of all the reactions to his news, this was one Mishka had never conjured. The boy was killing those who knew. The logic was inescapable. Logic told him the boy would kill him, too.

Kill his own father? How was such a thing even possible? But then, Mishka had never really been a father to Nicholas. Necessity had dictated that he give that role to another man. The boy and his surrogate father had always seemed close. Losing his parents had been very hard on Nicholas. Mishka had falsely believed he could simply step into the role. Circumstances had proven how wrong he had been. Nicholas had loved his foster parents with a strong and deep attachment, and now he suspected that Mishka had killed them.

So Mishka found himself flying through the night in a piece of shit Polish wreck of a car.

Dawn was just lightening the black sky when he pulled to a stop at the checkpoint outside Gdansk, Poland. He displayed the identification of a KGB general, credentials in another name he'd maintained as current for years against this very moment.

Mishka had no intention of waiting for the axe to fall. He'd cast his lot with his son, with his own blood, and been betrayed. He had so many enemies himself that the boy need only recruit one of them to silence him. No, the time had come. He would begin a new life in the West. And from that new life, he would wage a relentless campaign to place himself on the throne of Russia.

The guards cleared him with a salute and "yes sir'd" him through the border post. He arrived at the ferry port early enough to catch the first boat to Stockholm. He'd always made certain he had timely documents authorizing this trip out of the country. Sweden was traditionally neutral, and, in recent years, there had been more and more commerce and contact between it and the Soviet Union. No one questioned a senior official whose papers and identification were in order.

Mishka ate his lunch on the ferry, paying for it with American dollars. He felt as if a great weight was lifted from him. He'd always dreamed of doing this, then flying to London, where he'd be greeted by his old friend, Julian, the earl of Carlisle. After that, he'd be introduced to the finest social circles of Britain, where he would begin to make his case. He'd pictured the events to which he'd be invited time and again in his mind, even allowing himself the luxury of imagining an audience with the queen in his position as legitimate czar of All the Russias. It had been intoxicating.

And now Julian, the gateway to his dreams, was dead, Julian's reputation in shreds, and by no less than Nicholas's hand, Mishka's own flesh and blood.

Just off the pier in Stockholm, Mishka instructed the taxi to take him to the American embassy, certain the driver would have no idea where it was, but the man simply nodded and put the car in gear. A few moments later, Mishka stepped from the taxi, approached one of the two U.S. Marines standing guard, and, in distinct though accented English, declared, "I am a KGB officer. I wish to see the representative of your Federal Bureau of Investigation. Under no circumstances am I to be seen by your CIA man."

With those words, Mishka defected from the Soviet Union.

CHAPTER THIRTY-EIGHT

1991
Day Nine
Kingston Surry

Major General Raymond Philips finished his exercise, wiped sweat from his forehead, then turned on the shower and stepped in. Even at his age, he was a remarkably fit man. His daily regimen of nourishment and exercise never varied, and he was proud of the fact that his weight had not increased more than five pounds since he'd been at Sandhurst as an officer cadet.

Philips lived in Kingston Surry on the River Thames, a thirty-minute drive from the company office. It was a commuter area for the upper class and a section of Britain's wealthy. He owned a six-bedroom house sitting within a five-acre garden. His only luxury was a small stable of horses, and he rode whenever circumstances permitted, which was usually several times a week. An English gentleman, he believed, must be a superb horseman; and, of course, in his dreams, he imagined himself moving in only the best of social circles, where his riding skills would stand him in good stead.

Philips lived alone. The help arrived each workday to maintain the garden and tend to the house. He took breakfast at home, but rarely dinner and never lunch. The only other resident of the house was a young male Pilipino he'd recruited in Manila. The boy was devoted to Philips's personal needs and was available to service Philips between his periods of debauchery. It was an arrangement with which Philips was quite satisfied, as his position made it impossible for him to frequent gay bars in Britain.

His single failing in his social life, he believed, was his disdain for the company of women. He'd tried, on several occasions, to overcome it with no success. He'd always found women to be silly, frivolous creatures, not entirely human, in his opinion, more like an alien species dispatched to earth merely to distract men from a normal life. He'd never understood the attraction most men had towards women and wondered if they were not, in fact, secretly inclined as was he, but compensating by feigning this endless, obvious lust for the opposite sex. Philips believed this was in all ways a man's world.

For the present, he focused on his career and, in that regard, was almost giddy with anticipation. Once his military service had come to an undesired end, he'd switched his ambition to IMSS. In most ways, this had been—for him—a good fit. He'd performed every task given him with military precision and, he was certain, had played an important role in improving the company's performance. Discipline had been lax when he'd come on board. In that regard, the boy had not been the equal of the father. Such was no longer the case, and, in that, he took great pleasure.

As he toweled off, Philips wondered if the Arab, Khaldun, was doing what he'd promised. These brown people could be so untrustworthy. It was certainly in the fellow's interest that he did, but one just never knew.

And the gall of the man! Ten percent! It was absurd. Once Philips was in the driver's seat, he'd ring down the curtain on that kind of extortion.

As he dressed for the evening at his club, Philips replayed in his mind the events of Wednesday evening. He'd never killed up close like that before. As a young officer, he'd taken lives at a distance and he'd ordered his men to kill, but never before had he bloodied his hands personally. It really was not that difficult, he reflected.

He'd waited outside the love nest for her. When Evelyn had emerged, looking all prim and proper, he'd felt only disgust. She was, after all, a married woman. She deserved exactly what she got.

"Mrs. Hardaway," he'd called out softly from the shadows, moving slightly so she could see who was calling her name.

Evelyn stopped and looked. "Yes? Oh, it's you. I'm so sorry, but I've forgotten your name, Mister—?"

"I have a message for you from your husband."

Evelyn walked to him. "Yes? What is it? Surely, he's not sent you to—"

The moment she was within reach, Philips plunged the dagger into her stomach, throwing his free hand across her mouth as he did so. He could smell the sex on her, not entirely masked by her perfume. With the blade still in her, and his hand across her face, he threw her against the brick wall, away from sight, dragging the knife up into her body, stepping back at once to avoid her blood. He'd watched the life leave her eyes, then walked away.

After one hundred steps, he'd discarded the knife into a storm drain, in the gutter. There was no connection to him; he'd picked it up in India years before. A bit later, he removed his gloves and did the same with them. In the men's room at the underground station, he examined himself, then removed and carefully folded his bloodied topcoat. There was blood on his shoes, as well, which he carefully wiped away. He walked to where his car was parked and drove home without incident, the plastic sheets he had placed on the seat and floor of the car rustling as he moved. Once at home, he burned all the clothes and the shoes he'd worn in the fireplace, staying to stir the flames until nothing was left but ashes. Afterwards, he scattered the ashes on his rose beds and, following a large brandy, went to bed.

Before the murder, Philips had considered how he could make it look as if Christian had done it, but decided every idea that came to him was too obvious. In the end, he settled for the fact that her death would occur just across Hyde Park from Christian's townhouse, and that would be enough to cast suspicion on him. And Philips had taken nothing from the woman, so robbery would obviously have been ruled out as the reason for the attack.

Philips did not believe Christian would be charged with her murder, but that had not been his objective. He wanted only to create more confusion, to put greater pressure on the man. If things failed to develop as he envisioned, the Italian whore would go next. Philips would make certain Christian looked guilty in that one.

Philips was surprised that he felt no strong emotion after killing someone in such a personal way. He was amazed at his own steady hand, how well he had slept, and, even now, twenty-four hours later, he was cool and calm.

CHAPTER THIRTY-NINE

1972
Virginia

Mishka woke with a start. He had not slept well in the weeks since he'd arrived in America. The safe house in Washington was even suspect in his paranoia, every word and movement probably recorded. He waited there nervously, day after day, chain smoking cigarettes and drinking coffee, while the agents in charge kept him entertained with cards and American movies and promises to meet J. Edgar Hoover any day.

That day came on a Thursday, when he was taken to FBI Headquarters in a black Lincoln with dark-tinted windows. From its slow acceleration and heavy sway, Mishka could tell that the vehicle was armored. He was driven down a ramp at the side of the building, then to the furthest most wall of the under-ground parking area. There, he stepped out of the car, and was ushered to an elevator he had not noticed; it was in a dark corner and appeared to be for service use only. The elevator took him with surprising speed to the top of the building and, when the doors opened, he found himself in a small lobby with a pair of male secretaries and three rather obvious bodyguards sitting on chairs in scattered corners of the room. There were also two men in dark suits sitting on a sofa, pretending to leaf through magazines. One of the secretaries led Mishka through a door into a conference room.

And there he was, J. Edgar Hoover himself.

The seventy-seven-year-old Hoover, who, at that moment, had only a few months to live, took almost no time for pleasantries. Hoover assured Mishka that the Russian was in the care and under the protection of the Federal Bureau of Investigation, and Hoover personally guaranteed Mishka's safety. He introduced two special agents—those Mishka had seen outside—and told Mishka that they would handle his debriefing and see to all his needs.

"I am not satisfied with the house where I am kept, Mr. Hoover," Mishka told Hoover when invited to speak.

Hoover squinted at him, then spoke to one of the agents. "Move him to Virginia. Be certain he is satisfied with arrangements." Then he leaned forward and said in a near whisper, "You should be concerned. You can never be too careful; but these men can be trusted, I assure you. You were right to come to me and not those other people," which Mishka took to mean the CIA. Then Hoover leaned back in his chair and said expansively, "So, what finally prompted your decision?"

"It was time. Had I stayed, I would be dead. What have you heard of my defection?"

"Nothing. Perhaps the other people have learned about it, but we don't talk to each other much. It's good you are with us. Those boys at Langley are well penetrated. But then, you of all people knew that, didn't you?"

Mishka smiled. "Of course. Your FBI is the only government agency no one has yet penetrated. You are to be complemented on your achievement."

Hoover nodded his head in acknowledgement, his chest swelling a bit. "And what gifts have you brought to guarantee your application for asylum succeeds?"

"What do you have to offer in exchange?"

Hoover smiled. "U.S. citizenship, a new identity, a comfortable income for life. But first, we want it all. Everything you know."

"But of course," Mishka responded with a broad smile, intending to do no such thing. "Everything."

Hoover smiled. "We'll show those bastards, won't we?" And Mishka had no doubt at all who "those bastards" were. With that, the meeting with Hoover was at an end; in fact, Mishka was never to meet with him again. But Mishka's special agents became bonded to him as if by glue. Mishka came to wonder if they had families, as they spent so much time with him.

Over the next months, Mishka described details of the inner workings of the KGB—who was in, who was out. He also outlined several ongoing operations, providing invaluable details, though he withheld many more about which he knew. Their interviews were recorded, of course, and the transcripts were passed along to J. Edgar Hoover, who expressed his approval at the way things were going.

But such information was ultimately of greatest value to the FBI's rival, the CIA, and Hoover refused to pass it along. He had wanted foreign-intelligence gathering included in the bureau's brief and had never reconciled himself to the creation of the Central Intelligence Agency. The CIA director, who'd heard rumors of a high-level Soviet defection, had complained to President Nixon, but to no avail. Instead, Hoover used the information to expose the operations and reap the glory from the president, while casting the CIA in a bad light.

These might have been his final months on earth, but they were giddy ones for the old man.

Only after satisfying the need for information to assure citizenship and a new identity did Mishka turn to his real reasons for defecting. As he presented that, he'd given up in his effort to cause a coup from within the Soviet Union. He had to seek help from outside, from the Americans. He requested someone of high standing for the final and, in his view, most important stage of his debriefing.

He was given Chadwick "Mac" Macdonald, the former head of the FBI's domestic surveillance program during the most active days of the civil rights movement and the turbulent years surrounding it. A man who enjoyed Hoover's absolute trust, Macdonald was in his late sixties with a full head of silver hair and heavy-framed glasses.

Carefully, and with great precision, Mishka told Macdonald his true heritage. "I have worked all of these years within Russia to regain the throne for myself and my family. Throughout Russia is a network of supporters who, of necessity, must remain silent, but who will respond when I step forward."

Mishka told Macdonald of the ring he had secreted within a Swiss vault, of his birth certificate, and of the affidavit there from his mother. With modern testing methods, he assured Macdonald, there would be no doubt of his claim.

When Mishka was finished, Macdonald sat perfectly still. Mishka wondered if the man thought he was crazy. "Just who are these operatives who care so much about putting the Romanovs back on the throne? We don't hear about it from other sources in Russia."

"They exist, I assure you. There is a lingering love for the czar in Russia, just as there is of the church. Stalin could not crush it, nor can Leonid Brezhnev. I know the man. He has no imagination. All he wants is to cling to power until he dies. He does not care about the state. It will continue to rot from within. It will take very little to topple the Communists, when the time comes. If you help me in this cause, then a new czar, one eagerly awaited by the people, a czar obligated to you, will assume the throne. It can happen. It can!"

Macdonald assured Mishka that he would pass along this information, but Mishka heard nothing positive in subsequent days. When he attempted to speak again with Macdonald, Mishka was told Macdonald had retired. When he asked to speak directly with the director, his guards told him the old man was sick. But they were certain Director Hoover would see him as soon as he was back in the office.

This filled Mishka with concern, then fear. Was it really possible that the Americans would squander a chance such as this? He could not believe it. Had he suffered all those years for nothing?

In the end, Hoover was true to his word. Given a new identity, passport, and history as a Russian émigré from Israel—to explain his lingering accent— Mishka was relocated to St. Louis. Within weeks, he read that Hoover had died. Mishka pondered his alternatives, then made his decision. One month later, after taking precautions to make sure that he was not under surveillance, he boarded an airplane, landing in Zurich eighteen hours later.

* * *

Mishka, now known as Abraham Stephanovic, was amazed at the ease with which he gained access to his secret fortune. He had memorized all the required information that the bank would need. Julian had been a true friend, doing everything exactly as requested. In retrospect, Mishka marveled at his own willingness to trust the man, marveled even more that the trust had been honored.

Once he had control of the account, Mishka was perplexed by the idea of what to do with his money. His documents supporting his claim to the throne were safe, for all the good they might prove in the end. He briefly considered going to Britain with his story, but decided against it. The intelligence services there were rife with double agents and turncoats. He couldn't risk it.

No, if he were to succeed in overturning the Soviet empire, the only power on earth with the ability to help was the United States, and the only bureaucracy there that might be persuaded to assist him was the Central Intelligence Agency. The FBI had failed him. Perhaps the spymasters possessed the ability to see the possibilities. But Mishka knew he'd have to move carefully.

By now, Mishka had reasoned that simply contacting the Company would come to no good end. What did he have to offer them other than a story? And this was an organization used to hearing many, many stories. No, he needed to take them the means to accomplish what he sought, something that already existed, an effort behind which they could throw their considerable resources.

Mishka carried in his head the names and means for contacting more than one hundred agents, both those in the West and as many in the Eastern Bloc nations. These he had carefully recruited over the years or dispatched to their posts himself. Each of them had reported only to him and would have no other method of contacting their control. Many were sleepers, waiting for word from him to go active. They believed they were working for the workers' paradise; but they would be working, instead, to fulfill his own ambitions. The nature of their activities would be close to those the Soviets would direct, so there would be no suspicion.

In the almost two years from the date of his defection, it had been a very busy time for him, the busiest of his life, except for the war years. He had bought himself a small house in Fairfax County, Virginia, and hired two former Israeli Mossad agents to handle his personal security. He selected these men because not only were they very good, but because it advanced his cover as being an Israeli himself. He opened a small trading company office in downtown Alexandria, Virginia, a short drive from Washington, D. C.

Mishka drew from his memory the name of the American-based paymaster for the KGB agents within the Company, and made his contact, telling him the kind of man he was looking for in the CIA. A few days later, Mishka was informed that one of their double agents at the CIA was coming to meet with him.

Mishka arranged for this contact to meet at his office. Mitch Seaver had not long returned from his posting to London, where he had been recruited by Nicholas. The money he was being paid by the KGB had lifted his financial desperation, though the time in Britain had not done much, so far, to advance Seaver's career. This assignment to meet with Israeli businessman Abraham Stephanovic was typical of the kind of work Seaver was currently being given.

Mishka's private office was well appointed. Outside it were positioned six employees. Another dozen were scattered in offices in key cities around the world. Mishka met the young American with a hearty handshake and gave instructions they be brought coffee. After a few pleasantries, as each gauged the other, Mishka eased his way into business.

"How much do you know about me, my young friend?"

"Frankly, very little. I was just told to meet with you, and here I am. I have no idea why we are having this meeting other than I know that the person sending me thought it was an important matter."

"As you know, I come from Israel, but I am Russian and I have many Russian friends, men who hate the Communists, as do I. I have come to America to do business, but my true purpose is to work with the CIA. I want to give you information that perhaps you cannot get from other sources."

"Give to us? That's generous of you."

Mishka grinned. "In exchange, you will help me out. One hand will wash the other."

"Just what is your business?"

"I deal in arms. The name of my company is International Trading Partners."

Before leaving that day, Mishka had outlined in rough form what he had in mind. He would provide the intelligence; the Company would give business. It would work out well for both of them. To seal the deal, and give Seaver a help up the ladder of his career, Mishka provided Seaver with the name of a low-level traitor within the CIA.

"I give you this for nothing. They will not believe you at first. But, once you look, you will see that I am right. I know many other names and KGB operations. Once I see the Company is helping me, we will work well together. We will become great friends; and you, personally, my new friend, stand to profit enormously—if all goes well. And where would you like me to open your offshore account? From time to time, I will make deposits in it as a gesture of friendship. This will be between you and me, you understand?"

And so it began. Mishka was never bothered by the fact that Seaver was a KGB agent within the CIA, and Mishka made no effort to learn who his control was. He never once hinted to the man that he was anyone other than the man his cover story purported him to be. If he were to have a conduit to the Soviet Union, Mishka wanted it to be one he knew and one he could blackmail—if push came to shove.

In time, ITP grew far beyond anything Mishka had initially contemplated. As the company prospered, the CIA exercised greater and greater influence over it. He demanded complete freedom of action, but, he learned, that wasn't the American way. This was politics at its worst, which, he decided, was the primary reason the CIA was such a terrible intelligence organization.

Within a few short years, ITP was managed by a board of directors that included U.S. senators, three former congressmen, and a former vice president, along with a smattering of influential businessmen and the usual gaggle of political appointees.

Mishka despised the necessity of dealing with such men and remained in the background as much as possible. There were constant squabbles on the board, as lobbyists pressured for their clients to receive lucrative contracts.

Because the operatives were his own, and because of the wealth of information he personally possessed, Mishka was in a position to wield significant influence—where it most mattered, that being to maintain as much as possible in-house. While expensive to begin, once in place, the practice added to profits and enhanced Mishka's ability to exercise control over the fast-growing company.

His man within the Company, Mitch Seaver, proved very helpful, and, in time, Mishka asked the CIA to add Seaver to the board of directors.

As he could and as events permitted, Mishka pushed to bring the Soviet Union down. At the same time, he spent money and used his influence to advance his own cause without mentioning his claim to the throne. When the time came, he was prepared to call in his markers; that would be enough.

But the dying Communist regime tottered on as if on life support. Finally, at long last, a Communist official decided to take it on. When Boris Yeltsin began to make waves within the party, Mishka gave orders to his agents within Russia to support the man in every way possible. Yeltsin might be just the man to put a czar on the throne.

CHAPTER FORTY

1991
Day Ten
London

The grilling, for that was what Christian considered it to be, consumed five hours. He'd met with Detective Inspector Farragut and Detective Sergeant Connors at his solicitor's office, expecting that would make for an easier go of it.

He'd been mistaken. Farragut had been dogged and relentlessly pedantic, while Connors had been snide and unimaginative. Two hours in, they'd asked repeatedly if he'd not wanted a break, but Christian had refused, convinced it was they who wanted time to recoup and compare mental notes. Finally, the men had completed their enquires and said their good-byes.

The fact was, as Christian's solicitor reminded him moments earlier, the pair had nothing. They'd simply gone after him because he was the husband of the slain woman and because he was in the headlines. It was to be expected. "Unless they develop something more, I don't think you'll need to see them again," he'd informed Christian confidently, and Christian drew assurance from the man's opinion, as he was experienced at this sort of thing.

Christian thanked the man, then elected to walk to his townhouse, in need of fresh air and sunshine. He'd spent the previous weekend holed up with Hannah and, though that had its pleasures, the confinement had been difficult. Now, striding briskly along the street, he felt as if he'd been released from jail.

He walked that way for nearly half an hour, the streets busy as always at this time of day. He passed Westminster Abbey along Victoria Street, turned right down The Embankment, passing a pair of art museums along the way. It was comforting, familiar, and he'd miss it terribly if he were forced to take Hannah's advice and flee the country.

Christian had given instructions for his solicitor to see to Evvy's funeral arrangements. The service would take place the coming Saturday at the Hardaway estate. Christian wondered, for a moment, who would come and who would not. Not that it mattered. Evvy was dead and gone. Who attended her internment meant nothing to her and all but nothing to him. He refused to see the affair as a vehicle for measuring public perception of his predicament.

As he turned the corner to his townhouse, a man stepped forward to intercept him. *Damn reporter*, was Christian's immediate thought as he veered to avoid the man and picked up his pace.

"Young Christian," the man said in a familiar voice. Christian stopped in spite of himself. Only one man had ever called him "young Christian."

"Sir?" he said.

"Yes, young man. It is me, after all these years." There, in a well-tailored suit, with a neatly trimmed goatee beard and spectacles, stood Mishka, the Russian bear. Older and a bit heavier, perhaps, but the man himself was largely unchanged. His dark suit had an American styling to it, and the black shoes were definitely American made. Mishka's eyes twinkled as he took Christian in, and there was genuine warmth in the smile.

"My God!" Christian said. "Look at you. I thought you long dead. What's it been? Twenty years?"

"Since your father's death, yes. I am sorry to have been a stranger, but there have been reasons. We should talk. Not in your place. Old habits, you understand? Somewhere safe, like a park bench." Mishka gave that hearty laugh.

As they walked side-by-side, Christian sneaked more than one look at the man beside him.

He could not put a true age on him, but Mishka had to be somewhere in his seventies, Christian suspected, though Mishka looked fit and vigorous.

He had often wondered what had become of Mishka. The man had vanished at the same time his father had been killed. For all the intelligence that flowed routinely over his desk, and despite all the feelers he'd put out, there had been scarcely a word, and no reliable information for two decades. Two or three times sources had told him the bear had defected; but if that had been true, Christian was certain the Russian would have contacted him.

A few moments later, they were seated at the bench of a small municipal park. A nanny with a toddler sat across from them, absorbed in attention to her charge.

"I am sorry for your loss, young Christian," Mishka said.

"You mean Evvy? We'd not been close for some years; but thank you. It has been a shock. None of us is perfect, and she didn't deserve such an ending. Where have you been, old friend? Why haven't you contacted me?"

Mishka laughed. "Wait until you hear my story. You will not believe it. But you will understand why I have been such a 'stranger,' as you English put it." Pigeons flocked at their feet, so aggressively Mishka kicked at them finally. "Filthy pests." He scanned the park again, glancing at the nanny as she rose and moved off, then gazed at Christian for a long moment. "You've come to look very much like your father, young Christian. Very much. I have missed him over the years. Many times. Now, let me tell you how I came to be here and not in an unmarked grave outside Moscow with a bullet to the back of my head." The story took most of an hour—even with most of the "good parts," as Mishka put it, left out.

"*You* are Abraham Stephanovic?" Christian said in amazement. He had always been surprised to have never met his nemesis personally, and often wondered why the man was such a recluse, though in the armaments industry, that was not unusual.

"Yes, among others."

"And you manage ITP?"

"Not as directly as I'd like, but yes, I've been the primary director of it these years. The Americans have a strange system of management that I've never grown used to, not actually all that different from the KGB, frankly. Just not as deadly, I'm glad to say." He paused. "There is more I must tell you. Some of it shames me. The other you will find quite incredible; but it is all true."

Mishka then related his true life story. Part way into the account, Christian interrupted. "My father told me of your claim to the throne, just before his final trip to Warsaw. You're telling me it is true?"

"Of course." Mishka drew himself upright. "The documents exist that establish it. I have my birth certification, a notarized statement from my mother, the czar's ring, and other documents. Your father smuggled much of it out of Russia for me. And there are blood tests, if necessary."

"And all of these years you've worked to regain the throne for your family?"

"I have, but I am old now and see that it will never happen."

"Why did you defect? Surely, in your senior position, you could have done more within the Soviet system?"

"Perhaps. Perhaps not. I was in disfavor. But yes, I thought I could. My years in the West have been no more productive, unfortunately. The CIA and the FBI both see my claim to the throne as either the ravings of a mad man or an inconvenience. I expected too much." The old man paused, then said, "Young Christian, I know who killed your father and why." Christian braced himself. "It was Nicholas Rashidov. I believe you know him."

Christian thought a moment. "Of course. Your nephew, as I recall. I've not seen him since he was transferred to Moscow. He just resigned from the Communist party and has joined the government of Boris Yeltsin. We have him pegged as an up and comer in the new Russia, if Yeltsin manages to pull this off. Why on earth would he kill my father?"

Mishka patted Christian's thigh. "Because I was a very foolish man." He paused "Nicholas is my son." Mishka told the story. "I thought when he knew who he really was, what his proper place in history should be, he would help me. Together, we could have done it. I am more certain of that today than ever. *He*, not Yeltsin, should be leading this revolution in Russia. But I misjudged him. Blood is not thicker than water. When I innocently told Nicholas that your father knew and that I hoped to use your father's influence in the British government and with the royal family to advance our claim when the time was right, he asked to meet with Julian—your father. I realized only later it was to kill him."

"And that is why you defected."

"My own son would have killed me had I remained. It is also one reason why I have been such a recluse since then. I have been forced to hide from my own flesh and blood."

A wave of emotion swept over Christian. It was a long moment before he could speak. "I've always feared that my father was killed in my place. I was to have gone on that trip."

"It was not you. I brought your father to Warsaw because my son asked me to. I unknowingly set him up to be killed."

"Why are you telling me this?"

"It is time you knew the truth. I have been ashamed all these years that my own son would murder my best friend. You are entitled to know. Now, there is more. This trouble you have. Perhaps I can help."

"I don't see how. I'd say the noose is pretty well fitted about my neck."

"Young Christian, I am old now. My time is very short, and most of my life has been wasted. Christian, I loved your father, and I love you. You were both more loyal and honest toward me then even my own son. Saving you, saving the son of my best friend, is the least I can do." From his pocket, he extracted a thick envelope. "This should be helpful."

"What is it?"

"Pay records for a KGB agent in the CIA, along with other documents and tapes. The Company will change its tune once it knows you possess this. Use a trusted emissary to contact them. The mole is very senior. And he is one of the men they have been using to destroy you. It will make their position untenable."

Could it be true? Christian thought. Could this envelope be his salvation? "Who are we talking about?"

"A member of my own board. Mitchell Seaver."

CHAPTER FORTY-ONE

1972
Alexandria, Virginia

It was a lovely fall day, some months after his first meeting with Mitch Seaver, when Mishka's secretary informed him that a strange man was asking to speak with him. Mishka moved so he could look into the waiting area. There stood a very comfortable and prosperous-looking Ahmet Yuksek.

"I'll see him. Bring us some Turkish coffee."

After pleasantries and a sip of sweet coffee, Mishka said, "I won't ask how you found me. But tell me if others can also do it."

Yuksek smiled. "It was by providence, my friend. You are safe, I assure you."

"So why have you come to see me? How can I be of service to you?"

"It is I who can be of use to you. I have left my previous employer, but continue to provide tidbits of information here and there for a fee. I can be a trustworthy conduit for you, when you wish to distance yourself from the information. I can also be your eyes and ears on the ground when you need someone outside your new organization. Occasionally, I will run across information you might like to know first. I can prove a great service to you in your new endeavor." Yuksek lifted a biscuit to his mouth and took a bite with an approving eye.

And so the association was made, and, over the years, the little Turk had proven good to his word. Mishka had never been comfortable that the man knew who he really was and, more than once, considered killing him; but, in the end, Yuksek was too valuable for that. In any event, in America it was not so easy to eliminate threats as it had been in the Soviet Union.

In time, Mishka saw less and less of the little man. But Mishka was not surprised when Yuksek knocked on the door of his Istanbul hotel suite a few days before Mishka met with Christian in the London park.

The Russian suggested that they speak on the balcony, with its panoramic view of the Bosporus. "What brings you to Istanbul?" Mishka asked as they waited.

Yuksek lit an American cigarette. "It is my home. I am now advisor to the director of intelligence. It is a very good position, I must say. He is my father-in-law, you see. You have done well since we last spoke."

"What brings you to my door? Surely, not old time's sake."

"I have valuable information for you," Yuksek said.

"What information?"

"Understand why I am here, first. My director despises the Americans, especially the CIA. We were speaking a few days ago, and he expressed regret at the troubles IMSS is having. We have always done business with them, and he prefers the British to the Yankees, you see?"

"Of course."

"I casually mentioned that it was no doubt a CIA operation, and that the man central to it was a KGB operative. You do know that Mitch Seaver is part of this operation to destroy IMSS?"

"Of course." Mishka had observed these events, deeply troubled by them, knowing he would have to do something but uncertain as to what.

"And we both know to whom Seaver really reports."

"Of course."

Yuksek patted his coat pocket. "I have proof here, proof that will destroy Seaver."

"Why would you give it to me?"

"My father-in-law wishes the CIA embarrassed, your ITP disgraced, and IMSS rescued. He believes Mr. Hardaway will be quite grateful in future dealings with him. I agree."

"I understand his reasons, but why would *I* want to do that?"

"Because your time with ITP is nearly over, because you love Christian and do not want to see him destroyed." Yuksek smiled. "It will cost you one million dollars."

CHAPTER FORTY-TWO

1991
Day Fifteen
London

It was, Christian told Hannah by telephone that morning, a good day for a funeral, if there were such a thing. It was a bright and sunny day with a cool breeze blowing. The church service had been somber, and, in the end, it had all spiraled down to standing at the graveside, watching the coffin carrying the remains of Evelyn Hardaway slide into eternity. Christian was bombarded with memories—of the good times and then of the bad.

Christian wondered how many of the crowd would have come if he'd still been a murder suspect and presumed traitor, instead of a freshly minted national hero. As quickly as his world had come crashing down, just as quickly had it all been resurrected. The article exonerating him had run that morning in *The Times*, but the story had been the major news the night before on the BBC evening news.

On Friday reporters had been alerted to a major development. PM John Major was asked by a Conservative backbencher who'd been fed the question, "Mr. Christian Hardaway, son of Julian Hardaway, formerly the earl of Carlisle, and one of this nation's valued counterintelligence agents during the Second World War, has been accused of selling timers and other proscribed military equipment to terrorists and of systematically violating our export laws. But now it seems that he was working for the British Secret Service all along. Could the PM please clarify this situation?"

Prime Minister Major replied, "It is not my custom nor the custom of my predecessors to speak about the work of the Secret Intelligence Service or to comment on their activities. In this case, however, I will confirm with the greatest of pleasure that Mr. Hardaway has been closely associated with our intelligence services for some years, as was his late father, and that it was necessary, for reasons I cannot explain, for him to appear to be cooperating with terrorists. Mr. Hardaway, in fact, was the essential element of an ongoing and vital national security investigation and has provided invaluable information that has been and is of enormous benefit to Great Britain and her friends. While I cannot say more about what he has done, I would like to make it quite clear that Mr. Christian Hardaway is a hero, who put country before self and has performed invaluable service for Her Majesty's government at great personal cost."

The Times article that morning had included more details, the gist of which was that Christian had allowed his reputation to be attacked to uncover a KGB operation, the details of which were closely held. There was the suggestion, though no specifics were provided, that the American Central Intelligence Agency was at fault, and had been compromised by the Russians.

The reporter, the same Tim Barclay who'd been so quick to condemn Christian, had apparently written the piece in a state of glee, since any occasion when the American agency was brought into disrepute was deemed a triumph for Britain and her often-beleaguered intelligence services. Lawrence Skinner, deputy director of SIS operations, was quoted confirming that the scandal had been part of an ongoing investigation, "the results of which have been a triumph for the service, thanks to Mr. Hardaway."

Christian had been aware of the pending exoneration and had calculatingly spent the night secure on his estate. A cordon of police had been provided and were keeping the reporters and cameras at the road.

* * *

Following his meeting with Mishka, Christian had driven directly to see Ian Cathcart. The Russian's full story had explained a great deal to him; and, en route, he re-played it in his head repeatedly, comparing it against the events he knew. It was not a pretty picture.

He'd been surprised, initially, that he'd not been shocked to learn that Mitch Seaver was a long-time KGB mole within the CIA; but at some level, Christian realized he'd been suspicious of the man for years. Seaver had always been too slick and had risen too rapidly for it all to be strictly on merit. Christian had assumed influence and such could have as easily come from the dark side as not.

Ian had shown no surprise at Christian's arrival late that day. It was one of those marvelous March afternoons in England, the sun painting the surrounding land and river in lavish colors.

"I take it you have news, my boy," the man said as they shook hands on the deck of the boat.

"I do. Good news, I believe. You tell me."

Together, over tea and cigarettes, the men had read through the documents and listened to the tapes. It had taken the better part of four hours. "So," Ian observed when they were finished, "Seaver's been a traitor all these years. The Company won't like that one bit. And they won't like that anyone else has this information."

"There's nothing they can do about that. Mishka was of the opinion this would clear me."

"Oh, I quite agree, old boy. Obviously, Seaver was out to destroy the venerable IMSS that has served Her Majesty faithfully for so many years in order to position ITP to take over. You were being destroyed by false information planted against you. The CIA was being used as a tool of the evil KGB. But now, the truth will win out."

"How do you see it?"

"Greed, my dear boy. Greed. Seaver saw a way to greater riches. With the fall of the Soviet Union appearing imminent, he could not be certain his role as a spy for the Ruskies would not be revealed at some point. The new rulers of Russia might like nothing more than to open the KGB files to the West, as a show of good faith, if nothing else. He'd want a bundle with which he could disappear. He subverted your man Philips to plant the evidence. He then got the Company to lean on the home secretary and the secret service. Skinner wanted you done in for his own reasons and was only too glad to cooperate, based on the "facts" Seaver gave him. Now we can show it was all a Russian operation; and we can threaten to reveal the most highly placed mole within the CIA in its history. You're a hero, my dear boy—a hero."

Christian never felt less like a hero. In fact, he felt as if he still stood planted before an onrushing train. "Now what?"

"Just leave it to me. Spend the night, if you will at the hotel by the entrance to this marina, so we can talk this through at length. In the morning, I'll make a call, then you can drop me off in London. I don't own a car any more, I'm afraid. I'll have good word soon enough. I'm certain."

And so it had been. While Christian waited with Hannah, Ian had met with Douglas Hurd, the foreign secretary, who'd been delighted to receive the information. The wheels had been set in motion and, as quickly as certain parties had been to disgrace him, those same parties were now Christian's dearest friends. The CIA retreated so fast it made Dunkirk look like a summer-long campaign.

* * *

There was no reception following the funeral service. Christian shook a few hands to be polite, subsequently excusing himself, followed into the house by Ian. The staff had prepared a pleasant fire, and, before it, Christian and Ian Cathcart sat with brandy and cigars.

"Somber business, this," Ian said. "I still vividly recall your wedding. I've never seen a lovelier bride."

"Yes. She was a beauty."

"Have the authorities decided who killed her?"

"No. Just made the official statement that I am not a suspect. I'm prepared never to know.

There are just too many possibilities." He took a sip. "Any word on Mitch Seaver?"

"Ah, yes. Word spread very rapidly through the Company, and he was alerted. He was arrested at Dulles Airport, however, attempting to leave the country on a false passport."

"Now what?"

"That is it. The Americans have already issued a statement, denying any role in what has occurred here. Our side has agreed not to pursue the matter further, and Fleet Street has been advised to let the matter drop. We'll have a bit of gloating from the rags, just to show no one can tell them what to do. Then the story will vanish."

"What happens to Seaver now?"

Ian cleared his throat. "He's done for. I understand he's already being imprisoned in a federal facility on an army base in Utah. It's one used exclusively by the Company. His name has been changed, and he is under permanent administrative detention. There will be no trial. He knows too much."

"Surely, someone will notice. He was, after all, pretty high profile, and he has an ex-wife and children."

"My guess is that, in a few months, a star will appear on the CIA wall and his name will be added to the list of those who have fallen in service to their country. Ironic, isn't it? He will be a dead hero while spending the rest of his life locked up. But what about you, dear boy? What are you going to do?"

"I don't know. It's too soon. My business is no longer of interest to me—I've had enough. It has been damaged. Of course, I could rebuild it, if I had the heart and were willing to give it the time. I have neither. I'm pretty angry, actually. Skinner should be skinned alive for his part in this, if you'll pardon the pun."

"He's been shown the door—quietly, of course. There will be no knighthood for him. Perhaps they'll offer you a settlement through friendly parties and take IMSS over."

"I suppose. Any word on Raymond Philips?"

"Not as yet. He's out of the country, but I suspect he's about to discover it's a very small world, indeed."

CHAPTER FORTY-THREE

1991
Day Sixteen
Bangkok

Raymond Philips glanced at the boy again. They always lied about their age, claiming to be even younger than they were. This one said he was eleven years old, but Philips was certain he was at least thirteen. Still, what was he after? The reality or the fantasy? If he couldn't tell the difference, what did it matter?

The boy caught his look, smiled, and stretched out beside him. As Philips caressed the boy's flank, he ran through the sums in his various bank accounts once again. The total was distressingly small; but, in Asia, it would adequately support him. It would have to. Her Majesty's government would stop his retirement check, now that he was on the run.

It had all come apart so suddenly, and he could not imagine how. He'd been certain everything was set. The key to an operation of this sort was that the end result serve the purposes of other powerful people. He'd had Seaver and Khaldun. Indirectly, he'd had that man, Skinner, who positively drooled at the thought of dismantling IMSS.

Now it was abruptly over. There wasn't a word about Seaver he could find anywhere, but *The Times* article on the involvement of the CIA could have only meant Seaver, coming as it did on the back of Hardaway's exoneration. That boy certainly had all the luck.

Still, Philips observed, he'd not been lacking a bit of luck himself. He'd been home when word broke. He'd reached Heathrow within a couple of hours and arrived in Bangkok eighteen hours later, traveling on a Kuwaiti diplomatic passport given to him by Khaldun two years earlier. His mustache was gone but would grow back. He'd tossed away the wretched tourist clothes he'd worn in flight. All told, he'd made it.

He'd set up household near a border or two, then move back and forth, keeping his head down, enjoying the endless stream of young boys this part of the world provided. There were worse lives, he reminded himself. At least he'd taken his shot, hadn't he?

The boy looked up and said in accented English, "You like orgy?"

"An 'orgy,' dear boy? Why, yes! Bring some of the chaps along. There's a lad."

The naked boy rose and went out the door. Philips was tired, having come to the brothel straight from the airport. He'd find a hotel room shortly, then follow the news for a time before making preliminary decisions about his fate. He wondered if he'd moved too soon with Khaldun? He couldn't see how; but, perhaps, that was where he'd erred.

The boy returned with three other youngsters—six to ten years old, they seemed to Philips. My God! he thought. Thailand is paradise!!

But before Philips could begin to properly enjoy himself, there was a commotion outside.

The boys scattered into the bathroom or closet, like rabbits fleeing a fox, when in burst three Thai police officers brandishing nightsticks, shouting in Thai the only word that Philips understood: *farang*. It meant "Westerner."

"Now, just a minute," Philips admonished before the first club silenced him. The gaggle of boys watched wide-eyed as the officers proceeded to beat Philips into unconsciousness.

Kuwait City

The package had arrived at the emir's office the day before and received priority attention. Philips had arranged to send it to the emir through a front, so it would not be attributed to him. He'd been preparing the contents for years. There were photos of Moussa Khaldun with young boys of every persuasion; but most damning of all were the records of his finances—and, in particular, how payments were tied to contracts made by the emir on behalf of Kuwait.

The percentages were extraordinarily high, while some of the deals should not have been touched at all.

The decision was reached within minutes. Emir Jabir Al Sabah had spoken repeatedly of his unwillingness to abandon his British friends who, after all, had fought with the Americans to drive Saddam out of his country. Once he saw the bank accounts, he understood why his advisor had pressed him so hard. With the disclosure, through their own channels, that the man Seaver had been a Russian spy, Khalduns future was decided.

* * *

The Palestinian preferred to drive himself. He'd told the emir there was a family emergency in Beirut, where he maintained his household, and been given permission to take a short trip home. The truth was the publicity and the disappearance of both Seaver and Philips had rattled Khaldun. He'd decided it was time to end his years of devoted service to the emir. There was enough in his many bank accounts. If he stayed, he feared he'd never spend a pound of it.

Khaldun knew time was short, he'd gone out to his Mercedes with a few cases of personal documents. He'd considered having the houseboy start the car to cool it for the short trip to the airport, but the car would cool quickly enough.

As Khaldun settled himself comfortably into the leather seats he so enjoyed, he turned the key.

The car erupted into a ball of flames. The newspapers reported Moussa Khalduns "assassination" as, perhaps, the final violent act of the Gulf War.

CHAPTER FORTY-FOUR

1991
Day Twenty
Paris

Mishka sat facing the street at Place St. Michel, wondering why he'd answered the summons. Surely, no good could come of it. Before him, the street was busy with Parisians, students rushing to the nearby Sorbonne, seasonally early tourists taking a chance on the weather to avoid the crushing summer crowds.

Mishka drank his coffee. He knew why he was here. He had to try, even if this proved to be the last time. It had all begun that distant day when his mother had extracted the promise from him. He was the heir. The only purpose his life could possibly serve was to reclaim the Russian throne for his family. In pursuit of that goal, he'd shed an ocean of blood. He'd forfeited any chance of a normal life. The only real friend he'd ever had had been an English gentlemen who'd been murdered because of their friendship, murdered by Mishka's own son. And, in the end, Mishka had been forced to flee his native Russia and live among strangers out of fear that same son would kill him. Now, he sat outside a Paris café, waiting for that son, or perhaps the murderers that son was sending.

What difference did it make if he was killed now, Mishka realized. His life was all but over. He'd done his best for a lifetime and had failed. This was his last chance to succeed, and he had no choice but to take it. If this ended in his death, what of it? Everyone died.

And there he was, the so-called Nicholas Rashidov, walking confidently, wearing a well-cut dark-blue Italian suit, seemingly alone. Mishka gestured with a hand, but it was not necessary. His son had already spotted him. Nicholas crossed the street, stood at the table, and said in Russian, "Let us speak elsewhere."

"Here is very good," Mishka said in English. "And I suggest we will attract less notice in English. Sit, my son, sit, and tell me what you've been doing these past years."

Now in his early fifties, Nicholas was an attractive man, very closely resembling the late czar.

His hair was thinning a bit, with traces of gray, but he was otherwise trim and appeared fit. There was something of the predator about his eyes, but that was to be expected of anyone who'd survived a climb through the senior ranks of the KGB and had the courage to break with the party.

"You tell me. I'm certain you know." Nicholas hesitated, then sat, as Mishka gave an order for coffee.

"You are now a senior aid to Boris Yeltsin, no longer in the party—though, of course, you will always belong to the other organization. Like the Mafia, there is no getting out, except to defect."

Nicholas gave him a wry look. "How do you assess our chances?"

"The rotten mess is about to collapse. Mother Russia will at last be free of the Bolsheviks."

"And Yeltsin? What of him?"

"The liberator. What matters, of course, is what comes next."

"What will that be?"

"That is to be decided. The masses will yearn for the old days, I think, I hope. They will, if properly prepared. The right man, in the right place, could make his claim to history." Mishka eyed Nicholas steadily.

"Those days are over. It will be a new Russia."

"Don't count on it. Our people have never known freedom. They will be lost in it, like a bit of flotsam in a tempest. Someone will inevitably assume the heavy hand. Why not you?"

Nicholas glanced around them, then said in a low voice, "Not here. Please."

Mishka tossed money on the table and stepped off with his son. Not far away was a small park with a view of Notre Dame that offered a bit of privacy. "You must make your bid now," Mishka advised as they sat down. "Now is the time I have waited my lifetime for; but I am too old. You are not, and you are well placed to accomplish it. Stick with Yeltsin, but get control of the media.

Prepare the public for the return of the czar. You know how these things are done. In the meanwhile, be certain you have power over the security apparatus. It will be your key. I have money, if you need it. Money has long been the only god in our Russia."

"What are you talking about?" Nicholas retorted sharply. "Haven't I taken enough of a risk just leaving the party and state security? No one knows how this will turn out. You're talking insanity!"

"Insanity? Insanity was my years under the Man of Steel. I never went to sleep knowing if I would wake up. Towards the end, it took an entire bottle of vodka just to find a bit of rest. Insanity was the Great Patriotic War and the risks I took to help the Germans. *That* was insanity. What I urge is simply politics."

"Don't you understand I am well placed already? I'm to be first secretary in the new Russian government in a few months. I will be just a step away from president, when Yeltsin's time is over."

Mishka snorted. "Don't be a fool. I agree that Yeltsin will pull this off and become president, but the KGB will not allow that to continue. One of their own will take over, and they will be the true power in your new Russia. You have only this short window of opportunity to prepare your way before they can organize themselves." Mishka took his son's arm. "I will help. I have only a few years, yet. I know how these things are done. The time will come, soon enough, when I can return to Russia. I have money. I have influence there. You will see. No one knows we are related. I can clear the way for you."

Nicholas jerked his arm free. "Do you think I would ever trust you? You're one of Stalin's butchers! You and your kind should have been shot!"

"What are you saying, Nicholas? I am your father. We are heirs to the throne of Russia. It is yours for the taking. All you have to do is—"

"Shut up, old man!" Nicholas snapped. "The time for all that is past. Can't you see it?"

It took a long minute for the words to sink in. "What are you saying? I did all of this for you."

"For me? Your murdered my parents for me?"

Mishka drew himself up. "Your mother died because she gave you life. I am your father.

Those others were temporary caretakers, nothing more."

Nicholas looked around, then leaned forward until he was touching his father. "You are a threat to me. And you murdered my mother and father." Nicholas leaned over so that his shoulder was touching Mishka. His hand, which had already passed through the slit in the lining into his pocket, was grasping the butt of his Makarov. He pulled the pistol with its long silencer clear of his trouser band and pressed the trigger once, then again and again. Three shots fired, Nicholas stood and walked steadily away without looking back.

Mishka felt no pain, only the force of the bullets. He watched the retreating figure of his son until Nicholas was lost in the crowd. Then Mishka pressed his hands to his jacket and saw the bright blood. He'd killed so many thousands. Now his own time had come, and at the hands of his own son. It suddenly started to get very cold, and it grew dark quickly.

With all the force Mishka still possessed, he stood erect, wanting to die on his feet. He looked towards the blue sky, and in the distance saw a smiling face. "Mother," he said as his legs collapsed under him and he fell, dead before he reached the ground.

CHAPTER FORTY-FIVE

St. George, Bermuda

The waves lapped on the brilliant white beach. Christian moved slightly to a more comfortable position, turning a page of the novel. Hannah finished rubbing suntan lotion on her calves. "Where do you want to eat tonight?" she asked idly.

Christian looked up. "How about room service?"

"Again?"

"I like room service. We put the dishes outside and get straight to it."

"Men!" A bit later, she said, "Are we buying the house on Harbour Road?"

"Unless you don't want it."

"No, no. It's lovely. It's right on the beach. But almost five million pounds seems a bit much."

"We don't have to walk to the beach. It's right there. And I can afford it. Think of it as an investment."

They lay in pleasant silence for some minutes. Hannah asked, "Is it over, you think? Or is another shoe about to fall?"

"It's over. The consortium has taken control of IMSS. The money has cleared my Swiss account."

"Out of curiosity, how much?"

Christian chuckled. "Just over one hundred eighty million pounds, after the government took its bite."

"Too little."

"Probably. But I don't care. I'm out of it."

In the months since his crises and the reconciliation of his reputation and that of the company, the Soviet Union had fallen. Communism, in any meaningful way, was now a relic. The newspapers all agreed that the Cold War had ended in victory for the West.

Christian wondered about that, recalling his conversation with Mitch Seaver those many months before. A traitor Seaver might have been, but his observation that a leopard doesn't change its spots seemed prescient. How much of the

Cold War had been a struggle with Russian expansionism and how much with Communist ideology? Time would tell, he decided.

Two weeks after Evvy's funeral, he flew to Zurich and accessed Mishka's Swiss account. He'd received a letter by post which read, "I am meeting my son in a last attempt to persuade him because he is my blood, but I believe he has come to hate me and fear the outcome. I am sending you this as I loved your father and he never betrayed me, though without realizing it I betrayed him. Do with what you find as you will. Mishka." In the letter was the information he required to access the account.

Christian had no idea what he'd discover. The private bank had been so discreet; he walked past the entrance before noting the very, very modest sign. Once admitted, he found himself within a palatial entry room, not unlike a few royal palaces he'd seen.

The guard resembled a Coldstream Guardsman in dress and stance. Further within, additional guards wore green blazers with gold braid and all but stood at attention, scattered among the tellers' windows and bank officers' desks.

A young woman accepted his application for access. Blond, blue eyed, she might have easily been a fashion model. With a slight accent, she said, "There is fifty-two million pounds in the account." She waited for his response.

So much! Christian thought. He'd had no idea. "I'm closing the account. I'll take it in a banker's check." He'd leave the next day for his offshore bank to deposit the sum.

She nodded. "Very well, sir. There's also a security box."

"I should see it, I suppose."

"This way then, sir." She escorted him into the bowels of the enormous building, taking him into a long, narrow room lined with deposit boxes. She found his, entered and turned her key. Swinging the thick door open, she withdrew the box, then carried it to a private room. "Summon me when you are ready," she said as she left, executing the slightest of bows.

Inside, Christian found nearly £200,000 in various currencies, Mishka's emergency stash. Christian had brought a gym bag in this eventuality, unfolded it, and placed the money inside, along with a small package he found there. Later, in the privacy of his hotel room, he'd sat on the edge of his bed and carefully unwrapped the package. The paper was heavy and old. Inside, he felt a hard object within a wrapping of purple felt. He unfolded the cloth, and a heavy, gold ring spilt into his hand.

Christian lifted it to his gaze, turning it slowly in the light. It was ornate and bejeweled, bearing a double-headed eagle with a single enormous diamond dominating the center. The lettering was Cyrillic and quite old. It took him several moments to realize what he held.

My God! he thought. So that was it. It is the most ostentatious proof of Mishka's claim. He'd have to go to his own Swiss bank before leaving. This wasn't something one could lug around.

* * *

On the beach, Hannah leaned towards him. "What about the knighthood and sinecure on the board of that oil company? That might have been something."

"I passed. I've had enough of all that. I take it you won't mind not being Lady Hannah?"

"No, I'm content to be Mrs. Hardaway, if the offer's still good." She was silent for a minute, then asked, "What about that cretin, Philips?"

"The report was right. He was picked up by the Thai morals police. He's been sentenced to ten years. If he's still alive after that, the British will extradite him."

"Good for him. You know, Christian, they should have paid more just to shut you up. You're the real man who knew too much."

"I'm shut up. They don't have to pay me for that. I forget more every minute I lie here."

"What about Pauline? She certainly saved your Lordly Bacon for you, didn't she?"

"She will never have to worry about money again; I took care of that for her." Christian resumed his book.

"And Mishka? Was it really him?"

"I'm afraid so."

"Why Paris?"

"Who knows? It could as easily have been Istanbul, or Cairo, or London, for that matter."

"Another question."

"Yes, dear." Christian put down his book. "What is it?"

"What about the estate?"

"What about it?"

"Are you keeping it?"

"I haven't decided. The National Trust would take it, I suppose. I doubt we'll visit very often."

"You should keep it."

"You think?"

"Yes, I do. Let your heir decide its future."

"What heir?"

Hannah gave Christian a warm smile.